Walking
with
Dinosaurs

Rediscovering Colorado's Prehistoric Beasts

Anthony D. Fredericks

JB

JOHNSON BOOKS

AN IMPRINT OF BOWER HOUSE

DENVER

To the memory of my grandfather

Wirt B. Dakin, M.D.

Who always had what every good scientist has:

A twinkle in his eye!

Walking With Dinosaurs: Rediscovering Colorado's Prehistoric Beasts. Copyright ©
2012 by Anthony D. Fredericks. All rights reserved. No part of this book may be
used or reproduced in any manner whatsoever without written permission except
in the case of brief quotations embodied in critical articles and reviews. Bower
House books may be purchased with bulk discounts for educational, business,
or sales promotional use. For information, contact Bower House P.O. Box 7459
Denver, CO 80207 or visit BowerHouseBooks.com.

Printed in Canada
Cover and Text Design by Rebecca Finkel

Library of Congress Cataloging-in-Publication Data
Fredericks, Anthony D.
  Walking with dinosaurs : rediscovering Colorado's prehistoric beasts /
Anthony D. Fredericks.
     p. cm.
  Includes index.
  ISBN 978-1-55566-420-6 (alk. paper)
  1. Dinosaurs—Colorado. I. Title.
        QE861.2.F75 2010
        567.909788—dc22

                                        2009054083

10 9 8 7 6 5 4 3 2

Please Note: Risk is always a factor in backcountry and high-mountain travel. Many
of the activities described in this book can be dangerous, especially when weather is
adverse or unpredictable, and when unforeseen events or conditions create a hazardous
situation. The author has done his best to provide the reader with accurate information
about backcountry travel as of the writing of this book, as well as to point out some of
its potential hazards. It is the responsibility of the users of this guide to learn the necessary skills for safe backcountry travel, and to exercise caution in potentially hazardous
areas, especially on steep and difficult terrain. The author and publisher disclaim any
liability for injury or other damage caused by backcountry traveling, or performing any
other activity described in this book.

Contents

Introduction.. 1

1. In Touch with My Inner Lizard 7

2. Bake Slowly @ 103°F   MYGATT–MOORE QUARRY 19

3. Across the Border (Sorta)   DINOSAUR NATIONAL MONUMENT 36

4. Dinosaur at the Airport   RIGGS HILL 56

5. You Say "To-MAY-to" and I Say "To-MAH-to"   DINOSAUR HILL 73

6. Size Matters   FRUITA PALEONTOLOGICAL AREA...................... 93

7. Lost Souls Along the Purgatoire   COMANCHE NATIONAL GRASSLANDS .. 112

8. Stegosaurus and the "Bone Wars"
   SKYLINE DRIVE & GARDEN PARK FOSSIL AREA 137

9. Stepping Back in Time   DINOSAUR RIDGE........................... 163

10. Over the Ridge and Down the Trail   TRICERATOPS TRAIL.......... 188

11. The Queen of Dinosaur Poop   UNIVERSITY OF COLORADO, BOULDER ... 202

12. Return to the Oven   MYGATT–MOORE QUARRY DIG.................. 223

13. Not Quite the Last Chapter 246

14. Phenomenal Colorado Dinosaur Facts 261

Colorado Dinosaur Museums 266

Select Reading List... 270

Acknowledgments 272

About the Author.. 274

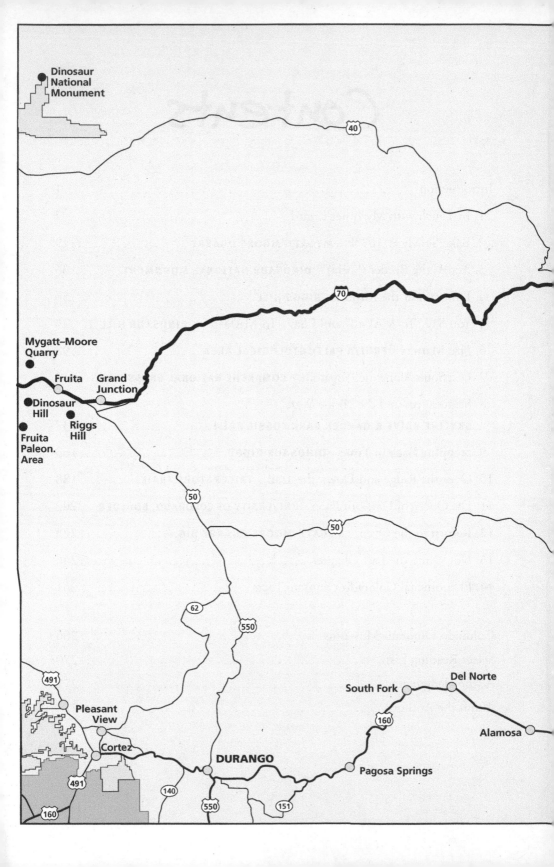

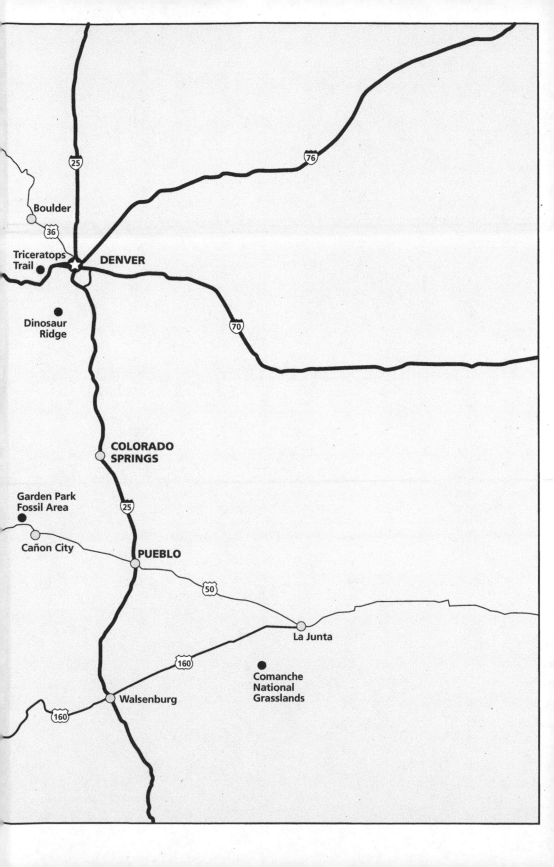

Introduction

I imagine that paleontology is similar, in many ways, to doing your income taxes each year. Sometimes you discover data in strange and unusual places; there's lots of mysterious information and bizarre forms; and a profusion of excessive sweating, labored breathing, and heavy lifting is always part of the equation. The singular difference is that, unlike taxation, paleontology is a relatively new pursuit of human beings.

While we know that dinosaurs existed for approximately 185 million years and that the last one probably died out about 65 million years ago, the study of dinosaurs is a somewhat recent addition to the catalog of scientific pursuits. For example, the first nearly complete dinosaur was discovered by one William Foulke in (of all places) Haddonfield, New Jersey, back in 1858. The bones belonged to a *Hadrosaurus*, an herbivore that lived during the late Cretaceous Period—about 80 million years ago. Currently, there is an eight-foot-tall bronze statue of this creature in the shopping district of Haddonfield (presumably poised to dissuade any shoppers who may be inclined to overextend their credit limits). It should also be mentioned that since 1991 the *Hadrosaurus* has been the official state fossil (a fossil is defined as the preserved remains or traces of animals, plants, and other organisms from the remote past) of New Jersey.* By comparison, Tennessee's state fossil is a clam and Oregon's is a leaf. Illinois' state fossil is—can you believe this?—a 300 million-year-old worm!

That paleontology is a relatively new science is a given. Nevertheless, it has yielded some of the most interesting information and fascinating facts about the world we live in than perhaps any other field. Paleontology has given us a peek into the past—a voyeur's view of life long before humans

*In order to maintain a modicum of journalistic integrity it should be mentioned that my wife Phyllis was born and raised in New Jersey. Thus, there are many things to love about the indigenous species of the Garden State.

ever invented *People* magazine or Twitter. Paleontology has provided us with an opportunity to examine the origins of creatures whose existence on this planet was far more dramatic and far more fascinating than the divorce of any spoiled celebrity or the release of any mega-million-dollar movie. Dinosaurs, while not the first forms of life on this planet, were arguably some of the most fascinating if only because of their stature (size does matter), their demeanor, and their longevity (185 million years). But, they are like a "difficult" sudoko puzzle—the correct solution is right there in front of us; it's just going to take some time and a lot of digging to unearth it.

However, this is not just a book about animals that have been dead for a long time. It is also a travelogue about my discoveries of things paleontological across the length and breadth of Colorado. I was surprised to learn that Colorado has more dinosaur fossils and more dinosaur sites than any other state in the Union (although why all those dinosaurs decided to move to Colorado, rather than Florida, to die is still a mystery to me!).

I am not a scientist—just a slightly past-middle-aged professor of education who has never lost his childhood curiosity about dinosaurs. My journeys across Colorado brought me into contact with dozens of real scientists, ordinary folks with a penchant for adventure, and amateur paleontologists who shared my passion for things prehistoric and for information best gathered on-site, rather than in dry and dusty tomes. With their assistance, I was able to obtain some rudimentary knowledge about ancient times and equally ancient beasts. I was also able to explore sites and "digs" with a keener eye for details. I certainly do not pretend to have discovered all the answers; perhaps I simply learned how to generate more learned questions.

It's equally important to note that I placed a restriction on my travels and on my investigations into the life and times of Colorado's prehistoric beasts. I chose sites where dinosaurs (and their remains) were in full view of any reasonably fit individual or intrepid hiker. That is, I wanted to focus on dinosaurs out in the open, rather than behind a shield of unbreakable glass in a museum case or barricaded behind polished stainless steel in the corner of a floodlit alcove. I have nothing personal against museums—they are wonderful repositories of artifacts, information, and reconstructions that would otherwise be unavailable to the general public. In fact, as you will discover, I often used them as valued resources to substantiate my investigations in the field. My journeys, however, were primarily to open-air "museums" easily available to fellow explorers. I wanted to traverse the same ground as did these great beasts and observe their remains in the actual places where they lived … and died.

During the course of this venture I would sometimes be in conversation with a seatmate on a cross-country flight or chatting with a new acquaintance at a cocktail party. The inevitable question, "What do you do?" would arise. However, when I explained to my new friend that I was writing a book about dinosaurs, I would inevitably get a look like, *He seems like a nice enough chap, but when is he going to write about grown-up topics like politics or sex or serial killers (or sex with politicians who are also serial killers)?* There would often be a pregnant pause in the conversation as the other person quickly tried to figure out why someone with slightly graying hair and a few extra wrinkles on his face was writing an adult nonfiction book about a seemingly juvenile topic such as dinosaurs.

The quizzical looks continued as I checked out reference books from my local public library or purchased "must-have" tomes from the bookstore in town. Titles such as *Extreme Dinosaurs, Graveyards of the Dinosaurs, The Last Dinosaur Book, Digging for Bird Dinosaurs,* and *Dinosaur Worlds* would not only raise the eyebrows of various librarians, but would cause bookstore clerks to cast decidedly strange looks my way (or ask strange questions) to see if I was (how shall we put this) "all right."

"Oh, these look interesting. Are they for your grandchildren?"

"No, they're for me!"

"Oh, my, that's … that's … nice! Hmmmm. Would you like your receipt in the bag?"

At times I would have to sneak into my office in the middle of the night to surreptitiously order books from Amazon just to avoid those questioning and persistent stares. Access to Google provided me with valuable research threads as well as the anonymity required of authors who seek to pursue topics that are sometimes perceived to be strange and weird (or juvenile) by the general population. However, I suppose that my reading of resources dinosaurian was validated in some small measure by the significant number of adults who accompanied me on treks, adventures, and excursions deep into Colorado's dinosaur country.

In 2001, Barbara Kerley wrote a very popular children's book entitled *The Dinosaurs of Waterhouse Hawkins,* which was illustrated by noted artist Brian Selznick. The book examines the life of a mid-nineteenth century artist and amateur paleontologist named Waterhouse Hawkins. First in his native England, and then in the United States, Hawkins devoted over three decades to building some of the first life-sized models of dinosaurs ever seen.

One New Year's Eve, Hawkins staged a dinner party for twenty-one of the top scientists of the day—inside a life-size mold of an *Iguanodon* dinosaur! For eight hours food was served, wine was poured, and speeches were given inside the concrete creature. By the end of the evening this fraternity of slightly-more-than-tipsy men were singing: "The jolly old beast is not deceased, the jolly old beast is not deceased." To this day I am convinced that the Rose Parade in Pasadena, California, and the Mummer's Parade in Philadelphia, Pennsylvania (both of which require liberal quantities of high octane spirits to ward off the heat [CA] and cold [PA] of New Year's Day), are in some way related to Hawkins' celebration inside an ancient and decidedly hard beast.

Hawkins was one of the first to bring dinosaurs into the public consciousness. He made them popular and he made them accessible. His models and molds were quickly followed by a rush of dinosaur discoveries in the western portions of this country—geography that was quite unfamiliar to those residing in the metropolises of the East. Paleontologists of every stripe were routinely pulling prehistoric beasts from deep canyons, scraggly hillsides, and long beds of hardened sediments. Dinosaurs were now and dinosaurs were popular!

But, why were they popular? How did they stimulate the senses or become such infatuating creatures? Noted evolutionary biologist Stephen Jay Gould, in his book *Dinosaur in a Haystack: Reflections in Natural History,* postulated that we tend to love dinosaurs because they are "big, fierce, extinct—in other words, alluringly scary, but sufficiently safe." This statement, of course, does not explain our innate fascination for things that are "big, fierce, and extinct." Why *do* we enjoy extra-large creatures or creatures with bad attitudes or creatures that have passed into that great dino quarry in the sky?

Suffice it to say, humans have long been captivated by dinosaurs. Michael Crichton and Stephen Spielberg certainly proved that true with the novel and subsequent film of *Jurassic Park* (a venture, I am sure, that raked in more money than is allotted to most paleontological studies of dinosaurs in the Centennial State). No matter our birth date, we are drawn to dinosaurs much like many of us are drawn to stores overflowing with decadent chocolate truffles, tall bags of semi-sweet cacao, and shelves of rich bon bons.*

So, like the feline who continually experiments with each of its nine lives, I too have an innate sense of curiosity. I enjoy posing questions for which I have no idea of the possible response—and then going out and seeking an answer. I'm fond of discovering topics that have little to do with my career as an educator, but which provide me with a broad range of experiences that I might not otherwise explore. For me, life is a constant series of experiences—looking around the corner, peeking at distant sites, and gazing at the incredible. Sometimes my ventures take me to a nearby venue; other times they send me to a foreign territory—such is the way of science. For my dinosaurian queries I traveled to the only place that would provide me with sufficient responses and equally fascinating ventures—Colorado. And I wanted you, fellow adventurer, to join me in these magnificent discoveries—discoveries that are only available when you are *walking with dinosaurs.*

---

*Which, like you, I eat solely for its health benefits. It is only through sheer geographical good fortune that I live less than thirty miles from the chocolate capital of the world—Hershey, PA. Ahhhh—life is good!

CHAPTER 1

In Touch with My Inner Lizard

I saw my first dinosaurs in Santa Monica, California. I grew up in West Los Angeles—an enclave of the giant metropolis criss-crossed by long tree-lined streets, carefully mowed lawns, and a pervasive sense of 1950s Eisenhower comfortableness. As a young boy, I spent endless hours in our backyard exploring and investigating all the creatures, habitats, and ecological niches I could locate in a single verdant acre. One summer I spent several weeks constructing a three-story fort in the woods that stretched along the back edge of that yard. I hammered boards together, built planks out over the understory of plants and weeds, and put a few rudimentary chairs on the bottom floor to simulate the casual, though rustic, quarters of a world-famous (and, I might say, quite dashing) adventurer. Indeed, I would imagine myself as a pirate, or fighter pilot, or daring explorer ready to set sail for distant ports or far-away lands.

But, it was shortly after I got my first bicycle that the world around me expanded just a little bit more. On Saturdays my friends and I would occasionally ride our bikes over to the Aero Theater at the corner of

Montana Avenue and Fourteenth Street in Santa Monica.* There we would take in the latest western with its predictable plot of hero-assists-helpless-stagecoach-travelers-against-rampaging-Indians-and-wins-the-heart-of-an-innocent-yet-alluring-young-woman. We'd cheer as Steve McQueen and

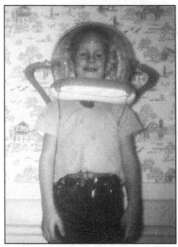

all his teenage friends would battle the most insidious protoplasm to ever invade any American city—*The Blob* (after which we would race over to the nearby toy store and load up on plastic eggs filled with Silly Putty® for our own backyard re-enactments of that movie).

But, my greatest thrill was when we pedaled over to the Aero to see one of the great movies of all time—the original (1933) *King Kong*. The movie was more than twenty years old when we first saw it,

A future scientist . . . ready for action.   but that didn't matter. Our 50 cents was going to take us on an adventure to see "The Eighth Wonder of the World"—a creature just this side of believable and a plot that just barely stretched the limits of credulity. All that mattered to me and my friends was that he was big, he was strong, and he was hairy. And (as we had heard through the neighborhood grapevine) that he would be wrestling some pretty awesome dinosaurs.

For us, the first twenty minutes of the movie was merely prologue (producer needs damsel for new film, producer finds damsel on street, producer takes damsel aboard a ship bound for an unknown island, yadda, yadda). The movie didn't really begin until the scene in which the great ape (with his terrific dental work) grabs neophyte actress Ann Darrow from the human sacrifice temple and lopes through the underbrush. The crew of the ship, carrying a convenient arsenal of weapons, quickly mounts a frenzied pursuit. They are led by (slightly arrogant) producer Carl Denham and (dashingly handsome) first mate Jack Driscoll. It's not long before they are spotted by a *Stegosaurus* who, as all Hollywood dinosaurs (irrespective of

*The Aero Theater first began showing movies in 1940. It is still in its same original location and is still showing flicks to a whole new generation of movie-goers.

whether they are carnivores or herbivores) are inclined to do, decides to attack them with reckless abandon.* The crew, in desperation, repeatedly fires their guns and throws gas bombs at the charging creature.** Finally, the brute tumbles to the ground, but then tries to get up. The crew continues their barrage of bullets and eventually the defeated *Stegosaurus* succumbs— most likely to lead poisoning.

It is not until several scenes later that our all-time favorite dinosaur shows up just like we knew he would. That's right—*T. rex*. Big, bad *T. rex*— the meanest, largest, and most dangerous beast ever to walk through any primordial muck.

In no time, the *T. rex* sees Ann Darrow safely ensconced in a tree (those Late Jurassic creatures sure had great eyesight!)—conveniently placed there by Mr. Kong. And, being a right and proper carnivore, *T. rex* decides to have

Tyrannasaurux rex (from Wikimedia Creative Commons under the terms of the GNU Free Documentation License)

himself a little snack. Ann screams (of course), and King Kong (who is trying to toss some unfortunate sailors into a very deep chasm) turns his attention to the girl and the inevitable fight—the fight of all fights—the fight that would rescue her and save the day! Wow, we were literally drooling over the edge of the balcony (sorry, sir). This was going to be so cool—King Kong vs. *T. rex*—the fight of the century, the fight of the epochs, the fight for the ages.

In less time than it takes to say "Rumble in the Jungle," the two beasts are engaged in a scuffle to end all scuffles. Finally, at the end of an unbelievable brawl Kong climbs onto the back of the *T. rex*. He grabs the carnivore's jaws in his hirsute hands and begins to pull them apart. He twists the jaws in opposite directions, and with one final snap the *T. rex* is dead—his mouth hanging open like a split watermelon.

We are literally jumping up and down in the balcony. Was that an amazing fight or was that an amazing fight? Sure, our all-time favorite dinosaur

*As I was to learn later in life, this was one of a rash of Hollywood miscues that perpetuated the persistent myth that dinosaurs and humans once existed together. There were other times, however, when I could have cared less about cinematic accuracy, as in the film *One Million Years B.C.* featuring Raquel Welsh in a fur push-up bra and form-fitting loincloth (a typical wardrobe, I was certain, for all prehistoric females).

**How do you stop a charging dinosaur? Take away its credit card! (Sorry, I just couldn't resist.)

had succumbed to the brute strength of one hairy beast … but what a fight! What a fight! I knew right then and there what I wanted to be when I grew up—a professional wrestling announcer!

Later King Kong fights with a *Plesiosaur* in a cave and a *Pterodactyl* on a ledge, but the movie is pretty much anti-climatic after that. Oh, sure, he goes to New York, appears on Broadway, and visits the Empire State Building, but all his big scenes were on the dangerous and treacherous island with all the dangerous and treacherous dinosaurs.

In my travels across the country or throughout Colorado I would regularly chat with companions at an adult birthday celebration ("Lordy, lordy, look who's forty!"), new acquaintances at a paleontological "dig," or even fellow passengers stranded at Chicago's O'Hare Airport or Denver's DIA waiting for a summer storm to clear out so we could resume our flights. Business cards would be exchanged, small jokes would be shared, and the usual political chit-chat would be bantered about. Then, there would be that inevitable small pause in the conversation, and I would rush in and ask my new-found companions: "I'm collecting some research for a new book. Could each of you please tell me what you think a dinosaur is?"

There would be the just as inevitable pregnant pause. A few people would nervously shuffle their feet. Some would stare at the pattern on the carpet. And, maybe one or two would find small pieces of lint to pick off each other's jacket sleeves. An uneasy cough, a faint smile, and a nervous twitch would punctuate the heavy silence.

There were a few brave souls who were willing to venture out into the conversational hinterlands and respond to my query. Either their cell phones had accidentally been left turned off or there was no more lint left to pick off their sleeves. The responses were as varied as the individuals who shared them. Here are some of the most typical:

Dinosaurs are:

- "Prehistoric creatures—some were meat eaters, some were plant eaters."

- "Very large animals that are no more."
- "An extinct reptile."
- "A prehistoric animal that died."
- "Dead animals from a long time ago."
- "Dead reptiles and other stuff."
- "I don't know. I do know that I need another drink."

So, I decided to go to the real paleontological experts—kids. I contacted one of my former students, who had just been hired to teach fourth grade. Hmmm, fourth grade, I thought, just the right age to know everything there was to know about a topic such as dinosaurs (at least, that was the case when I was in fourth grade). So, she invited me into her classroom and I asked the kids what they thought a dinosaur was. Here are some of their candid responses:

- "A dinosaur is an animal from a long time ago that has not been around for a while."
- "An extinct creature."
- "A dinosaur is a really big creature with sharp teeth."
- "A dinosaur is just like a big lizard, but they eat lots of meat and plants…"
- "Dinosaurs are creatures that lived a billion years ago."
- "A very old and tall animal."
- "Prehistoric animals that are huge and have gone extinct."
- "A dinosaur is a big, huge animal that lived back then."
- "A dinosaur is a plant or meat eater long ago."
- "Something that has been extinct for millions of years." (like "customer service" from the airlines)
- "A scaly looking thing that lived centuries ago."

In an animated conversation afterwards, the students told me that they all enjoyed dinosaurs enormously. Their reasons were as diverse as they were. They said that dinosaurs were "cool, awesome, and mean." They were fascinated with them because they were "mean and evil," and also because "they look scary." Several students ventured that dinosaurs were neat because "some are still a mystery," and "they are a mystery to scientists because they all disappeared and scientists don't know why." It would be safe to assume that these kids reflect the attitudes and persistent love affair that children have had with dinosaurs ever since the first dinosaur cartoon ("Gertie the Dinosaur," 1914) was shown on the silent screen. It was equally evident that kids today share the same devoted fascination with prehistoric beasts that my friends and I did decades ago. Jason (age nine) summed up the entire conversation that morning when he said, "Dinos rule!"

But still there was that persistent and ever-present question: What, exactly, is a dinosaur? The word "dinosaur" was coined in 1841 by Richard Owen,* who was the Hunterian professor at London's Royal College of Surgeons. Professor Owen was a widely published author who wrote articles on both living and extinct species. He tended to specialize in invertebrates such as shellfish, the nautilus, and certain human parasites.

Owen spent considerable time studying the fossils of several species of extinct reptiles, including *Iguanodon*, *Hylaeosaurus*, and *Megalosaurus*. He was especially taken with the size and stature of these creatures. Their anatomical features, too, seemed to put them into a category all their own. He quickly concluded that they were unlike any modern-day crocodiles, alligators, or lizards—they appeared to be part of a distinct and as yet unnamed class of creatures.

So, Professor Owen decided to coin a name for this new group of animals. He came up with the word *Dinosauria* for what he called "a distinct tribe or suborder of saurian reptiles." Owen created the name using ancient Greek—*deinos,* which means "terrible," and *saura/sauros,* which means "lizard" or "reptile." Thus, we now have the term *dinosaur* that literally means "terrible lizard."

But, the question still remains—what is a dinosaur? At the Museum of Natural History at the Smithsonian Institution in Washington, D.C., there is a small sign in the dinosaur exhibit that partially answers this query. It reads: "Dinosaurs are reptiles that walked with their feet directly under their body. They did not sprawl, nor did they habitually swim or fly."

What is most significant about this definition is that dinosaurs, quite simply, had legs that were relatively straight and positioned directly below

---

*Professor Owen had this curious habit of claiming the work of other professors as his own (one wronged associate went so far as to call him "dastardly and envious"). To add insult to injury, he regularly slandered his colleagues and periodically made false accusations against other scientists. As you might imagine, this did not endear him to the bulk of the scientific community, nor was he ever invited to contribute a piece to the book *How to Win Friends and Influence People.*

the body. Dinosaurs were reptiles, and most reptiles have cup-shaped hip sockets. Dinosaurs, on the other hand, had openings in their hip sockets and a unique stance. Most reptiles' legs (such as lizards, turtles, and crocodiles) sprawl sideways from their bodies. In fact, early depictions of dinosaurs (in the late 1800s and early 1900s) mistakenly illustrated creatures whose legs were sprawled out to the sides (as a result of the artists' familiarity with more common reptiles). Yet, because of its unique hip socket, a dinosaur had legs that extended straight down beneath its body, allowing it to support a greater body weight. There is considerable speculation that the upright posture and erect gait of dinosaurs was not only efficient and energy-saving, but may have been a substantial reason for their longevity.

While most people would state that there are two categories of dinosaurs—carnivores and herbivores—this is only partially correct. Yes, there are two subgroups of dinosaur. However, the subgroups are not carnivores and herbivores. The first subgroup is known as the *saurischians* or "lizard-hipped" dinosaurs. In these creatures, the pubis bone projects at an angle down and forward. The *saurischians* include all of the

> The physiological feature of straight legs is also a characteristic of modern-day birds, giving additional weight to the evolutionary connection between dinosaurs and birds. In addition, birds also have that defining dinosaur feature—hip bones with openings in the sockets. Scientists versed in comparative anatomy have counted more than a hundred features in common when comparing bird skeletons and dinosaur skeletons.* The primary difference between birds and dinosaurs is that the forelimbs of birds are considerably longer than their hind limbs. These longer forelimbs make much better wings.
>
> For a long time scientists thought that only birds had feathers. But newly discovered dinosaur fossils (particularly in China) show that some types of non-flying therapod dinosaurs also sported feathers. You might wonder why a creature might have feathers on its body if it didn't use them for flying. The answer could be that "early" feathers served a purpose other than flight. For example, they may have insulated the body, been used to attract potential mates, or offered a bit of lift when a theropod leapt at prey.
>
> * Birds are scientifically classified as theropods ("beast feet")—the dinosaur group that also includes *Tyrannosaurus rex*.

carnivorous dinosaurs, from some of the largest (*Giganotosaurus*—forty-three feet long, six tons in weight) all the way down to some of the smallest (*Compsognathus*—three feet long, six and a half pounds in weight). A very small number of herbivorous sauropods such as *Diplodocus* are also included in this group.

TYRANNOSAURUS

TRICERA

Some of my closest friends

The second subgroup of dinosaurs is known as *ornithischian,* or "bird-hipped" dinosaurs. Members of this group have a pubis that is roughly parallel to the ischium ("seat bone"). Both of these bones are directed down and back. The *ornithischians* are represented only by herbivorous dinosaurs and include *Triceratops, Stegosaurus* (made famous by his ill-fated decision to charge the crew of sailors in *King Kong*), *Iguanodon,* and *Apatosaurus.*

All of these creatures existed during the Mesozoic Era or "Age of Medieval Life"—a period of time that lasted for approximately 185 million years. Dinosaurs rose, existed, and became extinct from about 251.0 to 65.5 million years ago. Scientists divide the Mesozoic era into three separate time frames—the Triassic Period, the Jurassic Period, and the Cretaceous Period. These periods are represented in the chart below.

The Mesozoic Era*

Period	Time Frame	Geology	Representative Dinosaurs
Triassic ("Triassic" refers to the threefold division of rocks of this age in Germany.)	251.0 to 199.6 million years ago	All the continents were part of a single land mass called Pangaea. North America, Europe, and most of Asia comprised the northern part. South America, Africa, India, Australia, and Antarctic made up the southern part. Pangaea began to break apart near the end of this period.	*Coelophysis* *Torosaurus* *Eoraptor* *Plateosaurus*
Jurassic ("Jurassic" refers to the Jura Mountains—located between France and Switzerland—where rocks of this age were first studied.)	199.6 to 145.5 million years ago	The Atlantic Ocean began to open up between North America and Europe. Later, South America and Africa began to drift apart.	*Tyrannosaurus* *Diplodocus* *Allosaurus* *Brachiosaurus* *Apatosaurus* *Stegosaurus*
Cretaceous ("Cretaceous" refers to extensive deposits of chalk ["creta" in Latin] along the English Channel between France and England.)	145.5 to 65.5 million years ago	North America was separated into two sections by a shallow sea. The present-day continents began shifting into their present positions.	*Ceratosaurus* *Spinosaurus* *Oviraptors* *Ankylosaurus* *Iguanodons* *Hadrosaurus* *Triceratops* *Velociraptor*

 *(Adapted from "Divisions of Geologic Time—Major Chronostratigraphic and Geochronologic Units;" United States Geological Survey [USGS], March 2007.)

In any cocktail party discussions about dinosaurs or schoolyard banter about life in prehistoric times, there always seems to be some persistent and undeniable myths that surface. It is my hope to quickly dispel these misconceptions at the beginning of this tome so that we (both author and reader) can spend our valuable time in more scientific pursuits. The following "factoids" seem to be some of the most persistent dinosaur myths:

1. **Humans and dinosaurs existed at the same time.** Decades of newspaper comic strips (*Alley Oop*) and animated cartoons (*The Flintstones*), years of imaginative movies (*Journey to the Center of the Earth*), a plenitude of puffy purple prehistoric puppets (*Barney*), and library shelves bursting with liberally plotted science fiction novels (*Jurassic Park*) have long perpetuated the myth that humans and dinosaurs existed simultaneously. Here's the undeniable fact: humans appeared on the earth only after dinosaurs had been extinct for a very, VERY long time. While dinosaurs went extinct 65 million years ago, humans and chimpanzees diverged from one another about four million years ago, and *Homo sapiens* emerged about 500,000 years ago.

2. **T. rex was the most terrible dinosaur that ever existed.** It may be that *T. rex* has been part of the public consciousness far longer than other "brands" of dinosaurs. The first *Tyrannosaurus rex* fossil was uncovered by Barnum Brown at Hell Creek (a most appropriate name for a dinosaur site!), Montana, in 1902. Its pose in the American Museum of Natural History was characteristically predacious, with its dagger-like teeth, carnivorous stance, and fearsome stature. However, recent discoveries of *Giganotosaurus* in Argentina and *Spinosaurus* in Egypt suggest that there were other creatures with "badder" attitudes and a more predatory nature than our more famous friend, the *T. rex*.

3. **Most dinosaurs were carnivorous.** Typically, when most people (particularly children) focus on dinosaurs, they think of the largest or most predatory. Nevertheless, the majority of dinosaurs that lived during the Mesozoic Era were herbivorous in nature. They feasted on the ferns, cycads, and evergreen trees that covered the land during this time period. Some scientists have estimated that the ratio of carnivorous-to-herbivorous dinosaurs in some fossil deposits is on the order of three-to-one hundred. I suspect that although plant-eating dinosaurs seem to outnumber meat-eating dinosaurs, the carnivores just had better press agents!

4. **Dinosaurs were around for a very long time.** Here's a little known fact: dinosaurs were alive for only a very small portion of the earth's history—approximately 185 million years. Now, I realize that to us short-lived humans (we've only been here for a mere .011 percent of the earth's history) 185 million years may seem like a long time. However, the earliest evidence for life on earth comes from fossilized mats of cyanobacteria, called *stromatolites,* discovered in Australia and estimated to be about 3.4 billion years old, which means that dinosaurs were around for a mere 5.4 percent of the span of life on this planet.

5. **Paleontology and archeology are similar.** Well, yes and no. They are both sciences that examine stuff in the past, but from there they differ considerably. By definition, paleontology is the study of prehistoric life. Archeology, on the other hand, is the science that studies human cultures through the recovery and interpretation of material remains. Or, to put it another way, paleontology examines ancient critters and archeology examines ancient humans. The distinctions may seem minor, but if I may offer a kindly piece of advice —the next time you're at a cocktail party never get into the middle of a heated discussion between archeologists and paleontologists over whose field is more rigorous. Bones will be tossed, sacred urns will be hurled, and you may find yourself on the short end of a splintered martini glass.

And so, my venture across the plains, mountains, and deserts of Colorado began. I sought to discover not only the fossilized remnants of a long-dead group of animals, but the stories of individuals, both current and past, who have been at the forefront of this dynamic and exciting scientific pursuit. I generated questions, read shelves of books, and most important, immersed myself in a host of scientific pursuits in every corner of the state. I joined with other amateur paleontologists and would-be scientists who also sought answers to their equally perplexing prehistoric queries and conundrums. I was seeking new territories and new adventures—places where buried secrets were waiting to be uncovered by someone who, despite a potentially loose screw or two, was eager to probe the unknown and peek into the past.

Some Things I Learned

- I never met a dinosaur I didn't like—although I liked some more than others.

- Paleontologists are regular folks. (Well, there was that one guy on the Front Range—but I think it best he stays anonymous.)

- Train travel across the country has airline travel across the country beat six ways to Sunday. Take the train, see the land … you'll never regret it!

- The Colorado desert is really hot in the summer—particularly when you are down to your last two ounces of water in an unoccupied and barren territory (with absolutely no gas stations) somewhere south of Fruita.

- There is absolutely no comparison between digging for real dinosaur fossils in the wide-open spaces of Colorado and book learning.

- Standing inside a dinosaur track that was left by one of your all-time favorite dinosaurs is a sensual experience that is almost, but not quite, reminiscent of your first kiss.

- Holding a 65-million-year-old chunk of fossilized dino poop from a *T. rex* in your hands is absolutely the most wonderful thrill of a lifetime. (And, no, I didn't have to wash my hands afterwards!)

- Getting "up close and personal" with a *Stegosaurus* causes brain neurons to fire at a significantly faster rate than they would if, say, you were watching a re-run of *Days of Our Lives* while nursing a severe cold.

- Peering into a 100-year-old abandoned quarry where one of the world's great prehistoric beasts was excavated certainly beats the hell out of cleaning the garage or buying new socks at Wal-Mart.

- Dinosaurs are (still) cool!

CHAPTER 2

Bake Slowly @ 103° F

MYGATT–MOORE QUARRY

The city of Fruita, located on the arid (though aquifer-rich) landscape of western Colorado five hours of driving time from the big city life of Denver, is a remote outpost of some six thousand–plus hardy individuals. Previously known as Fruitdale, it was settled in 1883 by one William E. Pabor, who wanted to actively promote this fruit-growing region of the Western Slope. Fruita is also one of the very few towns anywhere to have an official dinosaur mascot. In this case it's *Ceratosaurus*—a large predatory dinosaur from the Late Jurassic Period. This beast is distinguished by a blade-like horn on its snout, along with a pair of hornlets over its eyes (its name means "horned lizard"). Remains of *Ceratosaurus* have been discovered not only in western Colorado, but also in Tanzania and Portugal (you must admit—it was quite a cosmopolitan creature!). Current research suggests that it was a voracious carnivore—feasting on crocodiles, fish, other large dinosaurs, as well as scavenging corpses. By the way, Fruita's official website (www.gofruita.com) also features a special page for "Mike, the Headless Chicken"—a historical avian celebrity with his own dedicated fan club.*

*This distinguished fowl lost his head (literally) on September 10, 1945, and, incredibly lived for eighteen more months. He toured the country and was featured in *Time* and *Life* magazines. At the height of his fame, Mike was making $4,500 a month. He has assumed cult status in Fruita (where he was born) and every May the town marks his passing with a "Mike the Headless Chicken" Festival. This annual celebration includes a car show, a "Run Like a Headless Chicken" 5K foot race, a chicken dance contest, and, of course, all the fried chicken you can eat. Let the good times roll!

First-time visitors might describe this arid settlement as "a drinking town with a desert problem." Here, fiery winds sweep in from the flatlands of Utah and across the high plains and sandstone mesas. The land is criss-crossed by canyons dotted with scraggly bushes and clumps of piñon trees. Meandering cliffs are rimmed with rich red rocks and enormous boulders. The town is home to the Museum of Western Colorado's Dinosaur Journey—a sprawling interactive museum that houses robotic displays of *Dilophosaurus, Stegosaurus, Apatosaurus, Triceratops, Utahraptor,* and the ubiquitous *T. rex.* Additionally, there

Utahraptor (courtesy Dick Hodgman)

are a variety of other displays, including real bones and cast skeletons of *Camarasaurus, Camptosaurus, Stegosaurus, Allosaurus, Velociraptor, Othnielia* and the rare *Mymoorapelta.* There is also an active paleontology laboratory, where visitors can watch paleontologists and volunteers poke around the skeletal remains of recent discoveries. Three-digit summertime temperatures are the norm in this town, as are overloaded RV's disgorging sun-baked tourists into air-conditioned curio shops brimming with "authentic dinosaur souvenirs."

Fifteen miles west of Fruita, and two miles from the Utah border, is the Mygatt-Moore Quarry. Discovered by two couples in 1981, it is a seemingly infertile expanse of abandoned wilderness—flanked only by I-70 and the whir of eighteen-wheelers and out-of-state convertibles speeding by. The couples, on an excursion through the area, came upon a sprinkling of dinosaur bones cached in the alkaline surface. They reported the bones to a local paleontologist, and in 1982 excavations began under the supervision of the Bureau of Land Management and the Museum of Western Colorado. The site was eventually named using the last names of the two couples—Mygatt and Moore.

Today, this area is vastly different than it was during the Late Jurassic Period (161.2–145.5 million years ago). Then, it was a lush floodplain with conifer trees and cycads spreading across the hills. The climate was warm and the atmosphere rich and humid, just right for a wide variety of sub-

The Mygatt-Moore Quarry at the "Trail Through Time."

tropical creatures. These included turtles, crocodiles, herds of herbivorous dinosaurs, and an occasional carnivore or two. Flying reptiles and prehistoric insects zipped through the moisture-laden air.

In the millions of years since that time, many rivers, streams, lakes, and seas have deposited thousands of feet of sediment over the area. Remnants of the plants and animals endemic to this prehistoric panorama were preserved through burial in the sediments. Over time, immense heat and pressure within the earth turned the sediments to rock and the plants and animals to fossils.

When paleontologists began excavating this area, they discovered a wide range of dinosaur bones, including *Allosaurus*, *Diplodocus*, *Apatosaurus*, *Camarasaurus*, and *Mymoorapelta*. Some of the bones had been severely crushed and scattered throughout the site. Other bones were parts of broken skeletons. A few bones had been well preserved in casings of thick mudstone, while others had been exposed to the elements. Trampled bones littered the site, an indication that they may have been walked on by other prehistoric beasts.

The hip bone of an Apatosaurus dinosaur being unearthed at the quarry. Note the size of the hammer.

Driving in from the verdant landscape of the Roaring Fork Valley just north of Aspen, my wife and I arrive in Fruita in the middle of a searing summer morning. Our time in town is brief—just enough to replenish our fuel, my supply of water bottles, and my wife's reserve of reading material. After departing the convenience store/gas station at Exit #19, we set out on the ribbon of sunburned highway that snakes over the buff-colored landscape and head toward the Utah border. Twenty minutes after leaving Fruita in my rear-view mirror, I swing off the Interstate and onto the #2 exit ramp. I make an immediate right-hand turn, and after less than a quarter-mile we roll into a stony parking area. Just before getting out of the car I note that the thermometer is already recording a temperature of 103 degrees. My wife, the smarter one of the duo, decides to remain in the air-conditioned comfort of the rental car. She leans back in the passenger seat, opens a magazine, and waves me goodbye.

I am covered with a pasty white layer of sunscreen (SPF50), my prematurely balding cranium is topped by a dashing safari hat, and I am fortified with three bottles of "pure mountain spring water" (from a spigot somewhere in Detroit, I suspect). I'm here to visit this dinosaur research site and walk the "Trail Through Time," a well-maintained path—with informative markers—that winds through the Rabbit Valley Research Natural Area and back to the pebbled parking area. The trail is administered by the Bureau of Land Management (BLM) and the Museum of Western Colorado. A cautionary notice in the BLM brochure advises visitors that, "It is illegal to remove, deface, or destroy rocks, fossils, artifacts, plants, animals, or site improvements. It is also illegal to remove vertebrate fossils anywhere on public lands." Since we are so close to Utah, I make a mental note not to transport any dinosaurs across state lines.

After a short stroll around a barbed-wire fence and up a dusty road, I amble into a section of the quarry that has been topped by an oversized tarpaulin to shield it from the blistering sun. There I meet Chuck, a vertically enhanced graduate student with waves of dirty blond hair and a jaunty "I've-been-wearing-this-sweaty-T-shirt-for-four-whole-days-devil-may-care" attitude. He has volunteered to assist with the excavations for the summer, yet is quick to pounce on any visitor as a break from his mundane and repetitive chores. With all the fervor of a young Indiana Jones, he gives me a nonstop monologue about the various discoveries taking place at the site. (I have a feeling Chuck has been sniffing way too many sedimentary layers of late.) He is quick to show me the hipbone of a large *Apatosaurus* dinosaur he has been picking at for the past several weeks. He lays his pickax next to the bone so I can have a frame of reference for the photos I shoot.

Chuck informs me that the discovery of certain types of plants along with the presence of freshwater snails suggests that this site was once a watering hole for thousands of dinosaurs over thousands of years. A number of dinosaurs died here, providing a convenient meal for visiting carnivores (sort of a reptilian prototype for the 24-hour drive-thru lane at your local Wendy's or McDonalds). Teeth marks and actual teeth of *Allosaurus* and *Ceratosaurus* found in the scattered bones of plant-eating dinosaurs show that predation may have been a regular and frequent occurrence. It depends on the cause of death for a given animal. Were they killed first and then eaten? Or, were they consumed (or scavenged) sometime after their demise?

Chuck is one of several volunteers who regularly work the quarry. These folks come from all walks of life—retired teachers, architects, lawyers, electricians, and just everyday folks with a general interest in paleontology. Under the guidance of a professional paleontologist, these volunteers engage in the backbreaking and often mundane task of carefully picking away tiny pieces of stone from around embedded fossils. They may also assist in mapping the location of various finds, and in the jacketing and removal of bones. A wide-brimmed hat, gallons of water (along with an iron-clad bladder), a desire for routine and precise tasks, and an ability to place your body in acrobatic contortions are the only prerequisites. Constant complainers are not welcome!

A group of German tourists arrives at the quarry and begins a discussion with the resident paleontologist, who is working the rocky slope just beyond the sagging tarp. I wish to join them, but I am now a listening post for Chuck's animated dissertation on the utility of various digging instruments, the scientific inaccuracies in the movie *Jurassic Park*, and the lack of a social life in Fruita. Eventually, Chuck takes a break to yell some instructions to a colleague emerging from the Port-a-Potty on an adjacent hill. I see an opportunity to escape his verbal clutches and aromatically enhanced clothing. I bid him a quick adieu and hasten my way down the road.

I arrive at a small BLM pavilion with its customary collection of notices, posters, brochures, and tattered business cards. Also included are warnings about the excessive summertime heat and the unique opportunities

The Museum of Western Colorado also offers some unique opportunities for the general public (i.e. paying customers) to become actively involved in these paleontological discoveries. They offer both one-day and five-day digs at the quarry throughout the spring and summer months. On the one-day dig, the museum provides transportation between the museum and the quarry, lunch, barrels of water or Gatorade,™ field instruction, and a whole day spent on your hands and knees in an ecosystem devoid of urban sprawl or volume-rich boom boxes (see Chapter 12). The five-day offering multiplies that (oven baking) experience exponentially and throws in a raft trip down the Colorado River, as well as an opportunity to cast dinosaur bones in the paleontology lab. For kids, it's an exciting opportunity to "get down and dirty" with real scientists and real dinosaurs (just imagine what they'll be able to bring to "Show and Tell" the next school year!).

hikers have to encounter wildlife with sharp fangs and irritating disposi-
tions (rattlesnakes), or invertebrates with mouthparts that pierce, probe,
and poke through your skin ("biting gnats are prevalent in May and June").
After a brief stop, I saunter along a rock-lined trail, make a left-hand turn
after about 150 yards, and begin a slow ascent up a rocky cliff face. I am
now on the trail—which, according to the brochure, is "a moderately strenuous one and one-half mile loop which takes approximately ninety minutes
to complete." Sorta like listening to Chuck.

I am just starting to break a sweat when I arrive at marker #2 (marker
#1 is a lichen-covered boulder at the trailhead). This spot identifies the light
gray neck vertebrae of a *Camarasaurus* dinosaur encased in a solid rock wall.
Barely noticeable is the front limb bone of this once lumbering giant.

Camarasaurus was a dinosaur of the Late Jurassic Period (161.2–145.5 million years ago). Its name means "chambered lizard"—a reference to the
holes in its vertebrae. There is some speculation that these hollowed spaces
in the spine saved weight, helping this beast lug its ponderous body over hill

The neck vertebrae of a *Camarasaurus* in the solid rock wall.

and dale. Yet, it was not even in the class of oversize dinosaurs such as *Supersaurus* and *Ultrasaurus*. Most paleontologists classify *Camarasaurus* as a medium-sized dinosaur weighing in at around twenty tons and reaching a length of about sixty feet. In size, it would be comparable to a modern-day humpback whale. Its life span, as was the case for most sauropods, was in the neighborhood of a hundred years.*

One of the most distinctive features of *Camarasaurus* was its enlarged teeth, each of which measured seven and a half inches in length (about the length of an average man's hand from the tip of the index finger to the base

Camarasaurus skull (Courtesy Dick Hodgman)

of the palm). These chisel-shaped teeth were evenly spaced along the entire jaw line and were extremely strong. As a result, *Camarasaurus* was able to eat a wide variety of coarse plant material. However, in order to sustain its twenty tons of body mass it would have needed to eat a tremendous amount of vegetable matter each day (by comparison, a seven ton African bull elephant needs to consume between 300 and 400 pounds of food every day just to maintain its weight). It's suspected that *Camarasaurus* swallowed leaves whole, stripping them off branches without chewing them. And it would probably have swallowed stones (gastroliths), like a chicken, to help grind food in its stomach. After a time, it would regurgitate the stones when they became too smooth. Unusually smooth stones have indeed been found in proximity to several *Camarasaurus* skeletons.

Like most sauropods, the front legs of a *Camarasaurus* were shorter than the hind legs. However, the high position of the shoulders meant that there was little slope in the back. In some sauropods, there were long upward projections on each vertebra, but the absence of such structures from the spine of *Camarasaurus* suggests that it was not able to raise itself on its hind legs.

*Recently scientists have found that some dinosaur bones have growth rings (called lines of arrested growth). These lines are only visible using a microscope. The bones have to be sliced into thin sections and viewed with a polarized lens in the microscope. It's similar to the science of dendrochronology, in which the age of a tree can be determined by its annual growth rings. For many dinosaurs, each year of growth leaves a trace in the bone.

Camarasaurus, like certain other sauropods, had an enlargement of the spinal cord near its hips. Paleontologists originally believed this to be a second brain, perhaps necessary to coordinate such a large creature. Modern opinion asserts that, while it would have been an area of large nervous (possibly reflex or automatic) activity, it was not a brain. This enlargement was actually larger than the remarkably small brain contained in the animal's box-like skull.

Based on its relative brain size to body size (referred to as an animal's EQ or Encephalization Quotient), the intelligence of the *Camarasaurus* was one of the lowest of all dinosaurs. *Troodon* (a relatively small, bird-like dinosaur of the Late Cretaceous Period, 99.6–65.5 million years ago), on the other hand, had some of the highest dinosaur EQs. *Tyrannosaurus rex*, certainly one of the world's most readily recognized dinosaurs, merely had

an average EQ. Perhaps the larger the dinosaur the lower its overall intelligence (overweight politicians take note).

Camarasaurus fossils have been found in groups with both young and adults together. This suggests that *Camarasaurus* may have traveled in herds and may have cared for their young. They probably hatched from eggs like other sauropods. Interestingly, fossilized eggs of other sauropods have been found in linear patterns as well as in nests. The implication is that

Camarasaurus (Courtesy Dick Hodgman)

the eggs were laid as the animals were walking. This suggests that some species of sauropods, unlike *Camarasaurus* whose eggs were clustered in nests, did not take care of their eggs or nurture their young.

After taking several photos at the *Camarasaurus* site, I make my way up to the fourth marker on the trail, which identifies several plant fossils embedded in stone. These twig and branch impressions were deposited some 135 million years ago. While they are seemingly unremarkable on the surface, they do offer paleontologists and paleobotanists valuable insights into the pre-historic environment and climate of the Late Jurassic Period. Paleontologist Kirk Johnson of the Denver Museum of Nature and Science points out that, "In most landscapes, it's the plants that make places look like they do, and the total biomass of plants vastly outweighs that of animals." He also points out that fossil plants "carry a signal of ancient climates and they show what ancient landscapes looked like." They are equally important in helping to understand the diet of several species of herbivorous dinosaurs that frequented the area.

I slowly meander up the trail and encounter a sheep fence traversing the parched landscape. The fence crosses the trail in front of me—from the top of the hill to my left and down over a precipitous ledge to my right. The BLM has wisely erected a walkover—a tired series of wooden planks that allows us bipedal wanderers to traverse up and over the fence without the need for a gate (which hikers are frequently known to leave ajar in their eagerness to get from one ecosystem to another). Presumably, four-footed livestock penned in by miles of barbed wire have neither the coordination nor inclination to make it up and over a wooden staircase. The walkover looks slightly worn and rickety, and I am careful to measure each step as I ascend up one side of this seemingly perilous ladder.

At the peak of the ladder and just as I am about to step down the back side of the staircase, I am aware that something or someone is watching me. I am sure I am being closely watched by some type of uncommon and/or alien creature. I am intent on keeping my eyes focused and my feet planted on the rickety wooden stairs, but now slowly … ever so slowly … I lift my head to survey my immediate surroundings.

Off to my left, three sheep are staring at me.

It's time to move on. I deliberately step down the other side of the staircase and back on to the trail. The rocks are jagged and rough, but I keep my pace at a constant rate of ascent. I amble upward, but I can't resist one last look. I pause and slowly look behind me and there they are—the triumvirate of sheep with their piercing eyes still focused on me. I turn and walk on, but can't get the inevitable newspaper headline out of my mind: Lone Hiker Ravaged by Sheep Gang on Federal Property!

The sun hangs overhead like an incessant heat lamp for which there is no switch. Not even the smallest clump of clouds scuttle across the sky for relief. I continue to negotiate my way up a slight incline and past some ancient boulders. Up on the right is an overlook and small shelter that affords travelers (particularly those still recovering from sheep-a-phobia) with a panoramic view of the Uncompahgre Plateau and the Colorado River canyons in the distance. I sit down and, in very short order, drain the contents of a single water bottle. Scanning this vast territory I am taken by its enormity—a seemingly endless stretch of a multihued landscape with burnt orange hillocks, sandy washes in shades of ecru and khaki, faraway mountain ranges jacketed in sepia and ochre, and, like a child's marble game, a splatter of pebbles, rocks, and boulders in shades of russet, umber, and beige.

Sprinkled across all of this is a menu of diverse flora: sandy, gravelly flats dotted with saltbush shrubs, meandering canyons of juniper, and a few thin patches of yucca and sagebrush randomly strewn in various directions. With the pulsating rays of sunshine directly overhead it is though I am observing an enormous slice of environmental pizza being roasted to a golden

The vertebrae of a young *Diplodocus* beside the trail. Note the light-colored disks.

crisp consistency. This is quite different from the conditions that existed when prehistoric beasts came to satiate their thirst at the nearby watering hole. I had the good fortune to bring my water with me. For most prehistoric beasts, hydration was not portable.

After a brief respite at the shelter, I follow the trail as it meanders downward through a brief section covered with bentonitic mudstones. Mudstones, with their distinctive greenish hue, often contain volcanic ash deposited along slow moving stream channels. It is speculated that they may be the result of nearby volcanoes or of volcanic activity elsewhere on the planet that deposited ash over extremely large distances. When wet, this surface becomes extremely slippery—similar, I suspect, to negotiating one's way across a garage floor covered with axel grease. I pick my way slowly over the greenish-gray slick.

Now the trail is sliding downward. This is its steepest section—winding in and among a collection of boulders, around a solitary cactus plant or two, and between a host of cobbled rock formations. Pebbles scramble under my hiking boots, and I feel as though I'm walking on an undulating sea of ball bearings. Small rounded stones repeatedly roll under the soles of my hiking boots causing me to use both hands to steady myself between trailside boulders as I make my way down the perilous slope. The trail is headed toward a sandy streambed. I swing around to the right and gain footing that is more level and sure.

As I slowly make my way down a modern-day streambed, I come upon the #11 marker, which clearly identifies the distinct and awe-inspiring remains of a *Diplodocus* dinosaur. Cemented into the side of a thick rock beside the trail are the vertebrae of a young *Diplodocus*. As I look carefully I can see the disks that separate each of these vertebrae (they are lighter in color). I quickly realize the parallels between the spine of this stone-bound creature and my own. Both dinosaurs and humans have interconnected vertebrae along their spines (humans have thirty-three vertebrae along their spines; *Diplodocus* had at least fifteen vertebrae in its neck)—each separated by a cushion of flexible material—the disk. I notice that along with the partial remains of the backbone are some ribs and a femur (leg bone) of the young specimen.

Diplodocus was a common dinosaur during the Late Jurassic Period. Its name means "double beam," in reference to certain T-shaped bones in its tail. It was one of the larger dinosaurs of this period, measuring up to ninety feet long. Twenty-six feet of that length was its neck and another forty-five feet was the tail. It might be safe to say that this creature was all neck and tail. It was for a long time one of the largest land creatures ever known. It wasn't until the discoveries of dinosaurs such as *Supersaurus* that *Diplodocus* was "shifted" from the longest to *one of the* longest.

If you think you've seen *Diplodocus* before, you probably have. It is truly one of the most recognized dinosaurs in the world. That's simply because so many *Diplodocus* skeletons have been unearthed over the years and placed in museums around the world. These include the Natural History Museum of London, the Field Museum of Natural History in Chicago, the Senchenberg Museum in Germany, and the Natural Science Museum in Spain, among others. *Diplodocus* has been featured in a raft of dinosaur movies, is a commonly seen figure in dinosaur toys and games, and has been "novelized" in James Mitchner's *Centennial.*

Despite its mass, *Diplodocus* was more lightly built than other giant sauropods—weighing in at a mere ten to twenty tons. It lived throughout what is now western North America. Its forelimbs were slightly shorter than its hind limbs, resulting in a posture that was more or less horizontal. Its elongated neck may have been used to poke into forests that were inpenetrable because of the sauropods' size. One recent study, however, suggests that the primary function of the extremely long neck of *Diplodocus* was for sexual display.*

The first *Diplodocus* fossil was discovered at the Marsh–Felch Quarry in Garden Park, Colorado. It was named *Diplodocus longus* ("long double-beam") by paleontologist Othniel C. Marsh (who has his own unique historical role—see Chapter 8) in 1878. Fossils of this animal are common throughout the Rocky Mountain region, with the exception of the skull, which is often missing from otherwise complete skeletons. Due to a wealth

*There is some speculation, at least by this writer, that the euphemism "necking" may have some prehistoric origins.

of skeletal remains from throughout the region, *Diplodocus* has been one of the best-studied dinosaurs in the world.

At this point on the trail, I am walking along a dry wash that sweeps down from the hill behind me. There is course sand and pockets of pebbles scattered about, the result of flash floods that barrel down the valley in the rare times when rain falls on this desiccated landscape. The trail at this point is largely undefined, but fairly easy to follow. I am careful to stop every so often to quench my ever-present thirst.

Marker #12 is ahead, identifying a scattering of fossil hash on this section of the trail. It is a dry streambed that courses slightly to my right. Scattered through the streambed are bits of fossilized bones and plants that were deposited in an "old" stream and are now being eroded out of a "new" streambed. The BLM brochure informs me that the original dinosaur bones were broken into fragments as they were swept along the ancient stream channel. I bend down to poke through the sand with the end of my pen and can see a few bone-like flakes scattered throughout the pebbled surface. Their journey through this streambed, just like the journeys of *Cama-*

Volunteers often help work the quarry.

rasaurus, *Diplodocus*, and other denizens of this prehistoric land, were, and will continue to be, left to the fates of nature.

Marker #13 identifies a location where a *Camptosaurus* dinosaur was discovered. Unfortunately, the fossils (including a skull and other bones) have all been removed from the site and are being studied in other locations. In essence, there is absolutely nothing to look at except another expanse of gray-brown rocks and sienna-colored dust.

I arrive at a Section Corner Survey Marker that indicates the edge of BLM land. The old trail (no longer recommended) goes straight ahead. There is another sign (which has been knocked down) pointing to the lower trail, which slides off to the right and down through a short ravine. I carefully traverse this section of the trail tredding on a blanket of rocks that litters the landscape.

As I'm walking along, I pass by an old mining claim marker to my right. It was apparently set up many decades ago, although what those prospectors may have wanted to mine in this area remains unidentified.

I'm about halfway along the lower trail. It has smoothed out considerably and would be easily accessible by wheelchair. Ancient rocks that have rolled down from the hills above litter the sides of the trail. Some have been partially eroded by wind and water. In short order I come upon another interpretive sign entitled "Dinosaur Pelvis." In the boulder before me are the fused vertebrae from the pelvis of a juvenile sauropod dinosaur. They are in an inverted position, requiring me (if I were so inclined) to stand on my head to view them in their correct anatomical position. Although the bones are the same color and texture as the rock, the pelvis is quite distinct. The course texture of the rock in which they are embedded indicates that this set of bones was probably washed down an active streambed before being buried and preserved.

I'm nearing the end of my cross-country journey—an odyssey into an environment quite different from interstate highways, fast food restaurants, and the latest journalistic revelations about spoiled and overindulged divas. At each of the designated markers, I would stop to take photos or record pertinent observations in my notebook. The unmerciless sun is the same sun that shone upon the incredible assembly of prehistoric beasts that long ago wandered this landscape. Perhaps it is the unrelenting heat that causes me to philosophize about this constant of time and space—the sun. But, it is strange that two completely different species of animals could walk on the same expansive landscape under the same celestial body—separated by several million years of existence. The footprints left by each of those two species may disappear with a westerly gust or they may be preserved in rock and stone for others—millennia later—to discover and reminisce.

However, after ninety minutes and three bottles of water, I am reduced to a slow and sweaty shuffle over a short rise and the last four hundred yards of my dusty journey through this prehistoric valley. I pass by the BLM kiosk, take a hard left, and amble down to the parking area. With both relief and satisfaction, I finally arrive at the terminus of the trail. My wife smiles at me from the interior of the air-conditioned car.

NEED TO KNOW ABOUT **Mygatt–Moore Quarry**

DIRECTIONS From Grand Junction, head west on I-70 for thirty miles. From Fruita, travel west for about seventeen miles on I-70. Take the Exit #2 off ramp (Rabbit Valley). Turn right at the stop sign and travel for about one-quarter mile directly into the gravel parking area. Walk through the open gate in the fence and up the trail for about one-quarter mile. The trailhead for the "Trail Through Time" begins at the BLM rotunda on your right.

CONTACT INFORMATION Contact the Museum of Western Colorado and obtain the trail map for the "Trail Through Time."
Museum of Western Colorado's Dinosaur Journey, 550 Jurassic Ct., Fruita, CO
(970) 858-7282

FEES None

HOURS Daytime. This is not a trail you want to hike in diminished light (unless, of course, you're looking for a convenient way to get rid of old Aunt Betsy).

BEST TIME TO VISIT Spring and fall—early morning or late afternoon. However, I have hiked the trail in the middle of the day in July (authors, as you are no doubt aware, don't always have all their brain cells fully functioning). If you visit in the summer, always remember five things: lots of water, lots of sunscreen, lots of water, a big-brimmed hat, and lots of water.

CAMPING/LODGING Fruita has half a dozen hotels and four campgrounds (check out www.gofruita.com). Grand Junction (www.visitgrandjunction.com) has nearly four dozen hotels, inns, B&Bs, motels, and campgrounds. There are plenty of accommodations in all price ranges.

SERVICES There is an enclosed pit toilet located at the Mygatt-Moore Quarry, which is about two hundred yards to the left of the trailhead. There is no water available.

ACCESS People with disabilities will need assistance on this trail. The restroom is not wheelchair accessible.

DIFFICULTY RATING Moderate to mildly strenuous. It will take between one and one and one-half hours to traverse the trail and read the informative signs.

NOTES This has long been one of my favorite places to visit in Colorado. It's great for couples, singles, family groups, or anyone who wants to get up close and personal with paleontology. Kids will love it because they can stop by and see what's being dug up at the Mygatt-Moore Quarry. It's usually being worked on through the summer months—check with the Museum of Western Colorado first. The kids can then tramp along the trail to see some bones embedded in rock (don't miss the *Diplodocus* skeleton), along with other delightful discoveries. It's great for adults, too! It offers some fascinating and jaw-dropping information, a very pleasurable outdoor hike (just keep your eyes open for marauding gangs of sheep!), and an opportunity to appreciate some dramatic desert scenery. I never tire of this site and I doubt that you or your family will either!

CHAPTER 3

Across the Border (Sorta)

DINOSAUR NATIONAL MONUMENT

The outlines of U.S. states are typically determined by one of two primary factors. In many cases, the geography of the land helped determine the border between two states. Mountain ranges, rivers, lakes, oceans, and other geographical features were frequently used by early surveyors to establish state boundaries.

The other determinant for state lines is a simple matter of cartography. Cartographers (map makers) have placed lots of lines on the surface of the earth. We refer to these as lines of longitude (north-south) and lines of latitude (east-west). If you glance at a map of the U.S., you will see any number of states whose borders are straight up and down or straight across (east-west). For example, the state of Pennsylvania has a southern border with Maryland that is an east-west line with an approximate mean latitude of 39°43'20"N. This line is more popularly known as the Mason-Dixon Line. Although the border between the two states was originally surveyed in 1765, it achieved its "notoriety" as a result of the Missouri Compromise of 1820, in which the Mason-Dixon Line was designated as the boundary between free states and slave states.

The West has fewer potential geographical boundaries (except for that pesky little mountain range that runs from Canada down into Mexico). As a result, surveyors made it easy on themselves (perhaps they were completely exhausted after all the geographical surveying they had to do in the East) and often relied on simple lines of latitude and longitude to help them out.

Now, let's go back in time to 1850, when the Utah Territory consisted of land wedged between latitudes 37°N and 42°N, as well as between the territories of Colorado and California. That was a lot of land for one territory to have, so pieces of that territory were doled out to a few other western states (it's not clear who was doing the doling, but you can be sure that it had something to do with the Federal government). One of the eastern pieces of Utah went over to Colorado, three western slices wound up as part of Nevada, and the "notch" in Utah's northeastern corner was annexed by Wyoming. Suffice it to say that by the time all this parceling and dividing and "giving away" was completed, Utah had a slight inferiority complex.

Then, in 1879, a group of surveyors entered the picture with their transits and compasses and chronometers and astrological readings. Their job was to establish the official western border of Colorado. They began their surveying venture at Four Corners, the only place in the U.S. where four states (Arizona, New Mexico, Utah, and Colorado) share a common corner. They decided to make it easy on themselves and head on a true-north line for about 276 miles to the Wyoming border. However, when they finally reached the border with Wyoming they discovered something very strange— they were about one mile west of where they were supposed to be.

About six years later, there was another survey of the border between Utah and Colorado. Those results confirmed that there was, indeed, an error of slightly more than one mile somewhere between eighty-one and eighty-nine miles north of Four Corners. And just to add insult to injury, still another survey in 1893 found an additional half-mile error between mileposts 100 and 110. "Oh, my gosh," the cartographers exclaimed, "this is a cartographical nightmare!"

Since Utah didn't become a state until 1896 you might be asking yourself, "Okay, now, why didn't certain government officials just go ahead and change the state boundary when they found the errors?" Of course, such a question would be the most logical one you and I might ask. But, keep in mind that we're dealing with an entity here known as "state government." And it is an unwritten rule that once a state boundary is marked on the ground and accepted by all interested parties then it is a true line—*even if it doesn't match the official written description* (please note my added emphasis). In order to change a boundary between two states the state legislatures of each of those two states must agree to the change, and the change would then have to be approved by Congress. All that means just one thing—lots of paperwork! And, since nobody was willing to do all that extra paperwork, the border between Utah and Colorado, to this day, remains slightly crooked.* Check out a state map of Colorado and you'll notice a little "jag" in the Colorado/Utah border just north of the line between San Miguel County and Montrose County in western Colorado.

Now, you're probably asking, "Okay, why this lesson on the cartography of the Colorado/Utah border?" (At least, that's what I'd be asking.) Well, you see this is supposed to be a book about my explorations of dinosaurs totally within the borders of Colorado. The book is not only about the dinosaurs that can be discovered by tourists to, and residents of, the Centennial State, it is also published by a Colorado publisher. And, as I explained to my very fine (and, I might add, highly intelligent) editor, I would totally confine my explorations and descriptions of those explorations to the borders of Colorado.

So, when I began my research on Dinosaur National Park I realized that I had a slight dilemma. About two-third's of the park is in the state of Colorado and approximately one-third of the park is in Utah. To add to the confusion, I learned that the part of the park that had all the dinosaur fossils was in the smaller Utah section, rather than in the larger Colorado section (even though the park straddled both states). Equally confusing, the town of Dinosaur, Colorado (with streets such as Brontosaurus Boulevard, Stegosaurus Freeway, Triceratops Terrace, Brachiosaurus Bypass, and

*Gentle reader: The use of the word "crooked" in the same paragraph as "certain government officials" is entirely unintentional and is certainly not meant to cast any negative aspersions on any specific or particular legislative individual. (Yeah, right!)

Diplodocus Drive), bills itself as "The Gateway to Dinosaur National Monument" yet it is far removed from any dinosaur fossils (all of which reside in the Beehive State).

So, I'm sure you can now understand my dilemma in writing a Colorado-based book in which I was inadvertently and unavoidably forced into considering another state. So, when I discovered that there was a slight "boo-boo" in laying out the boundary between Utah and Colorado (which may, or may not, have accurately bisected a national monument), I figured that I would be forgiven for considering an equally slight geographical "left turn" in order to continue my prehistoric investigations. Please keep in mind that the majority of Dinosaur National Monument is, indeed, in Colorado, so maybe I did cross the line and maybe I didn't. One never knows for sure. I guess you'll just have to take my word for it, 'cause, as everyone knows, you just can't trust those surveyors.

It's another crystal-blue Colorado day as I depart Grand Junction for Dinosaur National Monument early on a Monday morning. Behind me, sunlight is echoing off the maroon and crimson hills of the Colorado National Monument. Off to my left is a bank of dirty gray clouds left over from last night's sudden rainstorm.

After a few miles, I leave I-70 and begin my northbound journey on CO 139. In front of me is a long slate-gray ribbon of asphalt lancing toward a faraway mountain range and a bank of musty clouds that seems to hover overhead. CO 139 is like an arrow piercing great fields of corn, hay, and vast open-range ranches. After about a dozen miles the landscape transforms itself and becomes rolling hills of high desert with enormous vistas in every direction. A palette of cerulean blues permeates the sky above. Coupled with the multi-colored mountains in the distance, it makes for a delightful vista.

As I continue my journey, the clouds are becoming grayer and darker— more overcast—all the blue in the sky is slowly disappearing. This is a windy, twisty part of CO 139 and the road weaves back and forth like a drunken reptile splayed across a rocky hillside. The speed limit eventually reduces to twenty-five mph as I climb, back and forth, toward Douglas Pass

(8,268 feet). If you are unfortunate enough, as I am, to get behind a big belching lumber truck, the vehicular pace up the mountain tends to drop dramatically.

As I inch my way up to the pass, the road moves from high desert to spectacular alpine scenery. Finally, at mile marker 35, I crest the mountain and head down toward a distant flatland bereft of any sustainable crops. Throughout its length, the road is a constant parade of semis and other massive trucks carrying all manner of geological wonders—coal, gravel, stones, etc.

Slowly sliding down the back side of the mountain, I begin my traverse through the high desert of northwestern Colorado. This is an area punctuated by a smattering of low-lying mesas, rock cairns, scraggly grassland, and a series of flat-topped mountains. Human habitation is noticeably lacking in every direction.

After nearly two hours of driving, I pull into the town of Dinosaur, which bills itself as the "Gateway to Dinosaur National Monument." Just after passing by the sign for the Dinosaur Baptist Church, I come upon the Dinosaur Town Hall on the left. Next to the building is a deteriorating plaster model of a (supposedly) prehistoric beast with a sign saying "Stegosaurus—plant-eaters, Jurassic Period." The paint is peeling, the expression is almost humanoid, and it has obviously seen far better days.

Dinosaur is a scraggly outpost of sun-baked buildings along with a broad scattering of house trailers. There's also the Blue Mountain RV Park, the Pickle Shop (where, oddly enough, one can get an ice cream cone),

A multicolored *Stegosaurus* greets visitors to Dinosaur National Park. (Photo courtesy Jonathan Fredericks)

Christie's Liquor (an absolute necessity in this part of the world), the "Loaf and Jug" minute market, a Conoco gas station, and the Colorado Welcome Center (the only functioning public rest room for miles). After a quick stop at the welcome center to get some maps and use the facilities, I head west on US 40. I quickly pass by the Bedrock Depot Restaurant (ice cream, espresso, coffee bar) and the staple of every small town—a junkyard overflowing with rusting relics of every imaginable size and shape. The speed limit picks up and I'm soaring toward Jensen—another remote outpost twenty-five miles across the flatlands of the state I'm not supposed to mention in this book about *Colorado* dinosaurs.

After twenty minutes, I come out of the high desert into a rich and verdant valley—the strikingly pastoral setting for the town of Jensen. There is a profusion of trees, grass, and fields of green all around. This tiny town is adjacent to the appropriately named Green River.

Shortly after crossing the river I make a right hand turn onto UT 149. On the corner is a Sinclair gas station with its designated official (and slightly smiling) mascot (*Brontosaurus*) in front. This route sweeps along the left edge of the Green River and up towards the entrance to Dinosaur National Monument. After paying my $10.00 entrance fee, I turn into the large parking area for the temporary visitor's center and park next to an oversized RV emblazoned with a few dozen environmental, political, philosophical, and PG-rated bumper stickers ("If this trailer's a-rockin', don't come a-knockin'").

The dinosaur quarry is only one part of the enormous 210,844 acre Dinosaur National Monument, which straddles the boundary between Utah and Colorado. The park encompasses scenic river canyons, sweeping mountains, desert dry basins, and rich archeological sites. There are twenty-three exposed geological strata throughout the park—the National Park System's most complete collection. The environmental diversity just begs to be explored by tourists and residents alike. However, as Lindsey Lennek, one of the park guides working at the monument, informed me, "only 3 percent of the park is dinosaur bones, but 97 percent of the visitors come to see the dinosaurs."

The Quarry Visitors Center is a brand new building that serves as the visitor's center for the Monument (not just the dino stuff, but the whole park).

Upon entering the Center, you are greeted by a large *Diplodocus* femur. Once inside you will discover the Dinosaur Theater, displays on "Ancient Cultures,"

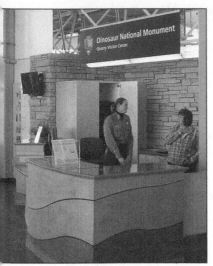

"Dinosaur's Rivers," and a unique tree sculpture. There is also The Dinosaur Store and a waiting area for the shuttle up to the Quarry Exhibit Hall.

The Center, along with the Quarry Exhibit Hall, is an homage to the work of paleontologist Earl Douglass, who was sent out to this remote region in 1909 by Pittsburgh's Carnegie Museum to scout for dinosaur bones. His excavations over the next fifteen years revealed a picture of prehistoric life that is almost unequaled in number of specimens or specimen quality. Many of those specimens are now exhibited in museums throughout the United States.

The Quarry Visitor's Center has lots of great information. (Photo courtesy Jonathan Fredericks)

Earl Douglass was first and foremost a paleontologist—and a pretty damn good one at that. He was born in Medford, Minnesota, in 1862. After graduating from high school, he worked on a farm, taught school, and studied at the University of South Dakota. After a trip to Mexico in 1890, he studied botany at Washington University in St. Louis. Later, he attended the South Dakota Agricultural College, as well as Iowa State College from which he finally received his baccalaureate degree.

From 1894 to 1900 he conducted some geological explorations in Montana and taught school in order to meet expenses. Later, he began his own personal collection of fossils with emphasis on mammals. He then attended the University of Montana, from which he obtained his Masters of Science degree in 1899. Then, in 1902, he became associated with the Carnegie Museum in Pittsburgh and continued his work in Montana under their auspices.

Beginning in 1907, Douglass was assigned the responsibility of exploring the fossiliferous (containing fossils) Uinta Basin in northeastern Utah. In September 1908, he was visited by Dr. W.J. Holland, who was

then the director of the Carnegie Museum. The two of them had heard stories (including one from John Wesley Powell, the noted explorer of the
Grand Canyon) about the possible presence of dinosaur fossils and decided
one day to set out across some foothills to see what they could find. They
came to an area that looked quite promising and agreed to split up and no-
tify each other with gunshots if anything was discovered. At this point I'll
allow Dr. Holland to take over the story.

> His [Douglass's] shotgun was presently heard and after a some-
> what toilsome walk in the direction of the sound I heard him
> shout. I came up to him standing beside the weathered-out
> femur of a Diplodocus lying at the bottom of a very narrow
> ravine into which it was difficult to descend. Whence this per-
> fectly preserved bone had fallen, from what stratum of the many
> above us it had been washed, we failed to ascertain. But there it
> was, as clean and perfect as if it had been worked out from the
> matrix in a laboratory. It was too heavy for us to shoulder and
> carry away, and possibly even too heavy for the light-wheeled ve-
> hicle in which we were traveling. So we left it there, proof pos-
> itive that in that general region search for dinosaurian remains
> would probably be successful.

Douglass returned the following year to try and locate the stratum from
which the fossil had come. If he could locate that stratum, then there was
a better than average chance that he could also locate fossils of other Jurassic dinosaurs. With a Mormon elder as his only companion, he began his
relentless search of the area. Occasionally they would turn up a few bone
fragments, but nothing of serious consequence. But, all of that changed on
August 17.

It was near noon when Douglass's keen eye caught the glint of a fossil
bone up the side of an east-west ridge running at right angles to the nearby
Green River. Scrambling up the side of the hill, he probed around in the
rocky soil where he soon uncovered the articulated vertebrae of a large dinosaur (the bones were arranged in the natural order in which they occur in

the skeleton). It was a definite clue that a larger, more complete skeleton might be in the general area. That evening, Douglass proudly recorded the following in his personal diary: "At last in the top of the ledge where the softer overlying beds form a divide … I saw eight of the tail bones of a Brontosaurus in exact position."

He quickly summoned Dr. Holland from Pittsburgh, and the two of them continued to survey the ridge. Each day additional fossils were revealed and significantly larger sections of the dinosaur were uncovered (Douglass later estimated that the entire animal had been approximately sixty feet long.). Not only was that specimen uncovered, but thousands of other bones were unearthed from the ridge. It was clear that 1) this would be a site rich with dinosaur fossils, and 2) it would be an expensive operation to uncover those bones and have them all transported back to the Carnegie Museum. As fortune would have it, Mr. Carnegie, the benefactor of the museum and a lover of all things paleontological, had more than enough money to keep the operation funded for a long time.

Douglass even went so far as to suggest that the *Brontosaurus* (now called *Apatosaurus*) would be one of the best ever uncovered. This prediction proved to be more correct than even Douglass could have imagined. After more than six years of excavation work and eventual restoration at the museum, the final mounted skeleton stretched to nearly seventy feet in length and stood almost fifteen feet tall. It was, and still is, one of the most complete *Apatosaurus* (*Brontosaurus*'s alter ego) skeletons known.

But as things turned out, this specimen was just the tip of the proverbial paleontological iceberg. More men and more quarrying revealed a rash of other skeletons. Tumbled in among the original bones were a partial *Stegosaurus*, three more *Apatosauruses*, an un-named plate-backed dinosaur, and dozens of bones from an array of prehistoric beasts. These discoveries alone kept the quarry humming for more than a year and a half.

Douglass soon deduced that this particular deposit of dinosaur bones was the result of an ancient river that had trapped, buried, and covered numerous dinosaur bodies. Douglass was able to calculate that the prehistoric river had flowed from west to east. As a result, he predicted that additional fossils should be located westward from this original quarry. His calculations were right on the mark, as additional skeletons and bones—the remains of both herbivores and carnivores piled on one another—turned up in great profusion. In the end, it took almost seven years to unearth all the bones in the western section of the quarry.

While Douglass was working the fossil-rich quarry, his friend and supervisor, Dr. Holland, was working back East, trying to get the site and the land around it declared "off limits" to any homesteaders or private developers. As a result of contacts with the White House, in October 1915, President Wilson proclaimed eighty acres at and around the quarry as Dinosaur National Monument. Shortly thereafter, Douglass and his crew began working another site slightly to the east. This, too, was an area overloaded with a cache of dinosaur fossils.

Nevertheless, the Carnegie Museum decided to divert the funds that had kept the operation going for many years (the museum's primary benefactor, Andrew Carnegie, died in 1919), in order to fund other potential projects with Carnegie's endowment. And so, in 1924, the last shipment of bones from the quarry was sent off to Salt Lake City (for the University of Utah) and the quarry was quietly shut down. In the end, more than 350 tons of fossil material had been extracted from the quarry by Douglass and his crews—an impressive total that is still being examined by paleontologists today.

Nevertheless, there were still large sections of the site untouched with still more fossils available that could be opened up for public viewing. In fact, shortly before the site had been designated as a monument in 1915, Douglass recorded in his diary a prophetic entry:

> How appropriate that [the dinosaur bones] be exposed in relief
> as they were buried … to reveal something of their lives and
> surroundings. How appropriate to build a fair-sized building
> over them to protect them … to help to appreciate nature and
> her wonderful ways!"

In 1953, the quarry was re-opened by the Smithsonian Institution. Using drill hammers and other excavation tools, the bone-bearing sandstone was slowly chipped away. A tin shed was constructed over part of the

The new Quarry Exhibit Hall is filled with paleontologial wonders. (Photo courtesy of Jonathan Fredericks)

site to protect the workers during the brutal winters. Shortly afterwards, the shed was replaced by a new Quarry Exhibit Hall. Then, in 1958, the august quarry building was opened to the public. From that time until 1991, when work on the wall was suspended in favor of other nearby sites, the public watched paleontologists conduct the demanding and precise work of exposing scores of fossil remains in their natural state. Scores of fossils are still embedded in the quarry wall, which is surrounded by the soaring glass walls of the Exhibit Hall.

In the cruelest of geological ironies, the famous Quarry Exhibit Hall that celebrated the distinguished work of Earl Douglass and opened up a quarry to the eyes of the world closed in July 2006. Constructed on expanding and contracting soil, the visitor's center experienced continuing problems with foundation movement. Door frames, walls, and floors were all warping. Tilting walls of the rotunda wing weakened supports to the ceiling and roof, and the east glass wall of the exhibit hall broke free of the foundation.

After the Quarry Exhibit Hall was closed down the National Park Service set about soliciting funds and obtaining all the necessary permits needed for a new Exhibit Hall. Extensive design work was initiated in order to resolve the many safety concerns and prevent "shifting" issues in the future. Then, between March 2010 and September 2011, the Quarry Exhibit Hall underwent a major deconstruction and total rehabilitation.

In the summer of 2010, crews installed special columns that penetrated the solid rock below the quarry. These "micropiles" extend to bedrock and allow the building to "float" above the problem soils. On the lower level inside the building, the floor is made with recycled and removable pavers that will allow for some movement to occur in the floor without damage. They will also allow the floor to be easily removed if a foundation repair is needed below.

During the planning process, monument staff felt that it was necessary to preserve the character of the original Exhibit Hall. During construction, the butterfly roof and steel support columns remained in place, forming the framework for the new structure. Today, just as before, walls of glass frame the quarry face, allowing visitors to look beyond the quarry to the surrounding landscape.

The renovation of the Quarry Exhibit Hall and construction of the new Quarry Visitors Center at the bottom of the hill together cost about $9,000,000, and was funded by the American Recovery and Reinvestment Act. The renovated building looks very much like the original with the same butterfly roof, and was built in the same exact footprint, but without the "rotunda," which housed former offices. The new Quarry Exhibit Hall, with its famous wall of fossils, reopened to the public on October 4, 2011.

Walking into the Exhibit Hall you are immediately taken by the spectacular quarry face. More than 1,600 bones have been left exposed on the face. These bones represent at least eleven different species of dinosaurs, including *Camarasaurus, Allosaurus, Stegosaurus* (at least 15 percent of the bones on the quarry face are those of *Stegosaurus*), *Diplodocus, Apatosaurus, Ceratosaurus,* and *Barosaurus* (among others). This diversity represents about five hundred individuals and approximately eighty million years of dinosaurs.

All of the bones in the quarry face were buried in a 145 million-year-old river flowing to the east. Eventually the river channel was covered by sand and gravel forming a sandbar. Over the millennia, thousands of feet of sand and mud from the Western Interior Seaway continued to cover the sandbar. This caused the sandbar to be compressed and solidified. Slowly, and over a long period of time, mineral-laden water seeped into the bones— fossilizing them. Then, about sixty-five million years ago the earth's crust buckled, which resulted in a tilting of the ancient sandbar. Wind and water erosion gradually brought the sandbar to the surface. That same erosion eventually revealed the bones, which were seen by humans (e.g. Earl Douglass) for the first time in 1909.

Some of the bones in the quarry face are articulated (still joined together). Articulated bones are quite rare and when discovered they indicate that the carcass did not travel far from the place of death. Paleontologists also assume that articulated fossils are an indication that the dead creature most likely did not experience great trauma from predators nor was it subjected to severe environmental conditions.

Most of the quarry bones, however, are disarticulated (mixed-up). That is, they probably received greater trauma than articulated bones and they may have traveled a greater distance from the initial place of death. Disarticulated bones often show evidence of round or smooth edges—the result of tumbling downstream during a flood or other water action. When lots of bones from lots of different creatures are all mixed together they present unique mysteries for paleontologists who must sort through them and assign each one to a specific individual. The bones in the quarry face, for example, represent seven different species of dinosaurs and include both adults and juveniles. Getting all those critters back together again would make the most challenging Sudoku puzzle seem like a cinch in comparison.

The Wall of Dinosaurs is incredibly impressive (it should be viewed from ground level as well as from the upper gallery), and the building perfectly captures the importance of the site. The wall is certainly the feature event, but there's more to amaze and inform. Shortly after entering the building there is a display of the late Jurassic's most fearsome predator—*Allosaurus*. Along with an eye-popping mural is a cast skeleton of an Allosaurus from east-central Utah. However, it is the encased skull that may be the most interesting.

You see, dinosaur skulls are very rare because they are so fragile (due to their cranial spaces) and rarely "survive" enormous geological forces over millions of years. Skulls also have this bad habit of disarticulating from their skeletons shortly after death. However, this particular Allosaurus skull is one of the best-preserved ever discovered. Even with its thin and delicate bones, the skull is remarkably uncrushed. Buried for millions of years, the skull is only minimally distorted (pay particular attention to its excellent dental work). Interestingly, fourteen complete dinosaur skulls have been discovered on this site.

One of the most intriguing dinosaurs unearthed in the quarry was the *Dryosaurus,* meaning "oak lizard," a reference to its oak leaf-shaped teeth. *Dryosaurus* was a relatively small dinosaur (eight to fourteen feet in length, five feet high at the hips, and an overall weight of around 170 to 200 pounds) that lived during the Late Jurassic Period (161.2 to 145.5 million years ago). Its diminutive size undoubtedly made it a likely target for large carnivores; however, some scientists believe that its strong legs made it an agile runner with the natural speed to escape any would-be attackers, much like an antelope. The *Dryosaurus* possessed a long, stiff tail that was most likely used as a counterbalance during escape maneuvers, and a horny beak that it probably used to snap off low-lying vegetation such as ferns and cycads. Some scientists proffer that a set of cheek teeth and the semblance of cheek pouches allowed this dinosaur to process food in its mouth at the same time it was ripping plants from the ground. There is also some indication that *Dryosaurus* was most likely a herding animal and that it protected its young for some time after hatching.

While several *Dryosaurus* fossils have been unearthed in Colorado, there are many more that have been found in Tanzania. Once again, this seems to suggest a strong terrestrial connection (Pangaea), and the eventual tectonic separation between two continents.

After you have consumed all of the mesmerizing features of the Quarry Exhibit Hall you may want to do as I did and set out for a short walk along the Fossil Discovery Trail. This easy-to-navigate trail offers several intriguing insights into paleontological features and discoveries. As I begin my journey, it is slightly overcast with a cool wind and a temperature in the mid-seventies. The trail is sandy with several "ups and downs." I'm doing the self-guided tour of the trail; however, depending upon the availability of staff it may be possible to have a guided tour by a park ranger explaining all the various sites.

The first stop along the trail is at the Mowry Shale site. The shale was laid down about 100 million years ago, when this area was an inland sea.

What remains for visitors to see today is a profusion of fossilized fish scales (fish scales?) from ancient aquatic creatures.

After exiting the shale site, I walk into an abandoned quarry surrounded by russet-colored cliffs on three sides. There's a fairly steep trail coming out of the canyon, and it begins to ascend up the side of a vegetation-less hill. Here, paleontologists discovered fossils representing ten different species of dinosaurs, ranging in size from about seven inches to seventy-six feet. Sliding across the rock face and joining up with the trail is a spur trail, along which are numerous fossils embedded in the hillside.

As I walk up the precarious spur trail, I come upon the vertebrae of some unknown dinosaur embedded in the rock face. The flyer I obtained back at the visitor's center does not describe this fossil (with a very distinctive white arrow pointing it out), so I'm left to my own imagination as to what creature might have owned it a few million years ago. I snap a few photos and then inch my way further up the side of the hill. There I encounter a femur embedded in the rock face. Once again, a very thoughtful

Over 1,600 bones are exposed on the Quarry Exhibit Hall face. (Photo courtesy of Jonathan Fredericks)

individual has been kind enough to paint a very large white arrow on the side of the cliff pointing to the femur so that photographically inclined visitors can easily identify it and take any number of photos (of real dinosaur bones!) to impress their friends back home. I'm no different.

While picking my way up the narrow trail etched into the side of the cliff face, I encounter a couple coming down. We carefully slide by each other on the precipitous footpath (avoiding physical contact, as is the usual custom in crowded theaters, filled-to-capacity airplanes, and along dinosaur trails in Utah). We exchange pleasantries and, as one of them passes, she points to the femur embedded in the rock face above us and says, "I sure hope I can get my old bones down this hill before they wind up like those old bones!"

At the top of the trail, where I have to make a precarious U-turn and ease back down the way I came, another leg bone is lodged in the substrate. It has been trenched (a small "canyon" has been dug all around it) so as to make it readily visible to anyone who passes near. Once again, I'm left to my own imagination about its original owner.

Shortly after my descent, I take another spur trail off to my right and into the Stump Formation. This area, too, was part of an enormous inland

A trenched leg bone waits at the top of the trail.

sea approximately 163 million years ago. The formation reveals additional evidence of aquatic life, including belemnites (a relative of the squid), snails, clams, and ammonites. Scattered across the face of several large horizontal rocks are numerous trace fossil impressions of small clam-like creatures.

I rejoin the main trail that ascends a steep slope along the side of the original visitor's center (this is where the tram drops off hikers for a reverse hike along the trail). I make my way down the asphalt road and back to the temporary visitor's center and the very cold bottle of water waiting inside the soda machine.

The monument is fairly quiet for a summer day. Even though it's noon-time, there are only about twenty cars in the parking area. Most of the people I meet in the visitor's center are a mix of older couples and young families coming to see the site. Most people, according to the rangers, are aware that the main visitor's center is closed. Yet, still the dinosaurs—from tens of millions of years in the past—send out their siren call.

As I pull out of the parking lot, I can hear my own internal siren call—my stomach, in no uncertain terms, tells me that it's time for lunch. Since there is only a smattering of homes in Jensen, and no restaurants, I decide to head back to the town of Dinosaur back in Colorado.

I pull into the Bedrock Depot (214 Brontosaurus Boulevard) on the edge of town—a 50s-style roadside restaurant that has undoubtedly seen generations of tourists pass by on their way to the dinosaur fields. As I step into the interior, I am greeted by a large sign advertising a variety of di-nosaur-themed coffee drinks. These include Amerisaurus (espresso and water), Lattesaurus (espresso and steamed milk), Cappasaurus (espresso and foaming milk), and my favorite, Mochasaurus (espresso, chocolate, and steamed milk).

I grab a card to fill in my sandwich choice for lunch. ("We do not have any of these sandwiches already made. Each is prepared fresh—just for you.") I'm trying to decide between the "Allosaurus Delight" (chicken apple sausage topped with onion, roasted red pepper, grilled eggplant, Asiago cheese, and Drunken Goat cheese grilled on focaccia bread spread with sun-dried tomato pesto and basil pesto), and the "Pteranodon Treat" (oven roasted turkey topped with sprouts, onions, sauerkraut, almonds, Asiago

The Bedrock Depot Restaurant in Dinosaur, Colorado, where lunch is always a (prehistoric) treat!

cheese, roasted red pepper, and mozzarella cheese on focaccia bread spread with [Bedrock Depot] Pteranodon sauce). I realize that I'm probably going to cause some type of egregious dinosaurian gaffe by ordering the "Pteranodon Treat" (since Pteranodons were not dinosaurs); but at this point in the day my stomach takes precedence over the scientific protocol of my journey.

I am not disappointed! The sandwich, when it arrives steaming hot fifteen minutes later, is a delectable indulgence ($7.95). The blend of ingredients and the tang of spices is an amazing sensual pleasure. The cheeses are electric with flavor, the red peppers caress the palate, and the almonds (surprisingly) are a toasty delight. From my perch at an outside table, I savor each mouthful with delicious abandon and gaze out to the high desert (and decidedly prehistoric) vistas that surround me. I will definitely come back to this slightly out-of-way, but definitely epicurean, restaurant on a return trip to the (future, and hopefully soon to be opened) new visitor's center at Dinosaur National Monument. My taste buds will be ready!

NEED TO KNOW ABOUT **Dinosaur National Monument**

DIRECTIONS Okay, okay, you just might have to slide over to another state (whose name I can't remember right now) in order to view one of the country's best-known dinosaur sites. But, then again, maybe we shouldn't trust those folks at Google or Rand McNally. For all I know, they may have used the same surveyors that were used to determine the original western boundary of Colorado. I don't know—it's just all too confusing for me right now.

That said, the most direct route to Dinosaur National Monument is to travel west from Denver on I-70 to Rifle, Colorado (approximately 183 miles). Take the exit for CO13 and follow it north toward Meeker. After about 40 miles, take a left on CO 64 west toward Rangely (about 78 miles). Go through Rangely and follow CO 64 west to Dinosaur, Colorado. In Dinosaur, turn west (left) on UT 40 to Jensen, Utah. Shortly after crossing the Green River and just before Jensen, turn north (right) on UT 149 and follow the signs for the visitor's center. Driving time from Denver is about five and a half hours.

From Grand Junction, head west on I-70. Take the Loma exit (Exit #15) and head north on CO 139 to Rangely. The road ends at CO 64. Make a left (heading west) on CO 64 and go through Rangely. Follow CO 64 west to Dinosaur, Colorado. In Dinosaur, turn west (left) on UT 40 to Jensen, Utah. Shortly after crossing the Green River and just before Jensen, turn north (right) on UT 149 and follow the signs for the visitor's center. Driving time from Grand Junction is about two and a half to three hours (depending on how many [very slow] trucks are going up and over the [very high] Douglas Pass on CO 139).

CONTACT INFORMATION Dinosaur National Monument, 4545 E. Highway 40, Dinosaur, CO 81610-9724; Quarry Visitor Center-Utah (435) 781-7700; Canyon Visitor Center-CO (970) 374-3000; http://www.nps.gov/dino/index.htm (NOTE: For information including Directions, Operating Hours and Seasons, Fees and Reservations, Campgrounds, Rafting Permits and Weather, please log on to the web site.)

FEES Private vehicle: $10.00; Motorcycle: $5.00; Individual (hiker, bicyclist): $5.00

HOURS New Quarry Visitor Center
Open daily, 9 a.m.–5 p.m. except Thanksgiving, Christmas, and New Year's Day; Quarry Exhibit Hall: 9:15 a.m.–4:45 p.m. (last trip up to the fossils is at 4:15).

BEST TIME TO VISIT
Year-round, except for Thanksgiving, Christmas, and New Year's.

CAMPING/LODGING   There are six developed campgrounds at Dinosaur National Monument—three on the Utah side of the monument (Green River, Split Mountain, Rainbow Park) and three on the Colorado side of the monument (Echo Park, Deerlodge Park, Gates of Lodore). Reservations are available only for group sites during high-use season.

There are no lodging establishments in Jensen. However, thirteen miles west on UT 40 is the town of Vernal—a town where there is no shortage of inns, hotels, motels, B&Bs, and dinosaur-themed accommodations of every imaginable shape and size. There is no lodging in the town of Dinosaur, but you may contact the Colorado Welcome Center in Dinosaur (970-374-2205) for additional lodging information throughout the area.

SERVICES   There are rest rooms and water at the visitor's center at Dinosaur National Park. There are soda machines and snacks available. A well-stocked gift shop has all manner of dinosaurian souvenirs available for sale.

ACCESS   Quarry Visitor Center: Reserved parking spaces are available with accessible walkways to the visitor center. Canyon Area Visitor Center: Reserved parking spaces are available with accessible walkways leading to the Canyon Area Visitor Center. The exhibits, bookstore, and restrooms are accessible.

DIFFICULTY RATING   The Fossil Discovery Trail is moderate. It will take between forty-five minutes to an hour to complete.

NOTES   There's a lot to learn here—for both adults and kids alike. Take the time to savor all the informative displays in the visitor's center and look at the array of books and souvenirs in the gift shop.

The hike along the Fossil Discovery Trail has three areas for observation—including some Indian rock art at the Mowry Shale site, the dinosaur fossils embedded in the Morrison Formation site, and the Stump Formation. This trail can be traversed on your own or you may elect to take a ranger-led hike (if available) through this landscape.

I particularly enjoy the short side hike up the side of the cliff at the Morrison Formation to see the embedded dinosaur fossils. The trail is a little tricky at times (hold on to Grandma's hand), but you'll get a rare opportunity to get up close and personal with some impressive (and well-labeled) fossils (be sure to take lots of photos).

CHAPTER 4

Dinosaur at the Airport

RIGGS HILL

United Airlines flight 268 from Harrisburg arrived at Terminal B of Chicago's O'Hare Airport on time. I had about two hours to kill before my connecting westbound flight and began to stroll down the concourse observing the scurrying parade of frantic businesspeople, perpetually lost tourists, and iPoded teenagers. I was hungry and needed something to eat before squeezing myself back into a tight-fitting airplane seat with no snack service (and a very bad movie) for three hours.

As I wended my way through the concourse looking for a meal appropriate for a humanoid carnivore, I could see an enormous dinosaur skeleton looming in the distance. It was "stepping" through a secure area of the airport like some animated creature from a 1950s science fiction movie preparing to snatch up any weaving taxicabs or screaming debutantes. Swooping down from the head was an elongated series of vertebrae attached to an enormous skeleton. A long bony tail whipped out behind the beast—the entire assembly extended to nearly seventy-five feet in length.

Arriving at the base of this prehistoric skeleton I noticed a small sign which read:

An ancient traveler strolls through Chicago's O'Hare Airport

This replica of the plant-eating dinosaur Brachiosaurus is based on bones in the collection of the Field Museum. This dinosaur lived 150 million years ago in what is today Colorado and Utah and was discovered in 1900 on a Field Museum Expedition. This discovery reintroduced the world to these long-extinct giants.

Underneath the left side of "this replica" was a Field Museum store with the requisite displays of dinosaur T-shirts, books about Chicago, videos, stuffed toys, candles, hand gel, playing cards, necklaces, and other curios commonly associated with dinosauria and paleontology.

As I surveyed this gargantuan creature, I noticed that the skull, which loomed forty-five feet above the passing crowds, was "looking" to its left and down the concourse at an eclectic array of fast food restaurants and snack purveyors.*

Then I asked myself, "How did a 150-million-year-old dinosaur from Colorado get itself posed standing over the United Airlines Customer Service Desk at one of the world's busiest airports?" The connection between dinosaurs (ancestral relatives of modern-day birds), birds (winged creatures able to fly), and airplanes (winged machines able to fly … while entombing humanoid creatures for extended periods of time) was not lost on me. However, the complete answer to my question required an investigation into the life and discoveries of Elmer Riggs.

Elmer. As much as I would like to, I simply can't remember ever meeting an individual with the name "Elmer." I have certainly been to my share of cocktail parties, "power lunches," conferences, and various social functions without once meeting a person named Elmer. It may be because I run in circles that exclude Elmers, or perhaps it's because Elmer is not as common a name as Brittany, or Brad, or Tiffany (names which certainly get more press in *People* magazine than any "Elmer" ever would). As part of my research

---

*I imagine that, just like every prehistoric herbivore, this particular *Brachiosaurus* was probably thinking to itself (assuming it had a brain to do so), "Gee, I sure am getting tired of eating nothing but cycads and other vegetable matter every day. I could sure use a caramel macchiato or a caffe latte about now!"

agenda, I Googled "Elmer" and discovered that in 1880 "Elmer" was the thirty-seventh most popular name given to boys. However, by 2007 "Elmer" had fallen to the bottom of the nomenclature pool—residing at 866th place among names given to American baby boys.* That seems particularly odd when you consider that this Germanic name actually means "noble and famous." One would think that given today's climate of celebrity adulation, more parents would want to name their newborn sons "Elmer" than say, "Cade" (round, lumpy; barrel-maker), "Mallory" (luckless), or even "Travis" (toll collector).

It may have been prophetic, but when Mr. and Mrs. Riggs crowned their son "Elmer," little did they know how accurate that name was to become in the annals of paleontology. For most of his early life, Elmer Riggs had an overwhelming fascination with science. However, it wasn't until he became the assistant curator of geology for the Field Columbian Museum (later renamed the Field Museum of Natural History) that he truly found his calling.

Curious about the prospects for fossil discoveries in the West, in 1899 Riggs sent letters to rural towns throughout the western U.S. He particularly selected towns that were close to the railroad, which would facilitate the transport of any heavily-jacketed dinosaur bones to the East after they has been discovered. Since plaster-entombed bones often weighed six tons (or more), this was a most intelligent decision.

He received one promising reply that sent him to southern Wyoming in 1899. He had also heard about the Grand Valley, but in an interview conducted several years later he stated that, "Before I went there I learned there was a publication by a man connected with the U.S. Geological Survey who'd been into the Grand Valley, and he came back and reported it was nonfossiliferous," meaning there were no fossils to be found. However, Riggs was sufficiently persuaded by several local residents that a visit might prove fortuitous.

One of the letters Riggs received was from Dr. S. M. Bradbury, a dentist in Grand Junction. Dr. Bradbury was also president of the Western Colorado Academy of Science. Bradbury wrote that "dinosaur bones have been

*The most popular baby name for boys in 1880 was John (God is gracious). The #1 name for baby boys in 2007 was Jacob (supplanter; held by the heel). Interestingly, Jacob was the most popular boy's name for eight consecutive years, from 1999 through 2007. According to U.S. voter registration records, some of the least common (least popular?) names for males include Burritt, Dainis, Sovandara, and Wattie.

known locally since 1885 and have been collected largely as 'curios' by local ranchers." This was just what Riggs had been hoping for, and he quickly mounted an expedition to the Grand Junction area in the late spring of 1900. Riggs later recalled, "We were eager to get into that man's office and see some of the things they had, and to ride out with him and see whatever he was prepared to show us."

The first place Riggs and his party began excavating was an area that is now part of the Colorado National Monument. Tucked deep in the crimson hills and eye-popping sandstone formations of this geologically intriguing area, Riggs discovered a shoulder and vertebrae of a *Camarasaurus*. These Jurassic Period creatures, whose fossils are plentiful throughout the West, are represented by juvenile specimens at a number of sites. As these juveniles were among the first of their species to be discovered, there was considerable speculation that this dinosaur was much smaller than it is now known to be.

Later, Riggs and his crew ventured a little closer to Grand Junction, specifically to a boulder-strewn hill overlooking the town (it's now known as Riggs Hill). It was here that they discovered the fossilized bones of a previously unknown dinosaur, *Brachiosaurus**—the same critter that now gazes longingly down Terminal B at the Starbucks store at O'Hare Airport.** As a matter of scientific precision, it should be noted that the actual bones of Riggs' *Brachiosaurus* are stored at the Field Museum; the United Airlines specimen is made of fiberglass due to the original skeleton's fragility and size. According to museum spokeswoman Nancy O'Shea, "An unwieldy amount of metal armature [around the original skeleton] would have been required to hold the actual bones in place."

Years later Riggs would recall, "This fellow was a record breaker for size for that time. It was a jim-dandy. I only wish I had the whole skeleton of him." Shortly after the bones were shipped back to Chicago, one Chicago paper bragged that the Windy City "has the largest land animal that ever

* *Brachiosaurus* means "arm lizard," a reference to its large size and the fact that its long humerus made its front legs longer than its back ones.

** In 1994, this skeleton was mounted in the Stanley Field Hall, the main lobby of the Field Museum in Chicago. At the end of 1999, it was disassembled and moved to O'Hare Airport in order to make way for "Sue," the world's largest and most complete *T. rex* (see Chapter 7) and the museum's (current) pride and joy. I guess that even 65 million-year-old carnivores still know how to throw their weight around.

lived." On October 14, 1900, the *Boston Journal* proclaimed it to be "The Monster of All Ages." In somewhat of a journalistic overstatement, the article went on to state that the dinosaur would have been over seventy-five feet tall—when, in reality, a height closer to forty feet would have been more accurate.

The discovery of the *Brachiosaurus* consumed most of the 1900 field season for Riggs. He returned to Chicago, but came back in 1901 to lead another expedition to the Grand Junction area. It was during this venture that he made one of the most significant and mind-boggling discoveries in the field of paleontology. But, dear readers, you'll have to wait until the next chapter (Chapter 5) to read what that was.

I began my journey to Riggs Hills by driving southward from Fruita on CO 340. This meandering road skirts the edge of the Colorado National Monument with its striking cliffs, dynamic rock formations, and deep shadows splayed across multi-colored boulders. The drama is simply eye-popping! On this day, the sunlight sprinkled down the eastern face of the sandstone formations making the vista even more impressive and spectacular. CO 340 eventually becomes South Broadway as it winds its way through a residential area of Redlands, an enclave of ranch-style homes and wood-rail fences. Directly across from Meadows Way is the entrance to Riggs Hill, a dusty gravel road with a sign that reads: "Private Property of the Museum of Western Colorado. Public visitation is permitted 7:00 a.m.–7:00 p.m."

I am the only visitor, and I ease my rental car into a space directly in front of a kiosk that has three tired and very empty display cases. There is little here to designate the location as one of the most significant paleontological sites in Colorado or even the fact that it is, indeed, Riggs Hill. Scattered across the face of the hill is a profusion of darkened boulders. I learn later that the black stain is known as desert varnish. It is the result of the oxidation of iron and manganese on the surface of the rocks.

I load up with my "necessaries"—two bottles of water, camera, tape recorder, insect repellant, and an extra-large economy-size bottle of sunscreen.

The start of the trail around Riggs Hill with the Colorado National Monument in the background.

It's early afternoon and the sun has taken its preferred position in the sky—directly overhead and pulsating with solar energy. I start my trek just to the left of the information-less kiosk. I quickly realize that the informative brochure ("Riggs Hill Trail Map") I obtained from the Museum of Western Colorado is a necessity, given that there are no interpretive signs anywhere along the trail. The brochure adequately explains each of the eight numbered posts along the trail.

Signs #1 and #2 point out selected geological features of Riggs Hill including a sandstone cap on the top of the Burro Canyon Formation, which acts as a protective barrier against the forces of erosion. I also note an enormous boulder that is covered with distinctive markings—the result of prehistoric stream channeling so common in this area.

Sign #3 indicates that the crusty gray material underfoot is bentonite. According to my geology colleagues, bentonite is described as an "absorbent aluminum phyllosilicate." While that description almost sounds like something I might use to spread over my increasingly balding cranium or on an extreme case of poison ivy, I did learn that bentonite usually forms from a weathering of volcanic ash. There's some higher-level chemistry involved here (most of which is far beyond my level of comprehension), but I also learned that there are two main classes of bentonite, both of which have industrial uses.

Sodium bentonite expands when it becomes wet. As a result, it is often used as a sealant in ditches and ponds, as well as a waterproofing material for walls and wells. Calcium bentonite, on the other hand, is an ingredient in Fuller's Earth, which was one of the first industrial cleaning agents. Curiously, bentonite seems to have myriad commercial uses including, but not limited to, adhesives, cement, ceramic glazes, cat litter, steelmaking, pyrotechnics (fireworks), and as a treatment for oily skin. In fact, the acne cream Clearasil® uses bentonite in order to absorb excess dermatological oil, or sebum. Not bad for something that spewed out of a volcano a couple of million years ago.

Carefully picking my way across the slurry of bentonite, I arrive at Marker #4 on the trail. Here I discover a small stone monument in which is set a bronze plaque that reads: "Brachyosaurus the Giant Dinosaur—first known skeleton discovered here in 1900 by Elmer S. Riggs and preserved in Field Museum." Sharp-eyed readers will note that in addition to a small grammatical error on the plaque (there's a missing "the" in front of "Field Museum") there is also a glaring spelling mistake ("Brachyosaurus"). One can only imagine the look on Mr. Riggs' face when he returned to this site in 1938 for the dedication of the commemorative marker—a marker that recognized one of the world's earliest and most significant paleontological discoveries—only to discover that some idiot couldn't even spell the name of his dinosaur correctly. And, to add additional insult to the injury, a corrected plaque has never replaced the original.

Right next to the trail and just across from the commemorative plaque there is a concrete cast of several vertebrae of Riggs' *Brachiosaurus* (please note the correct spelling). After taking several photographs of this cast, I use my hand to measure one of the vertebrae—which is two hands (sixteen inches) in length. Assuming that this is an accurate model* of a portion of the

---

*I suspect, although I can't confirm, that this model was placed on the ground in an effort to appease any irate grammarians or English majors who may visit this particular site. It does, however, show the location and approximate orientation of the skeleton.

The misspelled commemorative plaque celebrating the momentous discovery by Elmer Riggs.

Brachiosaurus vertebrae, it provides for an interesting comparison. According to one of my biology colleagues, an average adult human male who stands about six feet tall has thoracic (in the middle region of the back) vertebrae that measure approximately three-quarters of an inch apiece. Thus, a single *Brachiosaurus* vertebra is more than twenty-one times the length of a single human vertebra.

I walk a short distance up the hill—around the site of Riggs' discovery (marked by the concrete bones and monument). Large oxidized rocks litter the hillside, making it look as though all the boulders had all been in an enormous forest fire. As I look down on the original quarry, there are no other artifacts for visitors to consider. Nevertheless, the harsh conditions (the temperature is inching into triple digits) and remoteness of this location more than a century ago made Riggs' discovery of the first *Brachiosaurus* that much more amazing.

A reconstructed *Brachiosaurus* vertebrae near the quarry.

Brachiosaurus* was truly one of the tallest dinosaurs—not just during the Late Jurassic Period (161.2 to 145.5 million years ago)—but throughout the entire time dinosaurs roamed the land. Its browsing height has been estimated to be more than forty-five feet, higher than the fourth floor of an average apartment building (assuming, of course, that there would have been any condos or apartments around when *Brachiosaurus* was extant). This extreme height was advantageous in collecting food from the treetops (specifically conifers, ginkgoes, and cycads) that were out of reach for other, somewhat shorter, herbivores.

This critter was about eighty-two feet long. That would make it about five times longer than the Toyota Tacoma truck I drive. As a further comparison, the creature would be more than eight times longer than a BMW Mini Cooper (the vehicle I'd really like to be driving). Even more distinctive than its extreme length was the configuration of its body. Scientists, including Riggs, initially made the mistake of assuming that the front legs and back legs were of equal length. Take a look at a horse, or cow, or elephant and you will quickly notice that all four legs are of equal length. That same assumption was frequently applied to dinosaur fossils. However, later discoveries showed that the *Brachiosaurus* had front legs that were considerably longer than its hind legs. This discrepancy created a sloping back rather than a horizontal backbone. Riggs, like many of his contemporaries, assumed that the longer limb bones of his discovery were part of the rear legs—as they would have been with other sauropods. In fact, he initially identified the upper foreleg bone (humerus) as the upper hind leg (femur).**

In term of size, this behemoth weighed in at a staggering fifty to eighty tons. Early estimates pegged its weight at around seventy to eighty tons, but more recent discoveries have downscaled this approximation by about twenty tons. As a weight comparison, the *Brachiosaurus* would weigh as much as eight African elephants, or 109 thoroughbred horses, or 10,000

---

*You may recall *Brachiosaurus* from the first *Jurassic Park* movie. It was the creature that sneezed on the little girl who, with her brother and the Sam Neill character, was up in a tree.
**In the "Riggs Hill Trail Map" there is a photograph of a six-foot, ten-inch femur (upper leg bone) that towers over one of Riggs' field assistants (H.W. Menke). This *Brachiosaurus* bone was part of a creature that stood forty feet tall and was seventy-five feet long.

domestic cats (like the gray mass of fur currently purring under my computer table). Interestingly, the *Brachiosaurus* would be less than half the weight of an adult male blue whale (150 tons), which is the largest animal

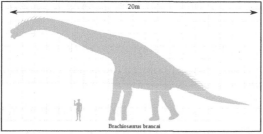

Brachiosaurus brancai

Brachiosaurus (from Wikimedia Commons under the terms of the GNU Free Documentation License)

(in total weight) known to have ever lived on the planet.

Early depictions of the *Brachiosaurus* showed a creature that spent its days partially submerged in large lakes or other aquatic environments. This was primarily due to the position of its nasal openings, which are located on the top of its head, above and in front of the eyes. It was initially believed that the critter used its long neck as a snorkel-like device as it foraged for food on the lake bottom. Later calculations of its rib cage and physiology indicated that water pressure would have made it nearly impossible for *Brachiosaurus* to breathe adequately. As a result, current illustrations have relegated the critter to a more terrestrial environment.

Given its extreme size, one might wonder why a dinosaur like *Brachiosaurus* was so large. There are several possibilities. First of all, an extra long neck would allow access to foliage that was out of the reach of smaller, less well-endowed critters. This provided a feeding advantage in the competition for limited resources. Its large size also provided the *Brachiosaurus* protection against predators, especially smaller carnivores. Although it had few physical defenses, its enormous size would have been more than a visual deterrent to any would-be attackers.

As I continue my journey, the trail undulates across the backside of the hill. It's rough in spots, and I have to watch my step across the bentonite layer. Eventually the trail begins an uphill ascent to Marker #5, which identifies an exposed sandstone layer in the side of the hill. According to geologists, this layer is indicative of a deposit left over from a flooded prehistoric stream channel. While it is seemingly unremarkable, it is an interesting counter-point to the checkerboard grid of suburban sprawl that flanks three sides of this paleontological site. Humans and their habitations are recent imports to this area—or, as I like to think about it: architecture is temporary, geology is forever.

The trail gets more pitched as I wend my way up to Marker #6. Here is another cache of rusty boulders and sienna-colored rocks. This marks the Holt Quarry, which is nothing more than a tumble of oversized boulders arcing down from the top of the hill. It was here in 1937 that a high school teacher by the name of Edward Holt unearthed the remains of *Stegosaurus*, *Allosaurus*, and another *Brachiosaurus* (and, yes, I double checked the spelling of all three names). According to the "Riggs Hills Trail Map," Holt wanted to leave "the especially well-preserved, articulated fossils intact hoping that they would become a natural exhibit." Unfortunately, what Mr. Holt did not consider was the tendency of humanoid predators to remove those specimens piece by piece for their own personal collections—thus robbing the scientific community of some of the most valuable prehistoric artifacts ever discovered. Although the bones were buried under a blanket of dirt by some local citizens, souvenir hunter after souvenir hunter plundered the site until every last relic of the past had disappeared from the site.

As the curator of paleontology for the Dinosaur Journey Museum in Fruita, John Foster knows vandalism well. He must contend with this issue on a regular basis (you'll have an opportunity to meet John in greater detail in Chapter 12). I asked John about the problem of site vandalism at various fossil sites.

"Yes, vandalism is a bit of a problem—and it's not just a recent problem. Ed Holt's site out at Riggs Hill had an articulated *Stegosaurus* in it that got plundered by Grand Junctionites over several years till nothing was left … and that was back in the 1930s. So it's not a new phenomenon."

John mentions that the vandalism occurs at quarries, along trails, and anywhere there might be the chance for some type of paleontological theft. In some locations, the fossils are exposed, which means there is not much that can be done to protect them. In other cases, the fossils are part of an active "dig" and must be buried and deceptively covered over every evening by the field crew in order to prevent any midnight robberies. John mentions that "sometimes the best approach is public education and trying to increase the traffic." To do that, the Bureau of Land Management works with paleontologists to put up signs reminding folks that it's illegal to remove fossils from public land.

There is also a concerted effort to make more people aware of a site and its potential treasures. As John puts it, "The more preservation-minded people frequent one of these sites, the more it will police itself through decreased opportunities to remove material." The overriding philosophy is that the busier a site, the less likely it is that vandals will try to get away with something. Since federal land management agencies don't have the law enforcement staff to patrol these areas, it's often up to the general public to act as a deterrent to any potential vandalism that might occur. As John states, "... [we] basically [rely] on the majority of honest visitors to scare off the poachers."

John told me about an incident that occurred at the Mygatt-Moore Quarry (see Chapter 2 and Chapter 12) a few years ago. It seems as though some vandals ripped out a jacketed set of bones from the quarry late one night. However, they neglected to see that only the top was jacketed. They proceeded to drag it down the trail to the gate (presumably to load it into a pickup truck). As they were dragging their loot along the gravely trail, rock and bones were falling out of the bottom, so that by the time they arrived at the entrance gate there was nothing left. When the field crew arrived the next day, they found the empty jacket and a trail of bones and rock all the way back up to the quarry. There was a cache of several wheelbarrows parked about twenty-five feet from the site—wheelbarrows that would have aided considerably in the theft of the jacketed bones, but which, for unexplained reasons, were not used by the thieves.

Suffice it to say, vandalism is a constant part of paleontology. During my travels throughout Colorado, I learned of several sites that had been intentionally buried by scientists working the site and essentially erased from the geological map in order to prevent any possible looting. The locations of these sites are known to only a few select individuals and they will remain in paleontological limbo until they can be adequately guarded and preserved—perhaps in another generation.

After departing the Holt Quarry, I continue my ascent up the hill. I pass by Marker #7, which provides a grand view of the peach orchard region of this seemingly arid environment. The rocky and steep incline continues its skyward ascent. It almost seems as though I'll never reach the top. I eventually reach a small flat area where the trail splits. Off to my left is an inviting ramada offering well-needed shade and a place to rest my now weary legs. Off to my right, the trail continues its ascent up to the top of the mountain. Which path would a logical person choose? Obviously, the sun has shriveled up any remaining brain cells and I elect to take the tortuous trail up to the very pinnacle of this hill.

After creeping and pulling my weary bones up the rocky face of this hill (which to my less than physically fit body seems more like an assault on K2), I arrive at a small plateau on the top. Just as it is described in the brochure, the view here is simply incredible. In front of me are the soaring sandstone cliffs of Colorado National Monument. Off to my right is a vast arid expanse of undulating hills and crimson outcroppings sliding past the town of Fruita in the distance. To my left is the spectacular Colorado River snaking its way past Grand Junction and on to its magnificent passage through the Grand Canyon. This is a view very few people get to experience, and I am glad I had the fortitude (or innate stupidity) to continue my final ascent up the hill.

Eventually, the direct rays of the afternoon sun bring me back to reality, and I realize that it's time to wend my way down off the hill and back to the parking area. As I pick my way down the slope, I pass by the ramada and head down a semi-steep slope covered with bentonite and small rounded pebbles. Keeping a close eye on my clumsy feet, I slowly descend the twisting trail.

Reaching my car, I grab a lone bottle of water unintentionally left in the back seat. I rip open the top and begin to guzzle this aqueous treat. It is only then that I realize that the water, over the course of the past hour, has been heated to a temperature only a few degrees shy of scalding. No matter ... it is wet and it is quenching.

NEED TO KNOW ABOUT **Riggs Hill**

DIRECTIONS   From I-70, take Exit 31 (Horizon Drive) in Grand Junction. Head southwest on Horizon Drive (the airport is northeast on Horizon Drive). Make a left on North 12th Street and head south. Continue heading south on North 12th Street, crossing over Patterson Road and North Avenue. Turn right (west) onto Grand Avenue. Pass through a major intersection (U.S. highway 50) and across the Colorado River. Grand Avenue is now CO 340. Pass Monument Road (on your left) and continue on CO 340 for approximately three miles. Turn left onto South Broadway (the road will be Vista Grande Drive on your right). Travel on this road for about one mile until you reach a parking area on the right side of the road.

CONTACT INFORMATION   Before starting out, be sure to obtain a Riggs Hill Trail Map brochure from Dinosaur Journey. The brochure is essential to understanding the eight numbered posts along the trail. Dinosaur Journey, 550 Jurassic Court, Fruita, CO, (970) 858-7282, www.dinosaurjourney.org

FEES   None.

HOURS   Open seven days a week, 7:00 a.m. to 7:00 p.m.

BEST TIME TO VISIT   All times of the year.

CAMPING/LODGING   Grand Junction has loads of camping sites, hotels, motels, inns, B&Bs, and other types of lodging. Contact the Grand Junction Visitor and Convention Bureau (www.visitgrandjunction.com) for the most up-to-date listings.

SERVICES   There is one shade ramada along the trail (after Sign #7). There are no toilet facilities or available water. There are no trash receptacles, so you will need to pack out your own trash.

continued next page

continued from previous page

ACCESS   The trail is not wheelchair accessible, nor is it appropriate for those with visual impairment.

DIFFICULTY RATING   Moderate to slightly strenuous. The three-quarter mile loop trail takes about one hour to walk.

NOTES   Although this site has considerable historical significance, there is not a lot to see or experience, particularly for kids. There are no interpretive signs, thus making the brochure—"Riggs Hill Trail Map"—an absolute necessity for any hiker. For those interested in putting a perspective on the *Brachiosaurus* at Chicago's O'Hare Airport, this would be an excellent exclamation point.

Mostly, this site will give you an appreciation for the rigors of paleontological work—particularly for those who set out in the early 1900s with little more than a dream and a few crude tools. If you decide to climb to the very top of Riggs Hill, you will observe a vista that few ever see. The view is simply incredible and will provide you with both perspective and appreciation for the diversity of geological formations and locations that are so much a part of this Western Slope environment.

Please keep in mind that Riggs Hill offers no dinosaur fossils, dinosaur illustrations, or dinosaur memorabilia (save for a single misspelled plaque and a lone concrete faux vertebrae). What you will get, however, is a moderately challenging hike, a series of incredible vistas, and the ghosts of a time long since gone.

CHAPTER 5

You Say "To-MAY-to" and I Say "To-MAH-to"

DINOSAUR HILL

It is said that one of the joys of growing older and having a fading memory is that you keep making new friends every fifteen minutes. If that's the case, then I can look forward to a whole raft of new acquaintances every time my wife and I go out to a social engagement or cocktail party.

I haven't forgotten anyone yet (have I?), but it is true that my memory of people's names is one of the constant challenges I face as my hair gets grayer and my wrinkles get more pronounced. But, you would think that scientists, who are all so young (and so highly intelligent), would have absolutely no problem with names. You would think that all of them would recognize that an animal that walks like a duck, talks like a duck, and looks like a duck should be called … a duck! That would seem to be pretty logical. Unfortunately, there seems to be disagreement in some scientific circles (but not in any duck circles) about the names ascribed to certain species—particularly certain species of dinosaurs.

Here's how the whole convoluted story began: Back in 1877, paleontologist Othniel C. Marsh (who was a central character in the infamous "Bones Wars" soon to be described in Chapter 8) and his crew unearthed an immature dinosaur skeleton at Morrison, Colorado. He decided to name this new species *Apatosaurus*—a name that means "deceptive lizard." He chose that name because the chevron bones (bones in the tail section) were quite similar to those of a prehistoric marine lizard known as *Mosasaurus*.

Then, in 1879, Marsh and his crew discovered a much larger, much more complete skeleton at Como Bluff, Wyoming. Marsh thought that this new discovery represented a new genus and so he named it *Brontosaurus* (which, in Greek, means "thunder lizard") due to its enormous size. At the time, this was one of the largest and most complete dinosaur skeletons ever discovered. Catching the public's fever for things dinosaurian, the Peabody Museum of Natural History at Yale University decided, in 1905, to create what was to be the first mounted display of a sauropod skeleton. The mounted skeleton, permanently tagged with the genus *Brontosaurus*, effectively cemented that name in the collective minds of the general public—particularly given its popularity at the museum.

However (and this is where it really gets interesting), study of the Wyoming specimen showed that the *Brontosaurus* was really something else. In fact, it was our friend Elmer Riggs who, in 1903, published a paper in the *Geological Series of the Field Columbian Museum* pointing out that *Brontosaurus* was not quite different enough from *Apatosaurus* to warrant its own genus (oh, shame, shame on Mr. Marsh). Mr. Riggs put it this way:

> The genus Brontosaurus was based chiefly upon the structure of the scapula and the presence of five vertebrae in the sacrum. After examining the type specimens of these genera, and making a careful study of the unusually well-preserved specimen described in this paper, the writer is convinced that the Apatosaurus specimen is merely a young animal of the form represented in the adult by the Brontosaurus specimen. ...In view of these facts the two genera may be regarded as synonymous. As the term "Apatosaurus" has priority, "Brontosaurus" will be regarded as a synonym.

In essence, we now had one animal with two different names—something of a scientific "no-no."

The case was taken up by the International Commission on Zoological Nomenclature (ICZN), whose task it is to "… create, publish and, periodically, to revise the International Code of Zoological Nomenclature" and to rule "on specific cases of nomenclatural uncertainty." It is the convention of the commission that "… if newly discovered fossils are ascribed to one genus and/or species, but then it becomes clear they actually belong to an existing, already described genus and/or species (are you still with me?), the first name takes precedence." The commission thus ruled that since the creature was originally named *Apatosaurus,* it would retain that name. As a result, the name *Brontosaurus* was officiously (and unceremoniously) deleted from official dinosaur lists.

But, as you might imagine, the story doesn't exactly end there.

You see, the ICZN—being a committee—took its time wrestling with this nomenclature stuff ("You say to-MAY-to and I say to-MAH-to.")—a couple of years to be exact. During that time the world became fascinated with, and almost obsessed with, dinosaurs of every size, shape, and disposition. Dinosaur fossils were turning up left and right, and the general public just couldn't get enough of them. In short, dinosaurs were the *American Idol*s of the early 1900s. And the bigger they were, the more popular they were (sort of like the gangly center on your hometown basketball team). *Brontosaurus* achieved near mythical stardom in popular culture—in newspapers and the growing movie industry.*

As a result, its name proved difficult to eradicate from the public consciousness. To legions of people the word "Brontosaurus" sounded much more dinosaurian than did "Apatosaurus." (Besides, it rolls off the tongue more smoothly … try it—say "Brontosaurus" three times in a row and then say "Apatosaurus" three times in a row. Did you notice how much easier it is saying the "B word" as opposed to the "A word"?) Interestingly, in 1989, the U.S. Post Office issued a set of four "prehistoric" stamps. Included was a stamp with an illustration of a *Brontosaurus.* A subsequent article in the *New York Times* (October 11, 1989) accused the Post Office of, among

*One of the most popular cartoon characters of the early twentieth century was "Gertie the Dinosaur"—often referred to (at least by her press agents) as a *Brontosaurus.*

other things, "fostering scientific illiteracy." The Post Office responded (in Postal Bulletin 21744) as follows: "Although now recognized by the scientific community as 'Apatosaurus,' the name 'Brontosaurus' was used for the stamp because it is more familiar to the general population."

Although *Brontosaurus* has been discredited in the scientific literature, it was—and still is—very much a part of the public's continuing fascination with things prehistoric. In essence, the name stuck then—as it still does today*—even though it is, and will continue to be, a scientific misnomer.

Elmer Riggs (our friend from Chapter 4) was, in 1900, knocking about the Grand Valley digging up dinosaurs—first in an area that was to eventually become the Colorado National Monument, and then on a hill just south of Grand Junction, which was to bear his name (Riggs Hill) several years later. Still itchy with "dino fever," Riggs was very reluctant to give up his search for dinosaurs and return to the cold confines of Chicago. So, he headed just slightly west to a site immediately across the river from the town of Fruita.

"I said to the boys, 'This seems to be a prosperous region. … We'd do well to prospect here for about three days,'" he recalled more than fifty years later. "And if we find things worthwhile we'll mark it and that will help to give us an urge to come back here another year."

Shortly after arriving at the hill that was to later become known as Dinosaur Hill, they located the skeleton of a very large dinosaur—one that in its life measured over seventy feet long and weighed in at more than thirty tons. But the season was drawing to a close and he couldn't begin his excavation. It wasn't until the following year (1901) that Riggs and his crew were able to return, intent on recovering the entire skeleton. However, they had to tackle another problem: getting any recovered bones across the Colorado River to the railroad station in Fruita for transportation back East.

"When we landed in Grand Junction, I went to a lumber dealer and gave him a sketch of a flat boat that was to be twenty-four feet long and ten

*Ask the next ten adults you meet to describe a *Brontosaurus* and they'll probably have very little difficulty doing so. Ask another ten adults to describe an *Apatosaurus* and they'll all draw a blank.

feet wide that I proposed to install on the old cable down at the river," Riggs said. "When we got the camp established, I got aboard my saddle horse— we had brought some saddle horses by that time—and rode back to Grand Junction and arranged to have the lumber delivered down on the bank of the river. And I fell to it and in two days I had nailed up that ferry boat."

After constructing their boat, Riggs and his crew had it fastened to a cable crossing the river, one that had been left over from a previous ferry. They scraped out a wagon road from the quarry site down to the edge of the river. This would allow them to transport any recovered bones down to the ferry landing by the river and eventually across the river and into Fruita for loading on an eastbound train.

The crew worked through the summer digging and blasting their way into the side of the hill. They used shovels and picks as well as some mining equipment borrowed from a nearby coal mining operation. By the end of the summer they had recovered approximately two-thirds of an *Apatosaurus* dinosaur that, encased in various plaster casts, weighed a total of six tons. The bones were from the back of the creature, and although they searched they could not find the head, neck, and front limbs—all of which (as Riggs surmised) may have been washed away in a prehistoric flood many millions of years ago.

Riggs' crew transported the bones very carefully and very slowly down from the quarry and across the hillside to the edge of the Colorado River. The plaster casts were loaded on the ferry and carefully carried across the sometimes unpredictable waters. Then they were unloaded at the railroad station in Fruita, where they were transported free of charge to Chicago (since they were scientific specimens) by the Denver and Rio Grande Railroad.

After their arrival in Chicago, the bones were mounted for display by a team of paleontologists at the Field Museum. However, Mr. Field, who was the founder and benefactor of the museum (and the man behind Marshall Field and Company, the Chicago-based department store), was quite adamant about having only real and actual materials on display at his museum. Thus, the original mount of the *Apatosaurus* was displayed missing the end of its tail (which may still be entombed in the mountain) and its front section. It was only after Mr. Field died (January 1906) that partly reconstructed bones for the front limbs, neck, head, and tail (found in Utah and Wyoming) were affixed to the original skeleton (sounds like the plot for a Frankenstein-inspired movie). The reconstructed skeleton of the *Apatosaurus* has been on exhibit at the Field Museum ever since 1908.*

After quarrying the dinosaur, Riggs rushed back to Chicago to supervise the reconstruction and eventual display of the skeleton. He later recalled, "It was the most important specimen that we found. It was one of the most important specimens that they have for the public at the Field Museum to this day." Visitors to the museum can still see the actual *Apatosaurus* (with a few added bones from various relatives) that Riggs and his crew extracted from Dinosaur Hill just south of Fruita.

Crisp Colorado skies and a cool breeze greet me as I leave my hotel and head out to Dinosaur Hill. I drive west on I-70 and take Exit 19 (Fruita) south. I quickly pass Dinosaur Journey Museum and the favorite restaurant of all carnivores—McDonalds. After approximately a mile, I come up to Rimrock Adventures on my left ("Rodeo Every Tuesday") and soon afterwards is the left turn onto the gravel road that leads to Dinosaur Hill. The short road terminates at a pebbly roundabout with plenty of parking for small cars or large RVs. My only company this day are two women who are power-walking the trail, performing body-twisting yoga exercises, and drinking large quantities of electrolytes as a defense against the soon-to-be punishing sun that is characteristic of the Grand Valley in summer.

I dress myself out as any professional explorer would do—bottles of water hang from my belt, my safari hat provides a small amount of portable shade, and I have liberally applied a large quantity of sunscreen on all areas of exposed flesh that I can reach. Notebook and camera in hand, I close up my car and walk twenty yards to the start of this prehistoric journey.

---

*In 1991 and 1992, the tunnel that Riggs and his crew had blasted into the side of the hill was re-opened by a team of local paleontologists. Inside they found tools that had been left behind by members of Riggs crew (apparently paleontologists are not as neat and tidy as one would suspect). They were also able to locate three tail chevrons (tailbones) and a rib segment of Riggs' original *Apatosaurus*.

The kiosks at the start of the trail around Dinosaur Hill have lots of good information.

Before me is a kiosk with all manner of informative posters, signs, and information. A brief history of the site and the discoveries made here is provided along with a note that Riggs' expedition was financed on just $800 for the entire field season. I also discover that while the party was crossing the river by ferry one day, the ropes to the boat snapped. As a result, much of their food supplies, and a half-ton of the cement needed to jacket any dinosaur bones, was lost to the ravages of the Colorado River. It was with a severely depleted storehouse of supplies that Riggs began his historic quest—putting him under enormous pressure to get his beloved *Apatosaurus* out of the hill and transport it back to Chicago with all deliberate speed.

In front of the kiosk are two beige-colored benches that are shaped, colored, and textured to look like a six-hundred pound *Apatosaurus* thigh bone. These replicas are based on photographs of bones uncovered by Riggs in 1901. I suppose that more than one photograph of kids sitting on these faux thigh bones has been taken by beaming parents and turned into a silly Christmas card with the likely caption: "Bobbie and Susie visit Dinosaur Hill in Colorado and sit on the lap of a very big dinosaur."

The trail that begins at the kiosk is well marked with concrete berms and a graded surface. The sandy path is easy to traverse, and I soon find myself at Marker #1, which identifies a boulder just slightly up the side of the hill. As I stare at the boulder I can see the mold of the femur (upper back leg bone) of a *Diplodocus* dinosaur. On the interpretive sign just below the mold is a 1930s photograph of amateur paleontologist Al Look with his arms extended around the ends of that same mold.

Unfortunately, the bone shown in the picture was later removed illegally from the mold. Again, the specter of scavengers and thieves removing scientific treasures from public lands raises its ugly head. I'm not quite sure what someone would do with a prehistoric femur (hide it in the attic, stuff it under the bed, turn it into a nifty table lamp beside the living room divan?) or why they would want to remove it from scientific exploration. But, still the thievery continues.

In order to get an appropriate perspective for the size of the bone, I climb the rock-strewn slope toward the back side of the boulder. As I examine the other side of the boulder I detect fossils of various freshwater clams embedded in the rock. This indicates that the boulder was once submerged in an ancient river channel. Slowly and carefully I scale the back of the boulder in order to reach the top. Being careful to maintain my balance, I reach down the front of the giant rock and use my right hand to measure the length of the femur mold. It is eight right hands long. Since my hand is eight inches long, this means that the femur is approximately sixty-four inches in length. A series of mathematical and anatomical calculations (which I always leave to experts, since my mathematical ability has always been highly suspect—especially by the I.R.S.) indicates that the creature to whom this femur belonged weighed approximately twenty-five tons and was about eighty-five feet in length—or longer than your average eighteen-wheel tractor-trailer.

I retrace my steps back along the trail to Marker #2, which provides information about the ancient streams that once flowed through this area. Nearby is a displaced boulder (which tumbled down the hill long ago) that shows a scalloped pattern grooved into its face. This pattern indicates not only the direction that the ancient stream flowed, but also how fast the water was

The mold of a femur of a *Diplodocus* dinosaur. The mold is over five feet long—its former owner was about eighty-five feet long.

IMAGINE A TIME ABOUT 151 MILLION YEARS AGO. *It is the Late Jurassic Period, a time when giant sauropods—thundering hundred-foot long behemoths such as* Supersaurus, *Seismosaurus, and* Ultrasaurus *roamed the land. Although the giants dominated, dinosaurs of every size and shape were common. But, it was also a time when small mammals began their evolutionary ascent. The first butterflies and moths took to the air, as did an array of flying reptiles* (Pterosaurs). *Leaf bugs, shield bugs, and plant-hoppers scurried about in the undergrowth.*

This was the time when the single landmass known as Pangaea, began to break apart. The northern part, called Laurasia, slowly, ever so slowly drifted away from the southern part, called Gondwana. A shallow, but ever widening sea began to form between these supercontinents.

Imagine a climate that was predominantly dry. The landscape was dominated by lowland valleys chocked with thick vegetation. Tall bundles of ferns swept across the hillsides. Cycads and Nilssonia plants spread out and around myriad shallow lakes. Ginkgo trees and conifers arced into the prehistoric skies—much as they still do today.

Just on the other side of a shallow lake, a small herd of Diplodocus *browses among the leafy vegetation. Adults are on the outside of this herd—carefully protecting a half-dozen juveniles, each of whom would make a tasty treat for wandering carnivores looking for an easy meal.*

Carefully observe as the adults use their long slender necks to reach the vegetation at a variety of levels. Their small, narrow skulls and spoon-shaped snouts duck in and out of leaf masses. Their mouths are filled with long, slender teeth, particularly in the front. These are appropriate for a creature who needs to strip branches quickly of their leafy vegetation—something it would do many times during the course of a feeding period in order to maintain its gargantuan weight. Like many herbivores (and modern-day birds) it swallows small stones (known as gastroliths) in order to help grind and eventually digest the vegetation it consumes.

> *Look again and you will notice that each adult has a long whip-like tail. Many millions of years later, scientists will speculate that these tails served two purposes—balance and defense. As you watch them whip those tails back and forth, you might well imagine that this behavior is enough to deter all but the most desperate of predators.*
>
> *The prehistoric sun looms overhead. A small herd of diminutive (five feet long)* Othnielias *darts through some thick-stemmed foliage. A flock of* pterosaurs *soars over the lake looking for a meal in the crystal clear water. An occasional carnivorous roar, the trickle of water flowing over a granite outcropping, and the hum of tiny insects punctuates the stillness of this prehistoric scene. The* Diplodocus *continues to browse and munch.*

moving. The etched ripples and the position of embedded stones are clues to the type of water movement that took place millions of years in the past.

As I'm reading the sign, I see a family of four climb out of their SUV and begin to read the information on the kiosk at the trailhead. The two parents and two very enthusiastic pre-adolescents begin their own journey up the trail and into another time.

I begin my ascent up to the next series of trail markers. This is a very well-maintained and well-marked trail, with a series of timbers lining the left-hand side and a series of posts with wire cable strung between them along the right. Marker #3 describes the sandstone outcropping on the ridge just in front of me. This sandstone outcrop is the remnant of an ancient river that once flowed along this ridge. The rocks, referred to as conglomerates, are composed of different sizes of pebbles and sand grains. This variation in size indicates that the ancient stream was a swiftly flowing one that carried rocks of many sizes.

I continue my ascent of the trail and am soon walking along a ridge that traverses the backside of the hill. Immediately below me is the Colorado River and the dusty town of Fruita. There are boulders of every size and shape sprinkled across the landscape. Brown grasses and green weeds poke

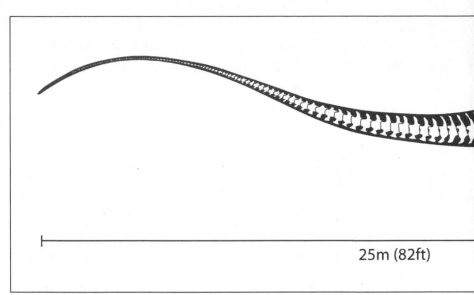

25m (82ft)

Diplodocus (from Wikimedia Creative Commons under the terms of the GNU Free Documentation License)

above the sandy expanse. Sagebrush litters the incline, spilling down over the sandstone outcroppings like concentrations of beige (and slightly deflated) beach balls.

I arrive at the top of the hill to a most remarkable vista—a 360-degree panorama that would make the Colorado Tourism Office proud. Just in front of me, to the south, are the red-rimmed cliffs of the Colorado National Monument, pulsating in the early summer heat. Off to the eastern end of the Grand Valley sits Grand Mesa, arguably the largest flat-topped mountain in the world, and, at an elevation of 11,000 feet, one of the most spectacular. It is a sight well worth a day trip for anyone who wishes to be awed by one of nature's greatest natural environments. Off to my left I can see Mount Garfield, which protrudes from the Bookcliffs, a natural geological formation that extends off into Utah. All around is a panache of color—ripe orchards, verdant farmland, crimson hillsides, cream-colored flatlands, and a conglomeration of geological formations that keeps the shutter clicking on my camera.

At this point, the trail begins a precipitous decline down the backside of the hill. A coating of bentonite and a scrabble of small rocks and pebbles

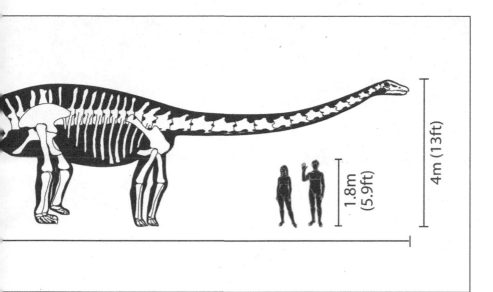

makes the descent slow and cautious. I must watch every step I take down this slope. The timber and ropes that marked the early parts of the trail are gone, and I must determine where to walk and where to place each step so that I don't turn myself into a one-man landslide (with no cell phone–equipped witnesses to rescue me).

This is a rugged landscape—both now and then. Note the Colorado River and the town of Fruita in the background.

The quarry where Elmer Riggs made his historic discovery.

At the bottom of the hill, the trail begins to twist and turn around several rocky outcroppings. Soon I'm at the bottom of a small ravine and can hear the sound of a freight train pushing its way through Fruita on the other side of the river. I look back up to the top of the hill and see the family of four considering their possible descent of the hill. After a few minutes of discussion they decide otherwise and begin to retrace their steps back along the trail to the parking area. Unfortunately, they will miss the best sight of all on this prehistoric journey.

As I begin a short ascent up the other side of the ravine, I can see Riggs' original quarry before me. I skitter (as much as one slightly-past-middle-age college professor can skitter) up the side of the short slope and can now see the original tunnel that was blasted into the side of the mountain. The tunnel is now closed off by a sturdy iron gate with another iron gate about twenty-five feet inside the first one. I suspect that these gates are designed to keep any would-be idiots from crawling down into the mountain and getting themselves trapped by a landslide or some other geological disaster, requiring fire fighters, ambulances, and all manner of other emergency personnel to extricate them from said stupidity (or as Forrest Gump put it so eloquently, "Stupid is as stupid does").

As I peer into the tunnel I can barely see a jumble of fallen timbers. It doesn't take long before I begin to imagine the workers out here more than a hundred years ago, who toiled inside this tunnel under less than ideal conditions. Rudimentary digging tools and the barest of safety precautions were the order of the day, yet the payoffs were incalculable. Sweltering heat, backbreaking work, and the long dusty days were the predominant working conditions. Yet Riggs, and each man in his crew, was driven by an insatiable desire to learn more, to discover what was around the next paleontological corner, to uncover a secret that had lain buried for millions of years. When I think of the skeleton looming over the exhibit hall back at the Field Museum in Chicago, I can't help but think how this tunnel was the gateway to a whole new world of scientific discovery and possibilities.

On the left side of the tunnel entrance is a cast of the exposed back vertebrae of the *Apatosaurus*. Although these are constructed of concrete, they are nonetheless spectacular and provide visitors with some comparative information of the overall size of the dinosaur. Once again, using my hands as measuring tools, I determine that a single vertebra is twelve inches in length. This means that the *Apatosaurus* found in the tunnel before me was approximately seventy feet in length when it was alive. Seventy feet would be equivalent to:

- The height of 4.6 giraffes—one on top of the other.
- The length of 177 compact disks lined up in a row side-by-side.
- 10.6 times the arm span of a male Olympic swimmer (79 inches).
- The length of 52.5 Eastern Gray Squirrels.
- The average height of the Capitol Christmas Tree in Washington, D.C.

To the right of the now-closed tunnel is a large stone structure with a bronze plaque set in the top. The plaque, dedicated in 1938, reads: "Discovered here 1901 a giant Apatasaurus skeleton by Elmer S. Riggs now mounted in Field Museum Chicago." Although quite brief (considering the enormity of the creature as well as its impact on modern-day paleontology), once again the name of the dinosaur was spelled incorrectly (you'll remember from Chapter 4 the egregious spelling miscue [Brachyosaurus] on the commemorative plaque at Riggs Hill).

This particular site puts many things into perspective: the extreme difficulty of digging for dinosaur bones with only the most rudimentary of tools; how many fossilized remains of dinosaurs may still lie beneath the sandstone strata of this wild and ancient place; and the harsh and equally demanding conditions that these early paleontologists, without the benefits of GPS, or diesel-powered equipment, or even sufficient funding, worked in without complaint or adequate compensation. Today the scenery is beautiful and the landscape is varied, but in 1901 this was nothing more than a remote and distant outpost forged out of the aridness of the Western Slope. There were no sprawling ranch homes, no ribbons of asphalt with eighteen-wheelers and top-down convertibles whizzing from one roadside convenience to the next, no air conditioning, electrolyte-replacing cold drinks, or La-Z-Boys to flop into at the end of a torturous day of digging and more digging and even more digging. Working here in the early twentieth century was more than challenging—it was a testament to the tenaciousness of scientific curiosity.

Just off to the side of the original tunnel is a litter of rocks and boulders scattered down the sides of a short ravine. I can only imagine that this is the debris left over from the tunnel blasting conducted by Riggs many years ago. The rocks are in all shapes and sizes, and there are portions of old plaster jackets tucked in between the rocks.

I decide to hike up this short ravine in order to position myself for some additional photographs of this historic site. I, of course, have the advantage of hiking up this rocky ravine with twenty-first century rubber-soled, ankle-bracing hiking shoes less than six months out of the box. Again, I try to imagine the workers in the early twentieth century and their rudimentary equipment trying to keep a foothold on this tumble of rocks and boulders. I'm certain that the footwear of 1901 was considerably less sophisticated than my own, providing little support and little traction, but certainly lots of slipping and sliding as one went up and down this rocky landscape.

Photographs taken, I arc my way down to the bottom of the ravine and up a gentle incline on the other side and just below the mouth of the tunnel. As I ascend the hill, two things happen simultaneously—a pale green lizard with a brown head scoots across the trail … and a single-engine airplane, heading southward, zooms overhead. I can't help but think of the surrealistic juxtaposition of these two events. A modern-day flying machine, based on principles derived from generations of birds, is able to fly overhead. Those generations of birds are the descendants of the ancient dinosaurs who once roamed this area many millions of years in the past. The tiny lizard, oblivious to its ancient history, and arguably a very distant cousin of those same prehistoric creatures, seeks safety and shelter from the cacophony of the small airplane. And, observing this surrealistic juxtaposition of past and present is a human explorer intent on discovering worlds—both ancient and new—in the twisting sands of northwestern Colorado.

I'm now departing the quarry area and am working my way back along the trail around the southern exposure of the hill. This portion of the trail does not have the neatly arranged wooden barriers and wired posts along the sides. Nevertheless, the trail is clearly defined in the pebbly expanse of this high desert area. The descriptive brochure ("Dinosaur Hill Trailmap") keeps me informed about the various geological features I encounter along this portion of the journey. I carefully examine a distinctive limestone layer that is etched into the side of the hill. Nearby are colored bands of fossil soils. Bands with a distinctive crimson hue are those that were laid down during arid times. Other bands, in shades of olive and jade, are those which were deposited during times of abundant water.

The trail continues through an expanse of bentonite and past a con-glomerate boulder that has broken off from a larger block higher up the hill. A slight bend to the right, a short downhill grade, and a quick hairpin turn to the left brings me to the terminus of the trail and my awaiting car (which is now doubling as a portable sauna in the triple-digit heat).

It is now past noontime and the punishing summer sun is brutal. Not a single cloud hovers over the nearby mountains. It's getting to be blistering hot—I imagine that the temperature is nudging its way past 100 degrees. One wonders if the semi-arid conditions of the late Jurassic Period were in any way similar to those I am now experiencing in this slightly (at least in geological terms) more modern environment. Not wishing to waste any ex-cess time in pondering that climatic conundrum, I come to the conclusion that there is only one thing left to do—quickly climb into my car and head back towards Fruita and the El Tapatio Restaurant for a large plate of cheese-dripping enchiladas, a tall basket of tortilla chips, and a very cold Corona (with lime) … especially the very cold Corona!

As I walk to the passenger side of my car to toss my backpack on the front seat, a silvery flash of light catches my eye. As I look down I see a foil wrapper for a condom lying among the detritus of the parking lot. I guess that just as certain prehistoric beasts used to frolic in this specific area—so too, do more modern species of creatures!

NEED TO KNOW ABOUT **Dinosaur Hill**

DIRECTIONS   From Grand Junction, head west on Interstate 70 and take Exit #19 (Fruita). At the stop sign, turn left onto CO 340 and head south. Go around two traffic roundabouts and continue driving south (a McDonalds and the Dinosaur Journey Museum will be on your right and a gas station/convenience store on your left). After about one mile look for Rimrock Adventures ("Canoeing, horseback rides, rafting, gift shop. Tuesday night—rodeo") on the left side of the road.

Just after Rimrock Adventures is a dusty gravel road on the left and a sign (on the right side of the road) for "Dinosaur Hill" (the entrance for Dinosaur Hill is 1.3 miles south of the entrance to Dinosaur Journey Museum). Turn left onto the gravel road, drive for one-quarter mile, and park in the spacious circular parking area (the parking area is large enough for RVs and campers). The trailhead and information kiosk is at the left edge of the parking area.

CONTACT INFORMATION   Before starting out, obtain a "Dinosaur Hill Trail Map" brochure from Dinosaur Journey. The brochure will help you locate and understand the ten numbered posts along the trail.

Dinosaur Journey, 550 Jurassic Court, Fruita, CO 81521, (970) 858-7282 www.dinosaurjourney.org

You might also want to get a copy of the BLM brochure "Dinosaur Trails in the Fruita Area," which describes Dinosaur Hill, as well as Riggs Hill, the Fruita Paleontological Area, and the Trail Through Time. Contact the local BLM office at www.co.blm.gov/mcnca/index.htm or (970) 244-3000.

FEES   None.

HOURS   Open seven days a week – sunrise to sunset

BEST TIME TO VISIT   Any time of year. If you come in the summer, plan an early morning or late afternoon visit (please note that summertime temperatures often soar to over 100°F).

CAMPING/LODGING   Both Fruita and Grand Junction have lots of accommodations—hotels, motels, inns, B&Bs, and various campgrounds. Check out www.gofruita.com or www.visitgrandjunction.com.

SERVICES   There is a picnic ramada at the base of the trail as well as two shade ramadas along the trail. There is a single restroom available.

ACCESS   Most of this tactile trail has been designed to include opportunities for hikers with visual impairments. The trail, however, would not be appropriate for wheelchairs (part of the trail is unimproved).

continued next page

continued from previous page

DIFFICULTY RATING   Moderate to mildly strenuous. The trail is approximately one mile in length and hiking time is about one hour.

NOTES   This is another of my all-time favorite hikes. I've visited on several occasions and always find something new to discover on each occasion. You should plan on completing the entire trail (even the slippery slope on the backside of the hill, and especially Riggs's original excavation site) in order to see and appreciate some remarkable vistas. I particularly enjoy looking at the quarry on the back of the hill and trying to imagine what it would have been like to dig in this area more than a hundred years ago.

   While the trail would be difficult for physically challenged individuals, the interpretive signs all have raised letters, making it relatively easy for visually-challenged folks to obtain important information. The trail is well-marked (except for a short downhill section of slate-gray bentonite on the backside of the hill) and is appropriate for both kids and adults (please hold hands) to traverse.

CHAPTER 6

Size Matters

FRUITA PALEONTOLOGICAL AREA

If you are considering a desiccated landscape—perhaps for a series of economically priced motel-quality paintings to be sold from the back of your van—you certainly can't beat the Fruita Paleontological Area. This expanse of scattered gray rocks, rugged sandstone outcroppings, parched rounded hills, deep gullies, and hardy vegetation peppering the red-brown ground is a classic desert environment. Any animals that reside in the area are safely hidden underground or beneath hard rock ledges—unlike the (supposedly intelligent) slightly-past-middle-aged explorer who is tramping over the landscape in search of information for a forthcoming book. (As most psychologists will tell you, there is little relationship between the cranial capacity of certain mammalian species and their ability to demonstrate something known as "common sense.")

Once again, I set out on a day that was to soar into the triple digits.

I was initially attracted to the Fruita Paleontological Area not just because of its abundance of large dinosaur specimens (such as *Ceratosaurus*, *Apatosaurus*, *Camarasaurus*, *Stegosaurus*, and *Allosaurus*), but also because it is one of the few areas of the world where an array of microvertebrates (small animals with backbones) have been discovered. Microvertebrates hold particular interest for paleontologists, not simply due to their small size, but rather because they can often reveal some fascinating information about prehistoric climates. The interpretation of ancient climates is often easier when examining smaller animals simply because the diminutive creatures do not migrate for long distances across a range of ecological zones. While larger dinosaurs seem to "get all the press," smaller specimens yield an incredible array of information both ecological and climatic.

Mesa County, Colorado, has a distinction that would make other counties—both in Colorado and in other parts of the U.S.—jealous (that is to say, if indeed, counties had the ability to be jealous). It has produced two of the world's biggest dinosaurs: *Ultrasaurus* (100 feet long, 50 tons) and *Supersaurus* (131 feet long; 40–50 tons). In contrast, it has also yielded fossils of one of the smallest (if not *the* smallest) dinosaurs ever found—the *Echinodon*.

Described in a recent edition of the *Guinness Book of World Records* as "the world's smallest dinosaur," *Echinodon* lived during the Cretaceous Period (145.5 to 65.5 million years ago). George Callison, a retired biologist from California State University at Long Beach, and someone who has worked the Fruita Paleontological Area for more than twenty years, says that the discovery of *Echinodon* "…was kind of startling" because a "lot of people think dinosaurs are all big. But we were able to demonstrate this was an adult."

The first fossil of this creature was originally discovered near Swanage, England, in the mid 1800s. Although it was initially mistaken for a lizard, it has frequently been compared to a modern-day chicken in terms of its size and leg structure (and, who knows, maybe even disposition). From the tip of its snout to the end of its tail, it measured twenty inches. It was bipedal (two-footed) with its hind legs longer than the front limbs.

After that, it is less a chicken and more of an enigma. For example, the *Echinodon* had a total of twenty-one teeth—those in front were fang-like in appearance. These fangs were small, almost blade-like, but well spaced and not close together (*Echinodon* means "hedgehog tooth" in reference to spines on its teeth). Then, life for this diminutive creature got a little more complicated when, in January 2010, it was assigned a new name—*Fruitadens*

("Fruita tooth"). This was the result of its reclassification as a heterodontosaurid, a worldwide group of dinosaurs (known from Europe and Asia) that had canine-like teeth at the front of their jaws, despite a diet consisting primarily of plants.

Tiny adult dinosaurs are rare, particularly plant-eating ones that supplemented their diet with insects. Small animals, including small dinosaurs, are high-energy critters and frequently need the extra calories from meat (insects?) in order to survive. Most very small dinosaurs were carnivorous; *Fruitadens*, however, was a rarity—a tiny omnivore. This creature is also unique because it is the first heterodontosaurid found in the Morrison Formation—the layer of rock exposed in the Grand Valley and elsewhere. A life-sized, fleshed-out reconstruction of *Fruitadens* is on display at the Dinosaur Journey Museum in Fruita.

I left my hotel in Basalt early in order to get a good start on the day. I headed down the Roaring Fork Valley, through Glenwood Springs, and out onto I-70 westward toward Grand Junction. The hills outside Glenwood pulsate with rich verdant colors—green, emerald, jade, lime, and olive spill down the mountainside and across Glenwood Canyon. It's been a very wet spring, and the heavy snowfall of the winter has turned the valley into a landscape rich with vegetation. Interspersed among all the greenery is a profusion of reds, burgundys, and cherries emblematic of the English translation of the word "Colorado." The landscape is like a living Christmas tree festooned with garlands of multi-colored lights.

Thirty miles outside of Glenwood Springs, the terrain turns desert-y. Greens are giving way to golds, and reds are transformed into siennas and ochres. There's a splattering of piñon and juniper trees on the mountains, and curtains of yellows and tans sweep up and down the hillsides on both sides of the highway.

At about mile marker 60, I enter Mesa County, whose slogan is "Monuments, Mesas, and Memories." As I look around I see a constant line of

The lumpy, bumpy parking area at Fruita Paleontological Area (as it was in 2008) fronts the wide open spaces. Note: The parking area has since been converted to a flat gravel parking lot!

arching mesas and flat-topped plateaus splayed out across the horizon. The speed limit has dropped down to sixty mph and I am very quick to lower my velocity.* The highway and train tracks parallel the Colorado River and there's a long line of coal-filled railroad cars weaving their way across the landscape.

I begin to knife through high palisades and soaring cliffs that choke the canyon. I sweep around a giant mesa to my right, over a bridge spanning the Colorado River, and into the high desert country that is symbolic of Grand Junction. On my left is the town of Palisade and the beginning of Colorado's famed (and not-to-be-missed) wine country.

As I slip by Grand Junction, it is about 10:30 in the morning and the sun has raised the desert air to a comfortable temperature of eighty-seven degrees. After another thirty miles, I take Exit 19 (Fruita) off the Interstate and head south. I make a quick stop for gas, load up on several bottles of Gatorade and bags of pretzels (in order to get my Minimum Daily Adult Requirement of sweetened juice, salt, and flour), and pull back out onto CO 340 (south).

After about a mile, I make a right turn on Kings View Road. Across the street is the large billboard proclaiming "Rimrock Adventures." Kings View Road parallels the Colorado River, and I wend my way through a small

*I once made the acquaintance of a Colorado state trooper on this long stretch of highway and did not wish to add another name to my "People with Very Starchy Uniforms (and attitudes)" list.

residential area clinging to the side of this asphalt ribbon. After about three-quarters of a mile, the road transforms into a graveled artery that leads into Horsethief Canyon. Two prairie dogs scamper across the road from my left (doing what prairie dogs do when the temperature creeps toward the top end of a thermometer). Soon after, I notice a sign indicating that I'm entering McMinnis Canyons National Conservation Area. Shortly thereafter is another sign: "Welcome to Horsethief Canyon State Wildlife Area."

After about a quarter mile of very slow passage down the pebbled road, I notice a very bumpy, very lumpy, very potholed parking area (since upgraded)—a muddy-hard twenty-five-square-yard pullout that looks like it has not been graded since before the Paleozoic era. I pull in, turn off the car, and begin to pack up my things. It's taken about two hours and fifteen minutes to get here from Basalt.

At the entrance gate, built into a menacing barbed-wire fence there is a sign:

> Welcome to the Fruita Paleontological Area. Fruita Paleontological Area—the FPA, a unit of Colorado Canyon's National Conservation Area is managed to preserve this rich topological resource and to provide for scientific study and research. This trail will lead you along ancient river channels where dinosaurs and other animals were buried during the late Jurassic period 151 million years ago. The trail interprets the FPA's fossil history and changing landscape. The FPA is half a square mile in area and was established in 1977.

Just inside the entrance is a metal box encasing a well-used Visitor's Log, where various visitors have recorded their hometowns and an assortment of personal comments about this site. Selected (and printable) comments include:

"Windy, well-marked spacious, nice area"

"Well done, informative."

"Nice!" (151 million years of incredible geological history and someone says it's "nice"!)

"Lovely"

"No comment"

"Happy Sunday!"

And, then there was my favorite comment—"Dinosaurs rule!"

The hometowns recorded also provide a glimpse into the range of visitors attracted to this remote and largely un-peopled site. Included are visitors from Juneau, Alaska; Chicago, Illinois; Phoenix, Arizona; Buffalo Grove, Illinois; Sacramento, California; Santa Clara, California; and Miami, Florida, among others.

As I enter the gate I can see a very brown, parched, and desolate landscape. Rocks jut from the hillsides, jumbles of boulders lie sprawled across the landscape like a concentration of errant bowling balls, and long stretches of auburn sand sweep out to the horizon. Off in the distance lies a red hill littered with juniper and piñon. Behind me is a denuded hill—a parched rise that stands like a slag heap at the edge of an industrial complex. There is absolutely no life to be seen anywhere on its flanks—any vestiges of vegetation have been permanently erased from its face as though they had been sanded away by an enormous hand.

The trail is well-marked with lots of informative signs.

The first interpretive sign I come to explains that this small area (about half a square mile in size) "preserves a greater diversity of prehistoric life from the Jurassic Period than any other known place on earth." That bold statement is supported by the enormous array of fossils that have been discovered in this region of the Western Slope. Most of the fossils are unique to the late Jurassic Period that occurred 161.2 to 145.5 million years ago.

Then, in an interesting aside for any youngsters reading the sign, a comparison is made between that period of time and the grandparents of the reader. The readers are asked to imagine that a single marble represents a hundred years (or, as the authors of the sign contend, the approximate age of one or more grandparents). If a hundred years is represented by a single marble (according to the sign authors), then 151 million years (a date also selected by the sign authors) would need to be represented by a line of marbles approximately sixteen miles in length. I went ahead and did the math. A single marble (Aggies or Cat's Eye are preferred) is about a half-inch across, so that would mean that a line of marbles sixteen miles long would contain approximately 2,027,520 marbles.*

As I continue along the trail, I learn about the geology of sandstone, how ancient rivers cut through this area, and how minerals and sediments were deposited over many millions of years. Also identified is a hardrock river bottom that includes remnants of the ancient Ceratosaurus River Channel. This river channel was named after the new species of *Ceratosaurus* dinosaur that was discovered within its boundaries.

Ceratosaurus (literally "horned lizard") is one of those scientific riddles that paleontologists keep turning up every so often. Its name refers to the large, bladelike horn set in the middle of its head. It's not clear exactly what this horn may have been used for, but there is some speculation that it had something to do with distinguishing the sexes, and that this was an "instrument" used in courtship rituals (similar, I suspect, to certain courtship "instruments" such as a dozen red roses, a box of chocolates, and an expensive dinner). It is not known whether the horn was useful as a defensive weapon.

*I'm sure that by now you have concluded that certain dinosaur book authors have, most assuredly, completely lost their marbles.

The first *Ceratosaurus* was discovered in 1883 in Fremont County, Colorado. Also discovered in the same quarry were remains of *Allosaurus*—indicating that these two dinosaurs probably were contemporaries of each other. They may have even competed with each other in hunting for food, which may have included sauropods, iguanodons, and other types of herbivores. It wasn't until 1884, however, that this creature received its current name from O. C. Marsh. Marsh was certain that, given the shape of its tail (long and thin), this critter was a relatively good swimmer—much like the crocodiles of today (with their equally long and thin tails).

That the *Ceratosaurus* was a fearsome predator is confirmed by its enormous jaws festooned with rows of blade-like teeth. Its forelimbs, although quite short, were powerfully built. Each of the forelimbs ended with primitive four-fingered hands and very sharp claws. Its body structure indicates that it was a theropod ("beast feet")—a suborder of dinosaurs that walked on their hind legs, and who were almost exclusively carnivorous.

Although *Ceratosaurus* was a contemporary of *Allosaurus* and may have hunted for the same food, it was somewhat smaller. An adult would have been about eight feet tall, twenty to twenty-seven feet long, and weighed in at somewhere around 1,000 pounds. (*Allosaurus*, its slightly more massive cousin, weighed in at around 2,000 pounds, and reached lengths averaging thirty feet.) Paleontologist Robert Bakker suggests that *Ceratosaurus* probably hunted aquatic prey, such as fish and crocodiles, although it had the potential to feast on large dinosaurs. Bakker also speculates that both adults and juveniles ate together, although the evidence for this is still tenuous.

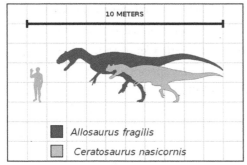

Ceratosaurus and Allosaurus (from Wikimedia Commons under the terms of the *GNU Free Documentation License*)

Although Colorado has produced some of the most compelling specimens of *Ceratosaurus*, remains have also been discovered in Tanzania and Portugal. *Ceratosaurus* was a creature of the Late Jurassic Period, a time when Pangaea was breaking up as northern Laurasia fragmented away from southern Gondwana. The early Atlantic Ocean was opening up between North America and Europe and, much later, between South America and Africa. Once again, we find a creature that has inhabited a broad geographical range.

As I continue on my way along the dry and dusty trail, I come to two more signs, both of which provide information about the history of this site. Although the area looks lifeless and desolate today, it has, over a period of more than a hundred years, produced some of the most unique and most varied prehistoric specimens of any site. Since the late 1800s, when this area was first explored,* the Fruita Paleontological Area has given up an amazing diversity of prehistoric plants and animals including:

- turtle and crocodile specimens
- the world's smallest dinosaur—*Fruitadens*
- carnivorous dinosaurs—*Ceratosaurus, Allosaurus*
- herbivorous dinosaurs—*Stegosaurus, Dryosaurus*
- long-necked giants—*Camarasaurus, Apatosaurus*
- fossils of spores, pollen, leaves, and wood
- fresh-water snails and clams
- crayfish, clams, and shrimp
- four kinds of fish, frogs
- three-toed dinosaur tracks
- various insects
- six types of lizards
- three types of lizard-like reptiles
- two- to three-foot-long "bunny" crocodiles
- ten types of tiny mammals
- dinosaur egg shells

*On May 30, 1891, the *Grand Junction News* reported that, "Agatized Bones of Mastodons" had been uncovered in the Grand Valley. In reality, those were dinosaur bones collected from the area that was to eventually become the Fruita Paleontological Area. Prehistoric specimens have been continuously collected from this site ever since.

The richness of the area, based primarily on these discoveries (made over many decades), resulted in the creation of an advisory group that included representatives of the Bureau of Land Management (BLM) and several paleontologists. Their discussions resulted in the official designation of this area as the Fruita Paleontological Area in 1977. The intent was to protect the area's fossils and to provide for continued scientific research.

The trail continues to snake across a hogback, back down into a ravine, and up and over any number of sandy tussocks. Sand and gravel spill across the landscape, and ridges splattered with sunburned rocks are everywhere the eye can see. Under rich-blue skies and an equally brilliant sun, I slowly tramp across layers of mudstone (fine grained sedimentary rock composed of a mixture of clay, silt, and sand particles) and deposits of claystone (a fine-grained sedimentary rock composed mostly of clay formed from floodplain deposition). The walk is easy, but the vistas are sufficiently compelling to cause me to stop periodically to compare "what is" with "what was."

During this part of the journey, I encounter additional signage that provides compelling information about the geology and geography of this unique region. There are lessons galore for any novice paleontologist or budding topographer. It quickly becomes clear that this landscape is considerably different now than it was during the Late Jurassic Period. The land all around me was part of a large shallow basin that extended from southern Canada all the way down to what is now Arizona. Flood waters and wind had carried nearly a thousand feet of sediment to this area, resulting in a generally flat landscape. Rivers and streams wound their way through this environment, and the land was covered with an array of sub-tropical vegetation. Just as important, an incredible variety of dinosaurs roamed the land.

For millions of years, sediments continued to pile up across the landscape as the result of overflowing rivers, the changing course of streams, the birth and death of lakes and other bodies of water, shifting winds, and the eruption of myriad volcanoes throughout what is now western North America. Then, about seventy million years ago, the earth's tectonic and mountain-making forces exerted their pressures on the land, forcing it upward and changing a nearly flat landscape to one pocked with mountain ranges and deep canyons.

The constant action of water, wind, and gravity has sculpted and shaped this land into its present form. Hills and ridge areas—capped by more resistant rocks—have eroded at a slower rate than the surrounding expanses. This erosion, accelerated by the constant and continual uplift, has exposed numerous rock formations, revealing a fascinating geologic story. The result is a profusion of dramatic landscape features that have been preserved along with any prehistoric fossils permanently encased in those features.

Here are the basic (and most fascinating) facts:

- The Grand Valley has lost more than 360 cubic miles of rock to erosive forces and uplift. (A cubic mile of rock and sediment is one mile high, one mile wide, and one mile deep.)
- About two miles of overlying rock material have been removed (through a combination of geological and climatic forces) from the Fruita Paleontological Area.
- The sedimentary rock moved by erosion at the Fruita Paleontological Area represents more than 10,000 vertical feet of deposition over a period of 100 million years.

My journey through this prehistoric wonderland continues along the well-marked trail. A green lizard slips out from behind a boulder and stops to consider me for a few moments (probably wondering what a humanoid is doing in this reptile-rich habitat). He waits in the punishing sunlight as I record my observations and take my requisite number of photographs. As I start to move on down the trail, he decides there are other places he'd rather be. He quickly scurries along across the boulder, down the side, and under a small ledge of sandstone. Once again, I am alone in this widening landscape. The temperature has risen into the nineties, but I am maintaining appropriate levels of hydration thanks, in large measure, to bottled products from the Gatorade Company.

As I walk along these ancient river channels, I am taken by the fact that, over time, more than twelve separate and distinct river systems flowed through what is now the Fruita Paleontological Area. It was these ancient rivers that were instrumental in preserving the ancient fossils from long ago, just as much as they were "responsible" for eventually uncovering those buried fossils for scientists to discover. In large measure, this site is like a very slow geological dance that covers and uncovers, reveals then hides. I learn that the trail has been designed to follow these ancient channels through the FPA—offering visitors unique opportunities to learn more about the deposits and their associated fossils.

The sun is now beating down unmercifully. It's close to noon, and the air temperature is approaching ninety-five degrees. That semi-tropical environment that I read about on an earlier sign is nowhere to be found. While draining an entire bottle of liquid refreshment, I pause to consider the slow forces that have, in a constant and measured way, exerted their influence on the shape of this landscape. I realize that what I am looking at will be virtually unchanged in a hundred years, and quite possibly in five-hundred

The vertebrae imprint of an *Allosaurus* in the rock face.

years. Its current configuration has been shaped by forces over periods of time that are far beyond the comprehension or experience of few the human intruders. Its history is measured in numbers that boggle the imagination.

I've now reached signpost #15 on the trail. Here I learn more about how flooding helped preserve the fossil record. It seems that during the Jurassic Period, flooding rivers would carry large amounts of mud and silt downstream. This accumulation of mud would create levees that rose up above the surrounding floodplain. With each new flood, old levees would be destroyed and new levees would be created. Sheets of sediment would be deposited and new channels for the twelve rivers that flowed through this area would be created. As new channels were created and old ones were destroyed, bends and twists would be created and the river would split and rejoin many times over many miles. These twists and turns would tend to trap animals as they came to drink from the stream.

Imprisoned by the mud and stranded by other debris in the river, animals would be buried whole as the river continued to deposit new layers—decade after decade and century after century. A quick burial was necessary in order to preserve those bones for scientists to discover millions of years later. The ribbon-like channel sandstones that were the sandy river bottoms deposited by these winding rivers are seen today as sandstone ridges sixty to one hundred feet wide, three to six feet thick, and extending for many miles. It is interesting to note that, due to the unique geography of this prehistoric environment, there was a significantly greater chance that more fossils would be preserved here than in most places around the world.

As I make a sharp right-hand turn on the trail, I begin an ascent up a slight slope. Soon after, I arrive at Interpretive Sign #17, which describes the vertebra of an *Allosaurus* imprinted in the rock face. The sign informs me that this fossil is from the middle section of the creature's back and is oriented upside down (since I'm the only visitor in this vast and lonely environment I'm tempted to stand on my head to get a better look. However, even in spite of the heat, a small dollop of common sense surfaces and I decide to let my camera do the necessary visual gymnastics). I also learn that this fossilized backbone has been weathered and vandalized (again!). There is, however, an illustration that shows visitors what the bone originally looked like.

Until the arrival of *Tyrannosaurus* during the Cretaceous Period, *Allosaurus* (meaning "different lizard") was unquestionably one of the fiercest and most vicious carnivores of the Late Jurassic Period. First discovered in Colorado in 1869, specimens of *Allosaurus* have been unearthed throughout the West, particularly in Utah (it's the Utah state fossil), Wyoming, and Oklahoma. It is postulated that this creature had an enormous hunting range throughout this region. In fact, the *Allosaurus* is the most common large predatory dinosaur found in the Morrison Formation (see Chapter 2) and makes up

about 10 percent of the dinosaurs found in the Fruita Paleontological Area.

Pound for pound, *Allosaurus* was one of the most powerful carnivores of its time—a virtual hunting machine. It reached a length of forty feet, stood fifteen feet tall, and weighed in at about

Allosaurus (courtesy Dick Hodgman)

two tons. Its rear legs were extremely powerful and exceptionally large. Like *Tyrannosaurus*, it had uncharacteristically short forelimbs ending in smallish hands. However, unlike *T. rex* (who only had two fingers on each hand), the better-endowed (hand-wise) *Allosaurus* had three digits. Each of the fingers tapered into ten-inch, dagger-like claws, which were probably used to capture and hold prey as it was being consumed.

The head of an *Allosaurus* was massive when compared to the rest of its body. Its oversized, powerful jaws contained incredibly large and razor-sharp teeth—teeth that also had saw-like rear edges. By working its upper and lower jaws back and forth to tear its food, an *Allosaurus* was able to turn its teeth into a perfectly coordinated set of dental steak knives. It is suspected that these teeth would have been more than helpful when taking down any large herbivorous sauropods that were abundant throughout the region, and which may have been the *Allosaurus*'s primary prey.

Allosaurus was, arguably, the strongest carnivore of its time. Even though its skull and jaws could bulge outward to grasp huge chunks of meat from any unfortunate victim, there is some disagreement as to whether it was a predator or scavenger (or both). Recently, Emily Rayfield of the University of Cambridge used computer modeling to suggest that *Allosaurus* attacked with its mouth wide open and, using its head as a battering ram, drove the teeth of its upper jaw into the prey. Then, with its powerful claws it would hold fast to any victim as it systematically tore away chunks of flesh and muscle. Some scientists speculate that *Allosaurus* may have hunted in packs to bring down larger animals—although there is insufficient data to confirm this hypothesis. Suffice it to say, an *Allosaurus* pack would have been a formidable and feared crowd on any Jurassic floodplain.

The next interpretive sign on the trail (#18) identifies a casted mold around the lower end of a leg bone. There is some speculation that this fossil may have belonged to a *Camarasaurus*—a herbivorous dinosaur common to the

The mold from the lower end of a *Camarasaurus* leg bone.

Morrison Formation. The sign also indicates that the mold was left after the bone was exposed on the surface and slowly weathered away leaving its impression in the harder rock.

I am curious how long it would take a dinosaur leg bone to completely weather away. I am mindful of the fact that the mineral content of the bone, variations in climatic conditions over time, and the chemical composition of the rock might all affect the weathering process. Yet, even allowing for those variables, I'm interested in finding out if there is an accepted rate of decomposition for exposed bone.

After my excursion through the FPA, I contact Dr. Bruce Schumacher, the Rocky Mountain South Zone Paleontologist for the USDA Forest Service (it's the Bureau of Land Management that administers the Fruita Paleontological Area). Bruce informs me that this is a question that is "obviously impossible to quantify [because]…there are many variables involved."

Bruce tells me that, "…assuming the starting point is when the bone first becomes exposed, and given a large bone (1–1.5 m in length), and contained in something as hard as that particular sandstone—vestiges of the bone could remain even after several centuries—and obviously the mold of the bone still remains today and may last for another century or so.

"[This is] very different for bones buried in mud, the rock type from which the majority of dinosaur materials are collected in the Morrison Formation. Mudstone, or shale, weather much more rapidly. A similar sized bone contained in mudstone could weather away completely in just a few decades—large chunks of it would likely survive for a longer period downhill from the point of exposure."

Bruce concludes by saying that, "… [he] can't offer … ballpark whole numbers, because there are just too many variables to consider." Perhaps scientists in the future, with more sophisticated instrumentation and a continuously improving storehouse of knowledge, may be able to provide additional data. Or, we may never have a definitive answer. While that may be frustrating to some, I find it to be one of the most intriguing elements of paleontology—simply that there may be questions that, like certain celestial objects, are just simply beyond our reach. The joy of this field, at least for me, is that it continues to generate questions and stimulate expeditions and excursions in constant search of potential answers and explanations.

The trail etches its way across the top of a dusty-brown hogback in the general direction of the lumpy, bumpy parking area. I come upon another interpretive sign that provides additional information about the Ceratosaurus Channel and the varied paleontological discoveries that have been made, and will continue to be made, in this fossil-rich region. The sign also reminds visitors that, *"... it is illegal to remove any fossil materials from the FPA. These materials have survived millions of years and your cooperation is essential to ensure scientists will be given an opportunity to study, interpret, and exhibit them for all the public to enjoy. A fossil's location and position tell a scientist as much about its past as the fossil itself. Fossils are extremely delicate and attempting to move one could destroy it."*

I'm now walking on a slight downward slope—rocky, but very easy to traverse. With beads of sweat trickling down my forehead from under my protective hat, I am convinced that the climatic conditions I now experience are considerably different than they were when *Allosaurus* and *Ceratosaurus* dominated this landscape. Their place, however, has been taken over by scores of grasshoppers hip-hopping all across the trail. It's an interesting evolution—fierce dominating carnivores have been replaced by very innocent herbivorous invertebrates. Of course, it took more than 150 million years for that "power shift"—but nature is constantly patient, if not constantly slow.

In short order I weave back through the entrance in the fence and over to my car. I grab a very warm sandwich and an equally warm bottle of water and lean up against the side of the car to eat my lunch and survey the surrounding environment once more. After about five minutes a man and his wife pull up in a massive SUV. As the man gets out of his car he asks me if I've seen Dinosaur Hill. Before I can answer, he mentions that he read an article in a magazine in a barber shop in Pittsburgh that described Dinosaur Hill, and he's been trying to find it. I quickly point him in the right direction and provide instructions on how to get back to CO 340 and the entrance to Dinosaur Hill.

Afterwards, he walks over to read the welcoming sign for the Fruita Paleontological Area. After considering its contents, he slowly and thoughtfully walks through the gate and gazes at the trail before him. He carefully surveys the parched landscape, the punishing solar energy all around, and the dusty trail sweeping across the hillocks and ledges. He considers them all, turns around to look at his wife drumming her fingers on the dashboard, and decides that he'd rather be someplace else. He quickly walks back through the gate, climbs into the comfort of his air-conditioned SUV, and pulls out of the lumpy, bumpy parking area to follow the road back to civilization.

It is now past 2:00 and the temperature has soared into the triple digits. I notice a small cloud cover scuttling in over the mountains to the southeast. There's a faint breath of cooling air and perhaps a hint of rain somewhere in western Colorado. As I slowly weave my car back along the gravel road, I note two buzzards floating in the dry desert air above me. They are apparently looking for fresh meat. Mindful of what often happens to humanoid creatures who stick around the desert too long, I turn up the air conditioning, grab another bottle of water, and put a little extra pressure on the accelerator.

NEED TO KNOW ABOUT **Fruita Paleontological Area**

DIRECTIONS From Grand Junction, head west on Interstate 70 for approximately nine miles. Take Exit 19 (Fruita). At the stop sign, turn left and head south on CO 340. Go around two traffic circles and past Dinosaur Journey Museum on your right (a good place to visit on your return trip). After approximately one mile, turn right onto Kings View Road (it's directly across from Rimrock Adventures). Follow this road for about three miles (the road turns into a dirt/gravel road after about half a mile). Stay on the main road (see the description at the beginning of the chapter) and you will come to a (now improved) parking area on the left side of the road.

CONTACT INFORMATION Obtain an informational brochure or current information from one of the following:

Dinosaur Journey
550 Jurassic Court
Fruita, CO 81521
(970) 858-7282
www.dinosaurjourney.org

Museum of Western Colorado
462 Ute Avenue
Grand Junction, CO 81502
(970) 242-0971
www.museumofwesternco.com

FEES None.

HOURS Open seven days a week—sunup to sunrise.

BEST TIME TO VISIT Early morning or late afternoon. I strongly advise an investment in "liquid assets"—the midday sun can be especially brutal out here.

CAMPING/LODGING There are lots of accommodations in the nearby town of Fruita. Check out the offerings at the town's official web site: www.gofruita.com.

SERVICES There are absolutely no services here—no shady ramadas, no benches, no cool water, no lemonade stands, no itinerant masseuses waiting to massage your aching muscles, no nothing! If you need something, please bring it with you—especially your own water (lots of it) and your own shade (wide hats are heartily recommended)—particularly in the summer. Note: There is now a single restroom (Yeah!).

ACCESS The first one-third of the trail is wheelchair accessible. After that the trail gets rough and rises and falls with the undulating landscape. Physically challenged individuals may find this trail particularly difficult. Visually impaired individuals may need some assistance with the reduced lettering on some of the interpretive signs.

DIFFICULTY RATING Moderate to slightly strenuous. The trail is about half a mile in length and can be traversed (including reading the twenty interpretive signs) in approximately one hour.

NOTES This trail will be exhilarating for some and "less than adequate" for others. If you're looking for lots of dinosaur fossils, then you might want to look at some of the other offerings in this book. However, if you would like an informative overview of the prehistoric geology and ancient history of this part of the world, then you are in for a treat. The signs are all scientifically accurate—in both the depth of their information as well as their illustrations. While some basic science background is helpful in reading the information posted on many of the signs, you don't have to have a Ph.D. in paleontology or geology to get an appreciation for the many forces—geological, climatic, tectonic—that shaped this area over hundreds of millions of years.

That said, this is probably not the best place to bring young kids. There won't be a lot for them to admire and, with few exceptions, there's not a lot of specific dinosaur information (or fossils) to appreciate (with the exception of the single *Allosaurus* fossil). Although research has been taking place here for more than a hundred years, youngsters may find that the one hour hike is more physical and less awe-inspiring than they would like. The focus of the interpretive signs is more on the geologic and paleontological history of the area than it is on the specific dinosaurs and other creatures unearthed here over the years. However, if you're looking for an area rich in paleontological treasures and prehistoric drama (over millions of years), then this is a good place to visit. Bring lots of water, a pair of sunglasses, and keep an eye on those vultures circling overhead!

CHAPTER 7

Lost Souls Along the Purgatoire

COMANCHE NATIONAL GRASSLANDS

S he was beautiful!
She was picturesque!
She was truly one of the most gorgeous individuals I have ever seen!

She had long graceful legs, a magnificently proportioned body, and a face so attractive that people would stare at it for hours on end. I simply could not get over her grace and her presence—she titillated the senses and made everything and everybody around her come to a standstill. She was, quite obviously, the center of attention and everyone in the immediate area was as mesmerized by her charms as I.

Her name was Sue. Sweet, beautiful Sue!

Unfortunately, she had been dead for more than sixty-five million years.

I had arrived at the beautifully colonnaded Field Museum in Chicago as part of a six-hour layover between trains on another westward journey. I

Sue, the *Tyrannosaurus rex* at the Field Museum in Chicago (from Wikimedia Creative Commons under the terms of the GNU Free Documentation License)

also wanted to pay homage to fossil hunter and theropod specialist Elmer Riggs, one of the Field Museum's first curators (see Chapters 4 and 5). It was during expeditions to Grand Junction, Colorado, in 1900 and 1901 that Riggs discovered the *Apatosaurus* fossil now housed in the museum (and the *Brachiosaurus* fossil that was once housed here, but which has now taken up residence at Chicago's O'Hare Airport). As you may recall, the *Brachiosaurus* Riggs found was one of the first of its kind ever discovered.

Entering the massive main hall I was greeted by two elephants (who, in their taxidermist-induced condition, completely ignored me). However, further down the ornate hall was a most impressive display of (according to a nearby interpretive sign) "… the largest, most complete, and best preserved *Tyrannosaurus rex* ever discovered. This combination of size, completeness, and quality of preservation makes Sue one of the most important fossils in the world. … Sue is the largest known specimen of *T. rex*. Her extreme size has set new records for length and estimated weight for her species."

Sue was discovered in the Hell Creek Formation of western South Dakota by Sue Henderson—after whom she was named—on August 12, 1990.* She soon became involved in a protracted court battle, which was finally resolved when the court ruled that she belonged to the owner of the land on which she was discovered. The rancher then decided to sell Sue at a public auction. With financial assistance from the McDonalds Corporation,** Sue was eventually purchased by the Field Museum for $8.4 million at Sotheby's auction house in New York.

Museum preparers spent two years (over 30,000 hours) cleaning and preparing the more than 250 bones and teeth in Sue's skeleton. Since a *T. rex* skeleton consists of approximately 321 bones, it soon became apparent that this was the most completely preserved specimen (over 90 percent complete) of *T. rex* ever discovered in the world. The fossil was only missing a few ribs, one foot, some vertebrae, one arm, and a few other small bones. Using computer-generated images, scientists were able to create very accurate replicas of those missing bones for the permanent display.

The railing around Sue was crowded with kids from a local school, who were all decked out in their white shirts, blue pants, blue dresses, patent leather shoes, and, of course, personal cell phones. In fact, the entire museum was a proverbial beehive (or massive anthill) of activity, with the ebb and flow of scores of kids milling around Sue under the ever-watchful eyes of their yellow named-tagged chaperones trying to keep them in tow.

Another interpretive sign indicates that Sue's real skull was far too heavy to place on this skeleton and is displayed on the balcony above this exhibit. I find my way up the ancient stairwell to the side of the exhibit hall and over to the skull. It is simply enormous. Most impressive are her teeth—serrated like steak knives—that remind me of elongated pirate daggers or middle-eastern scimitars. A *T. rex* normally had fifty-eight very large and very sharp teeth that were continually shed and re-grown during its lifetime (much in the same manner as modern-day sharks). Each of the teeth on display in this skull ranges in length from seven and a half to twelve inches. They would have certainly made for one hell of a weapon in any kind of face-to-face battle.

*Even though Sue was named after her discoverer, scientists are not positive about her gender. Determining the sex of most dinosaur fossils is, at best, an educated guess.

**I note, with just the slightest hint of irony, the fact that one of the world's greatest carnivores is sponsored by one of the world's greatest purveyors of meat. I'm not sure if I'm being manipulated by some crafty (and perhaps very secretive) advertising campaign, but I know I'll never look at a Big Mac in exactly the same way as I did before.

In my subsequent reading of the museum's publication, "The Ultimate Guide to a T. rex Named Sue," I learn some additional facts about this specimen specifically and about *Tyrannosaurus* in general.

- Since 1900, when the first *T. rex* was discovered, only seven skeletons more than 50 percent complete have ever been unearthed.
- Sue's brain was about the size of a sweet potato.
- Sue suffered several fractured bones during her lifetime, perhaps an indication of battles with other prehistoric beasts.
- Sue is forty-two feet in length (the length of two-and-a-half pickup trucks), twelve feet tall at the hips (slightly taller than a one-story building), and weighed seven tons when alive (the combined weight of 11.6 thoroughbred race horses).
- Sue had only two functional digits on each hand—most carnivorous dinosaurs had three.
- Sue's foot, with its three digits, is quite similar to a bird's foot, lending further credibility to the belief that birds are "living dinosaurs."
- Scientists have discovered that a large portion of Sue's brain was devoted to detecting and processing smells.
- *Tyrannosaurus rex* existed for nearly two million years—which is about twenty times longer than humans have lived on the earth.

I spend the rest of the morning touring Evolving Planet, the Hall of Gems, Plants of the World, and other exhibits in this not-to-be-missed museum. After about three hours, I realize that all this education has made me hungry and so I head downstairs to the museum's Corner Bakery Café. There I tear into a Chicken Pomodori sandwich with all the passion of any self-respecting and ravenous carnivore.

Sue would have been proud!

On this westward venture, I have decided to take the train across the heartland of America. The thought of being crammed into an undersized airplane seat, feasting on small bags of peanuts, and dealing with snoring seatmates and howling kids was sufficient inducement for me to book passage on the Southwest Chief rolling out of Chicago, across the Midwest, and into the small Colorado town of La Junta. As the folks at Amtrak proudly proclaim in their *Amtrak Vacations* guidebook, "If getting there is half the fun, why not get there the nicer way?" Amen to that!

The irony of taking a train to view dinosaurs is not lost on me. As trains were becoming an integral part of the American landscape in the late 1800s and early 1900s, so too, were paleontologists using those trains to transport their fossil treasures across the country. Of no less importance was the fact that dinosaurs were often paired up with, and compared to, the great locomotives that crisscrossed the land. As cultural historian W.J.T. Mitchell puts it in his hefty tome, *The Last Dinosaur Book*, "This linkage is reinforced by the common association of dinosaurs and machines with fossil fuels." To reinforce this concept it is interesting to note that one of the first animated cartoons to appear in this country was the 1914 short animated film *Gertie the Dinosaur.** "Gertie," a cartoon *Diplodocus*, interacted and played with several props in the film, including a locomotive.

I soon discovered what train people mean when they say that this form of transportation is definitely stress-free. I can get out of my seat anytime I want to visit the lounge for some liquid refreshment, stroll to the dining car for a first-class meal that involves something more than cellophane-wrapped (and expiration date-stamped) meals, read a book while spread across two very wide and very comfortable seats, and, best of all, enjoy the passing scenery of small towns, wide prairies, and occasional herds of wild animals feasting on trackside vegetation. Again, the folks at Amtrak summarize the entire experience in a single concise statement, "There's a certain amount of freedom that comes with taking the train."

We pull out of Union Station on a gray Friday afternoon. Rolling past the rail yards of Chicago, our pace is slow and steady. It is only when we reach the outskirts of the city that our speed picks up. Grimy apartment buildings and the weathered facades of abandoned factories eventually give way to rows of tree-lined streets, open expanses of crop-filled fields, and the well-named wide open spaces.

*In a survey of cartoon historians and animators conducted in 1994, *Gertie the Dinosaur* was named as one of the fifty greatest cartoons of all time (#6 on the list). Interestingly, *Snow White* only came in at #19.

We rumble by the towns of Naperville, Mendota, Galesburg, Fort Madison, and La Plata. By the time we slide out of Kansas City at 11:00 p.m. (after a forty minute stop), I am comfortably cocooned in my travel blanket. Soon after, the click, click, click of the rails lulls me to sleep, and the night—as well as the landscape—passes by me.

At 6:00 the next morning, after a nighttime passage through eastern Kansas, I arise to strong shafts of light peeking around the window curtain. A strong cup of coffee and a couple of breakfast bars, and I'm down to the observation car to gaze at the rest of Kansas rolling under the wheels of the train. Flatness and more flatness seem to be the theme of the landscape.* Vast acres of green fields, tall grain silos dotting the countryside, and the occasional stockyard filled with oceans of complacent cows are the order of the day.

At 7:00 we pull into Dodge City, Kansas—a town that seems so laid back and different from its heritage that it's hard to imagine that it was once a critical part of western history. Just before the train pauses at the station to unload and load passengers I note a sign pointing up an asphalted two-lane road to the infamous "Boot Hill." Shortly afterward, we roll past a Thai restaurant, a martial arts studio, a Comfort Inn, and a big building selling "Wholesale Fireworks." Ahhhh, the wild, Wild West, indeed!

Soon after, the train arcs it way into southeastern Colorado. Just outside of Lamar, four horses send up small clouds of dust as they gallop away from the approaching locomotive. This part of the state is a wide and wild expanse of short-grass and mixed-grass prairie. The landscape is dotted with rimrock canyons, splintered groves of cottonwood trees, riparian woodlands, and an endless carpet of grassland that stretches far beyond the horizon. Sharp-eyed observers can sometimes pick out bands of lesser prairie chickens as they engage in their elaborate mating dance in April and May, or flocks of sandhill cranes soaring overhead in October. Bighorn sheep, wood ducks, wild turkeys, and graceful raptors are some of the other indigenous creatures that inhabit these environs. An occasional mat of primroses in the late spring brings a palette of color to the dusty-brown

---

*In 2003, three geographers compared the flatness of Kansas to the flatness of a pancake. They used topographic data from the U.S. Geological Survey along with a pancake purchased from a well-known House of Pancakes. If perfect flatness were a value of 1.00, then the calculated flatness of a pancake would be 0.957, "which," they reported "is pretty flat, but far from perfectly flat." Kansas's flatness however, turned out to be 0.997—which, according to the aforementioned geographers, is "damn flat."

vegetation. It is certain that no airplane passenger, zooming overhead at more than five-hundred mph, could ever sense the remarkable spectacle of this thriving and vibrant ecosystem.

The train is a little tardy (but nobody seems to mind) as we pull into La Junta, Colorado. I disembark with my backpack and overnight bag and hitch my way over to Ruby's Auto Body on West Third Street to pick up my rental car. I have a hankering for some good Mexican food, and so with the recommendation of the good folks at Ruby's, I head to Mexico City Restaurant, located on Raton Avenue in a middle-class residential area of the city. As I enter, I'm greeted by multicolored tablecloths, sombreros, a portrait of a burro, neon beer signs, cactus plants, two plastic flamingos, a clay iguana, loud country music, and a brass bull on the wall with lighted eyes. In short order, my server, Ty, a local high school student (whose parents also operate the restaurant), takes my order—the #6 combo (tamale, enchilada, tostada, refried beans, jalapeño pepper, and a scoop of one of the restaurant's specialties—vermicelli!).

As I savor each delicious morsel of my lunch (along with the requisite bottle of Corona and its equally requisite slice of lime), the restaurant slowly begins to fill up. This is obviously a place where all the locals come—everybody knows everybody else. It's the kind of place where, when you walk in, six of your best friends greet you. In a subsequent conversation (they have a great dinner menu, too), Ty tells me that La Junta is quite a bit different than the big city life of, say, Denver. Here, everyone knows each other, like an enormous and very friendly family. Among other things, La Junta is a major agricultural area in southeastern Colorado, a place where the railroad is a vital economic link to places both near and far. Ty says that although he's planning to go to college, he also plans to return to La Junta to maintain those close ties.

Bursting at the (abdominal) seams, I exit the Mexico City Restaurant and head over to the Stagecoach Motel at the very end of West Third Street—my base of operations for the next two nights. A friendly hello and a very comfortable (and quite inexpensive) room greet me as I flop down on the bed for a quick nap. Tomorrow would be a long and busy day.

Saturday morning dawns with crystal blue perfection. I climb into my car and head over to the Comanche Grasslands Field Office for what I am certain will be the event of a lifetime. I'm here to take a guided auto tour of Picketwire Canyonlands, located on the Comanche National Grassland south of La Junta. This entire region has a long and most interesting history. It seems that sometime in the early 1600s a party of Spanish military explorers (the Spanish, by 1598, had already established the colony of New Mexico) ventured into these canyons seeking treasure. Whether due to the harshness of the terrain or the unforgiving nature of the environment, they all perished somewhere in these canyons. Since they died without the benefit of clergy, the river running through the canyon was named *El Rio de Las Animas Perdidas en Purgatorio* (the River of Souls Lost in Purgatory). Later, French trappers traveling through the area shortened the name to "le Purgatoire." When Anglo travelers arrived in the region via the Santa Fe Trail, they had difficulty pronouncing "Purgatoire" and further corrupted the name into "Picket Wire"—a name the area retains to this day.

But, perhaps just as important, is the fact that these primitive canyons are also home to the largest dinosaur tracksite in North America—a tracksite I was about to explore as part of a guided tour orchestrated by the U.S. Forest Service.

Approximately 150 million years ago (during the Late Jurassic Period) the climate of the area was tropical and considerably different from the arid conditions that characterize the landscape today. The dominant plants were cone-bearing trees and ferns. The geology was considerably different, too. The canyon walls and the rock layers making up those walls did not exist. The Rocky Mountains had not yet formed and the land was gently rolling with many stream valleys.

Hundreds of dinosaurs inhabited the land now known as the Purgatoire River Valley. These animals congregated along the banks of a huge freshwater lake—one that stretched for many miles in every direction. As the dinosaurs ate the foliage and drank the water, they plodded through the lakeside mud (primarily a sandstone/limestone mix) leaving behind long trails of footprints in the soupy muck. Those tracks paralleled the shores of the ancient lake. Later these muddy flats were buried and turned to stone. Then, about 85 million years ago, the continents began to shift, buckling the earth and causing the Rocky Mountains to rise. Later, rain and snow in

IMAGINE THAT IT IS MILLIONS OF YEARS AGO. *A blazing sun hangs in the late summer sky. Many animals, both large and small, prowl the edge of the flood plain looking for something to eat. The roar of an isolated carnivore or the stomp of great herbivores walking in a small group occasionally echoes across the landscape.*

This is a tropical environment that stretches out to the horizon. Clumps of low-lying plants are scattered around the edges of a large shallow lake. Clouds of dust are kicked up in the distance—a migrating herd of creatures is meandering along an unseen trail. There is a shallow stream that empties into the lake. Along its edges are clusters of bushes and tall leafy trees. Fallen logs and moss-covered rocks line the edges of the stream. The waters of the stream are populated by tiny clams, shrimp, and other invertebrates. Every so often, a band of sauropods, large ponderous beasts, plods along the shoreline of the lake. They, too, are looking for something to eat. Perhaps they will find a clump of succulent plants to devour.

Now imagine a few carnivorous theropods, each on its own journey, strolling across the mud flats. These three-toed meat-eaters would often patrol the shallow flats in search of small prey. Occasionally, they would wander across the stream to seek possible food sources on the other side.

A torrential rain falls, sending a flood of water down through the valley. Silt and mud sweep across the tracks burying them under a layer of mushy sediment. Each of the tracks is now entombed in a blanket of ooze—preserved for the ages.

Approximately 1,300 tracks are preserved in the dynamic and eye-popping landscape.

the mountains cascaded downhill creating the Purgatoire River Valley and eventually exposing the tracks. Today over 1,300 of these footprints are revealed at the Picketwire Dinosaur Tracksite.

This tracksite has yielded six track-bearing layers (about 40 to 45 million years of built-up soil) representing a minimum of a hundred animals. The prints are primarily those of long-necked sauropods (what we used to know as *Brontosaurus*), as well as two-legged carnivorous theropods like *Allosaurus*. According to Martin Lockley, who heads the Dinosaur Trackers Research Group at the University of Colorado at Denver, and a scientist who has studied the tracks extensively, this site is significant because it has revealed. "… some of the world's longest trackways, the world's first reported Brontosaur tracks, evidence of herding or social behavior, and evidence that brontosaurs trampled and extensively disturbed the soils beneath their feet."

As a paean to the notion that many great scientific discoveries (e.g. penicillin) are made quite by accident, so too was this site. Young Betty Jo Rittenhouse was a student at a school in Higbee, Colorado, about twelve miles downstream from the tracksite. Late in 1935, she discovered the tracks while walking beside the river. One day, her science teacher, Don Hayes, was teaching a lesson on dinosaurs. Betty Jo told him, "I know where there's some tracks." And, as adults do sometimes, he teased her a bit and quickly dismissed it. The next day her mother came to the school and said, "Yeah, we really do have some tracks and I know where the tracksite is."

So, in February 1936, the first documented expedition to the site was mounted. One of the initial newspaper reports of the expedition erroneously reported that both *Triceratops* and *Tyrannosaurus* tracks were discovered next to the river. What the reporter did not know was that those two Cretaceous creatures did not exist until nearly 80 million years after the tracks were left alongside what was now the Purgatoire River. Nevertheless, the newspaper report brought the tracksite to the attention of the world.

Although Betty Jo would discount her importance in this paleontological revelation, she would later write, "My first impressions … were that the tracks looked like a large turkey or bird that had walked across the river." It was an interesting statement to be sure; all the more so since current scientific thought is that there is an evolutionary connection between ancient dinosaurs and modern-day birds.

Roland T. Bird visited the site in November of 1938. Oddly, Mr. Bird was on his way to view a better-known dinosaur tracksite in Texas and decided at the last minute to take a small detour to the Purgatoire site. There, he correctly interpreted many of the tracks as those left by brontosaurs. His description, and subsequent letter in *Natural History Magazine,* confirmed that these were the first sauropod tracks ever reported. Unfortunately, Bird did not spend a lot of time at the tracksite, but devoted most of his attention to the more easily accessible Texas site.

Because of Bird's extensive work at the Texas site, the Purgatoire tracks were, almost overnight, erased from the public's consciousness. They were not "rediscovered" until the early 1980s when researchers from the University of Colorado at Denver began to examine them more closely and in greater detail. Thanks to a resurgent wave of "dinosauria" at that time, along with improved research methods, the tracks soon became more popularly known by the general public.

Now, about forty amateur paleontologists are gathered inside the board room at the Comanche Grasslands Field Office. There, Kevin Lindahl, the Visitor Information Assistant and leader of this tour, is explaining to us the prehistoric, historic, and natural features of the canyons. Besides the dinosaur tracksite, we will be visiting some examples of rock art, left on cliffside boulders by prehistoric visitors to the canyons. We'll also visit an early Catholic church and cemetery with 150-year-old headstones, as well as the nearby Rourke Ranch—which is on the National Register of Historic Places.*

After the orientation meeting we all climb into our respective vehicles—eighteen in all—and begin the one-hour caravan down to the river. I'm riding with Justin Simon (my rental car did not have the required high ground clearance necessary to navigate the primitive and very rocky canyon roads), who has been a volunteer with the Forest Service for the past three

---

*Several months prior to this venture, I was required to sign an official legal document absolving the U.S. Forest Service of any liability in the event of any physical harm to my person. I also had to attest to the fact that I had thoroughly read and understood the required *Safety Checklist*. Among other things, this two-page document (in very fine print) noted that, "You may encounter animals such as prairie rattlesnakes, scorpions, and centipedes. Encounters are very rare, but you should AVOID TALL GRASS, and WATCH WHERE YOU SIT AND PLACE YOUR HANDS AND FEET." The capital letters are theirs, not mine.

years. A maintenance technician for Conoco Phillips, he has lived in La Junta since 1991. As we head in a southerly direction over paved roads, I'm curious as to why he takes this trek on multiple Saturdays in May, June, September, and October. "I just wanted to do the dinosaur tracks for free," he tells me honestly.

Early in our sojourn, Justin warns me that, "I'm kind of a talker." And, indeed, it is true. In the space of a twenty-plus mile drive, we discuss professional basketball, cow manure, church music, the military, cows in general, electronics, jeeps, GPS, track and field, the dangers of cows on the road, CPR training, oil reserves, gas reserves, bicycles, global warming, more (damn) cows, Mexican food, religion, genealogy, hats, and, oh yes, dinosaurs. To this day, I'm still not sure if it was a nonstop conversation or a nonstop exercise in conversational listening.

After a brief trek on the asphalt highway we turn onto a dusty and pock-marked dirt road that rambles over a varied terrain. Here short-grasses are interspersed with several varieties of cactus, willows, sedges, salt bushes, juniper, tamarisk,* and piñon. The eighteen-vehicle caravan fills the sky with a perpetual cloud of dust that creeps into every nook and cranny of our truck (we are the last vehicle in this cross-country convoy). After another twenty minutes of travel, the opening and closing of two gates, and a bone-jarring descent into the canyon, we first arrive at the site of the ancient rock art. The images of cattle, horses, and other 1,500-year-old animals etched into the rock face is both compelling and awesome. Kevin explains to us how the rock images may have been created to ensure a successful hunt or a year of plentiful food. After snapping off a series of photos, we travel a little bit further to a picturesque overlook and stare across the valley to the dinosaur tracksite in the distance.

Then it's back into the vehicles and on to the tracksite. Upon our arrival, we all change into shorts and river shoes, which we'll need later for a short walk across a shallow river bottom to the side where most of the dinosaur tracks are visible. We briefly stroll (two-tenths of a mile) down a dirt

---

*In an effort to control excessive soil erosion, tamarisk plants were brought into the area in the 1930s. However, in an ecological twist of fate (and this is why it's not nice to fool with Mother Nature) tamarisk plants have proven to increase the risk of fire danger in these ecologically sensitive canyons. Moreover, each tamarisk plant has the capacity to take in from 200–300 gallons of water each day. Each year, the Forest Service regularly removes large numbers of tamarisk plants, particularly along river banks, in an effort to re-right the natural balance in the region.

road busy with springing grasshoppers and lined with golden wildflowers, and we arrive at an interpretive sign posted at the edge of the river:

You've arrived at the largest dinosaur tracksite in North America.
- *Use caution when crossing the river. Bottom can be slick and the current may be swift seasonally.*
- *The tracksite surface is fragile. Do not ride bikes or horses on the site or pour plaster into the prints.*
- *If you want to see live dinosaurs, you're about 150 million years too late.*

All forty of us gather around Kevin as he explains some of the paleontological and geological features of the site.

"What is really significant about this site," he says, "is that there are several sets of parallel tracks that go through it. There's a lot of tracks close together. When we walk, our steps are about three feet apart. But these guys were picking their foot up and setting them down sixteen to eighteen feet downrange the next time that foot touched down. So, the fact that we have long tracks close together indicates that there were several dinosaurs walking in line. And the parallel tracks they [the paleontologists] found, the larger tracks are on the outside and the smaller juvenile tracks are inside those, which made them think that there might have been a herding mentality. In other words they traveled in a group and the young were protected while they were traveling. Those were some of the things they had never seen before in dinosaur tracks until they got to this site. So that was pretty significant stuff."

Kevin proceeds to pass around a collection of three dinosaur gastroliths. "These were used to aid digestion," he explains. "They are similar to those found in the gizzard of a chicken or a bird. Paleontologists often look for these—which are frequently found in groups of up to three hundred or more. And usually that would be where the animal died and the gastroliths would be left behind."

Before we cross over to the other side of the river, where the main tracksite is located, Kevin points out a large flat rock area behind us with several tracks. One of the first things I notice is that the tracks are all from three-toed creatures—indicating that they were all probably bipedal (two-footed).

Some of these three-toed tracks, which are scattered throughout the entire site, are approximately six inches in length, while others extend to eighteen inches long. My "I'm-not-an-official-paleontologist-but-I-think-I-know-what-I'm-talking-about" mind quickly surmises that these may have been made by several different species of creatures. My assumption is confirmed later when I learn that some tracks may belong to a group of carnivorous dinosaurs known as theropods (meaning: "beast feet"), while others may have been left by a group of herbivores known as ornithopods (meaning: "bird feet").

My after-the-fact research also revealed that the size of a dinosaur can be easily estimated solely from the length of its footprint (or track). Paleontologists have a rule of thumb that states that, "…for most bipedal (two-footed) dinosaurs, the hip height equals about four to five times the foot length." Martin Lockley, who has studied this site extensively, postulates that the three-toed creatures that tramped across this now suspended sediment ranged in height from two to eight feet. And, while he can't pinpoint the exact species that left these tracks, he has been able to make an educated guess that the larger tracks were probably left by *Allosaurus* and/or *Ceratosaurus* and the smaller tracks were most likely the work of *Ornitholestes*.*

A line of us begins to ford the shallow (one foot deep) river. Although the river is not swift, there is a slick coating of mud and silt on the rocks on the bottom, so we each take our time in crossing. Arriving on the other side, we are greeted by an incredible array of rock-hard footprints in various patterns and concentrations. As I scale the shaley slope, I find myself in the midst of dozens of these prints, some clear and distinct, others less so.

The tracks are remnants of many different types of dinosaurs—some large, others small. They are indicators of not only the size of various creatures, but of how fast they walked, how they walked (one foot in front of

---

*I certainly do not wish to be a purveyor of the long-held myth—and most certainly it is a myth—among certain unmarried females who, when talking (in decidedly hushed tones) about potential mates, voice the maxim, "Large feet, small…(you know what)." I would not want you, dear reader, to draw any possible conclusions about my inclusion of that phrase in any discussion of foot length and, say, my obvious and considerable lack of intelligence.

the other signifying an erect gait or a sprawling gait indicating a semi-erect posture), how many creatures were in a specific spot, which types of animals were predominant in this area, and the direction(s) in which they were headed. It's sort of like taking a census of people in a rural town. Just a few facts can reveal a tremendous amount of information about habits, behaviors, and customs.

It is not unusual for paleontologists to refer to dinosaur tracks as "experiments in soil mechanics." That means that the tracks provide scientists with valuable information about the composition of the soil when the tracks were made, as well as the materials that composed that soil in prehistoric times. The ancient geography of an area can be reconstructed depending on whether a creature stepped into mud or sand, or whether it left a deep footprint or a shallow one.

What becomes clear about this site is a consistency in the direction of various sets of tracks. This lends further support for the idea that these beasts traveled along the edge of an ancient lake. I note that a majority of the tracks move in an east-west direction, suggesting that the ancient lakeshore was also in an east-west direction. A few sets of tracks are perpendicular to

The author's foot inside a sauropod track.

the flow of the river. This may suggest that some individual dinosaurs, or even a group of creatures, may have attempted to cross over to the other side of the shallow lake.

Most of the tracks are clogged with dirt and silt, suggesting that this river floods every now and then. Several of the tracks have short grasses and other plants growing inside them. This presents a decidedly surrealistic scene—modern-day plants taking root inside 65-million year old footprints.

A significant piece of information that turns up in my later investigations is that the rocks in which these prints are embedded consist of alternating layers of tough limestone and soft, gray shale. Both sandstone and shale are sedimentary rocks, indicating that the ancient environment was undeniably a lake basin or shallow waterway. The limestone layers have recorded features other than footprints, such as ripple marks and mud cracks—a further indication that those layers probably formed along the edge of a lake. Also embedded in the layers is a wide variety of small organisms such as shrimp, snails, fish bones, clams, plant stems, and the remains of fossilized algae. As you might expect, this offers scientists further information about life in this ancient sea—leading to the conclusion that this lake was a healthy and active ecosystem that sustained a wide variety of life forms, besides a bevy of dinosaurian visitors.

As I wander around this area, I can see the large rounded prints of sauropods side-by-side

A young member of the group is almost swallowed up by the size of a single sauropod track.

across the hardened surface. Kevin explains that this is one of the few places in the world where evidence of herding behavior of dinosaurs is preserved. In some places, the limestone layers contain clear trackways of sauropods. In other places, the layers have been heavily trampled. The prints of these big plant-eaters show that they were generally traveling in a westerly direction along the shoreline—often in groups or herds. The differences in size of those prints may be indicative of mixed groups of young and old creatures or males and females.

Near the western end of the tracksite, I come across a distinct three-toed track that may have been left by an *Allosaurus*. Next to it is a faintly outlined larger track, which could have been an adult dinosaur protecting its baby. As I look around I can see the tracks of these carnivorous dinosaurs spreading out in all directions—a sign that they may have roamed this lakeshore primarily as solitary hunters. Generally meat-eaters are less common than plant-eaters, but this site seems to indicate equal numbers of footprints from both.

Paleontologists have a number of mathematical formulas that they use to calculate the speed of dinosaurs, based primarily on the stride length of the tracks. Although my mathematical ability is severely limited (having never made it past basic geometry in college), I'll see if I can detail it in a way that won't cast any further doubt on my limited intellectual capabilities.

If you or I, for example, were to run (in wet bare feet) down a dry sidewalk, the distance between each of our footprints would be greater than if we were walking down that same sidewalk (with those same soggy feet). In other words, our stride length walking is considerably shorter than our stride length running. The same holds true for dinosaurs (although they didn't have any sidewalks to run on). The sauropod stride-length of the tracks at this site indicate that they were traveling at a speed of about two to four mph. On the other hand, the stride-length of the theropods shows that they were moving along the shoreline of the ancient lake at a speed of about four to six mph. Both of these speeds indicate that most of the animals were walking rather than running or galloping. It is likely, therefore, that they weren't being chased or that they weren't doing the chasing.

Newly formed mountains and long-preserved tracks provide an interesting contrast.

The sun is high overhead, and clusters of fellow paleontologists have decided to take a break and eat their lunches. One couple sets up an umbrella and lawn chairs (how the heck did they get an umbrella and two lawn chairs in their backpacks?) on a shale shelf beside the riverbank. Another couple lays down a blanket on an outcropping and pulls out some tiny hors d'oeuvres and a small bottle of wine. Others are sitting on rocks or standing in small conversational groups eating their bagged lunches. The mood is almost festive—it's like a picnic at the beach. It's a scene that is definitely in stark contrast to the prehistoric motif and equally prehistoric creatures that also used to lunch in this area. I, too, find a rock to sit on, whereupon I reach into my backpack to retrieve a slightly warm turkey sandwich and a bag of crushed mesquite-flavored potato chips. Sinking my teeth into the meal, I can pretend that I'm a fellow carnivore beside a shallow and familiar waterway.

Shortly afterward, we are summoned to head back across the river and on to the vehicles. I can't help but take one last look at this amazing site. My camera is filled with an abundance of photos that I will later stare at for hours—the geological and paleontological information revealed by these prints is almost beyond the imagination. This is a site that captures the imagination and just doesn't let go. It is engaging, it is fascinating, and it is incredible. But, as I learn later, it is also in danger.

It seems as though the Purgatoire River, the same force that unearthed this tracksite years ago, has since begun to erode it away. Kevin points out horizontal lines creasing the layers of limestone and sandstone (there are actually six distinct and different layers of dinosaur tracks at the site). When these layers were covered up, they exerted weight on the various layers resulting in stress fractures. Some of the underlying layers are soft and are beginning to erode. The force of the river water washing by these layers is causing some blocks of rock to break and fall into the river. Bit by bit, pieces of the site are being lost to the forces of nature.

Kevin points to a place that has eroded out about five or six feet in the past hundred years. Recently, the Forest Service has taken steps to ensure the

A set of tracks heads toward the Purgatoire River.

long-term preservation of the tracksite by installing erosion control structures. They've built some weirs out of the rock that's coming off the site. These are positioned to slow the river and its deposits of sediment. The intent is to create some natural sandbars. Ironically, these preservation measures are covering up some of the tracks, but at least those tracks are being preserved for future generations.

We return to the parking area, remove our river shoes, climb into drier clothing, and clamber back inside the cars. The day sparkles with an azure blue ceiling overhead—there's not a cloud in the sky. We are off to see a crumbling church and abandoned dwellings, the remnants of settlers who homesteaded this area in the 1870s and 1880s. We meander our way between rocky cliffs in colors of copper, beige, sienna, brown, tan, along with streaks of black. Coursing along the canyon rims is a sprinkling of piñon trees silhouetted against the skyline. Butterflies dart over the scrub brush.

After our visit to the church and cemetery, we head off to the historic Rourke Ranch, where we learn how this pioneering family was able to expand their 160-acre homestead in the late 1800s to an over 50,000-acre cattle empire that was maintained by descendants of the original owners until well into the 1970s.

After a "pit stop," we slip back into our cars and begin the long climb out of the canyon along the now familiar rough and rocky road. I am invited to travel back to the field office in La Junta with Kevin to obtain some additional information about the tracksite. I climb down from Justin's car and make my way over to Kevin's (apparently prehistoric) truck.

At first glance, Kevin appears to be an escapee from the 1960s. His long beard, pony tail, and genuine smile belie an intense devotion to this area and to the mission of the Forest Service in protecting it. Kevin first visited the site many years ago while on a car tour with some friends. During the next season he volunteered to help with tours. He was not only taken with the mystique of the canyon, but also with its prehistoric significance for visitors. "I want people to walk away with the uniqueness of the canyon. I want them to leave with a sense of awe, as well as how unique this place is."

Kevin works with a volunteer corps of five and a paid staff of two. This dedicated crew is responsible for maintaining an area of about 23,000 acres—of which the dinosaur tracksite is just one part. As he puts it, "[This is the] perfect job—minimal paperwork with most of the time spent in the field." It is clearly evident that he is equal parts passion and wonder as he describes the significance of the area for both scientists and the general public. He tells me that about 60 percent of the visitors are Colorado natives, while the rest are from other states and other parts of the world. By the end of our trek back into La Junta, I have the sense that this region is a Disneyland for the senses as well as for the intellect.

After returning to the Forest Service office, I toss my gear into my car and head back to the Stagecoach Motel. The Colorado sun has worked its ever-present magic, and all I want right now is a slow leisurely dip in the motel swimming pool. The icy water is a most refreshing accent to a day spent tracking dinosaurs in the remoteness and heat of southeastern Colorado.

The next morning, I'm up before the proverbial "crack of dawn." Today I'm off to Cañon City and another prehistoric wonderland. I load my backpack and supplies into the back seat of the car, climb in, and drive to the rear of the parking lot and my exit westward onto US 50. Looking up and down the road for any approaching traffic, I notice a Sinclair gas station across the street. There, perched on the roof above the gas pumps, is the company's iconic and ever-present mascot—a *Brontosaurus* (a.k.a. *Apatosaurus*).

I'm not certain, but I think he's smiling!

NEED TO KNOW ABOUT **Comanche National Grasslands**

DIRECTIONS To get to La Junta, head south on I-25 from Denver or Colorado Springs toward Pueblo. About forty-three miles south of Colorado Springs (just as you're entering Pueblo), turn onto US 50 (east) and head toward the town of La Junta, which is sixty-five miles east of Pueblo.

To get to the Forest Service office, stay on US 50 as it swings around La Junta. Just after the railroad tracks is a KFC Restaurant and a traffic signal. US 50 then begins to bend to the left, and West Third Street goes straight (look for the overhead sign). Exit (slight right turn) onto West Third Street. Continue on West Third Street through the downtown area of La Junta. You'll go through several stoplights, and the road then becomes East Third Street. Keep going, and just as East Third ends (back at US 50) you'll see the Forest Service/Comanche National Grassland building on your right. Pull into the small parking lot in front of the building.

Although the auto tour is the best (and most informative) way to see the dinosaur tracksite, it is also possible to drive yourself to the trailhead and hike or mountain bike down through the canyon to the tracksite. For that venture, drive south from La Junta on CO 109 for thirteen miles. Turn right (west) on County Road 802 (David Canyon Road) and continue for eight miles. Turn left (south) on County Road 25 and travel for six miles. Turn left at Picket Wire Corrals onto Forest Service Road 500A. Travel along Forest Service Road 500A for three miles, following the signs to Withers Canyon Trailhead. Park at the Withers Canyon Trailhead parking loop.

Starting your hike or bike trek at the Withers Canyon Trailhead, follow the trail east-northeast to a brown pipe gate. From this point, the trail descends 250 feet in elevation into Withers Canyon. Then, the trail follows a dirt two-track road (east) into Picketwire Canyon. Once in Picketwire Canyon, the trail turns south/southwest and heads up canyon. Markers are placed approximately every 1.5 miles along the trail. The hike from Withers Canyon Trailhead to the dinosaur tracksite is 5.3 miles one way (10.6 miles round trip). Be sure to get a detailed trail map ("Recreation Opportunity Guide") from the USDA Forest Service/Comanche National Grassland office in La Junta.

CONTACT INFORMATION Tours are offered through the Recreation Fee Demonstration Program of the United States Forest Service. Contact them at: USDA Forest Service, Comanche National Grassland, 1420 East Third St., La Junta, CO 81050, (719) 384-2181, www.fs.fed.us/r2/psicc/coma

continued next page

continued from previous page

FEES $15.00 per adult; $7.50 per child (Believe me, it's worth every penny ... and then some!)

HOURS The guided tour lasts for eight hours —8:00 a.m. to 4:00 p.m.

BEST TIME TO VISIT The guided tour is offered on Saturdays in May, June, September, and October. Check the website (www.fs.fed.us/r2/psicc/coma) for the actual dates.

CAMPING/LODGING There are a wide variety of lodges, inns, and motels in La Junta. These include the Stagecoach Motel (http://www.stagecoachlj.com) [my personal preference], Holiday Inn Express, Mid-Town Motel, La Junta Inn & Suites, Travel Inn of La Junta, and the KOA campground (http://koa.com/where/co /06119). Check out the La Junta Chamber of Commerce (http://www.lajunta chamber.com/) for the latest information.

SERVICES There is an outhouse available at the dinosaur tracksite and another available at the Rourke Ranch. There is no drinkable water in the canyon. Each person should bring a minimum of two quarts of water at all times of the year.

ACCESS Physically challenged individuals may need assistance in crossing the river to see the main tracksite.

DIFFICULTY RATING Easy. Most of the difficulty is in driving up and down the rocky, bumpy, and less-than-graded roads for getting in and out of the site. The Forest Service recommends four-wheel drive vehicles with high clearance. Take that more as a command rather than a suggestion (you'll remember this later—particularly if you suffer a broken axle and need to get a mechanic—literally, out in the middle of nowhere).

NOTES In a word (or more) this tour will simply blow you away. To have the opportunity to see and actually walk among the tracks of dinosaurs that traveled through this area millions of years ago is one of the most incredible experiences of my life. I was literally mesmerized by the array of dino footprints—and went through three rolls of slide film before I realized that I had taken photos of one set of tracks four different times from four different angles. This is a tour for the entire family—one the kids will talk about for years and one the adults will savor and tell their grandchildren over and over and over again.

  You don't have to be a dinosaur fanatic to enjoy this venture. It will get your attention and not let go. You'll get to experience something that few people have ever seen. And, shame on you if you forget to bring your camera (be sure to get the requisite photo of your foot placed inside one of the dinosaur tracks). Like me, you will probably groan and moan when it's time to leave the main tracksite and cross back over the river. But, you will always treasure this adventure!

CHAPTER 8

Stegosaurus and the "Bone Wars"

SKYLINE DRIVE & GARDEN PARK FOSSIL AREA

After sweeping around the perimeter of La Junta, US 50 rockets westward across the flatlands of southeastern Colorado like a shaft of steel. I've left my hotel behind and set out for a two-hour drive to Cañon City, where Skyline Drive and the Garden Park Fossil Area are located. The first part of my journey takes me past rich agricultural lands brimming with all manner of vegetable goods. I slip by the tiny town of Rocky Ford, which is known as one of the leading melon producing regions of the country (it's too bad they aren't in season at this time of the year—a fresh-picked cantaloupe for breakfast would sure make the three-day old donut I picked up back at the hotel go down just a little easier).

As the car follows the ribbon of asphalt toward Pueblo, I can see that it's a foreboding day. An enormous bank of gun-metal grey clouds rises up over the distant Rocky Mountains, signaling a potential morning rainstorm. I slip through the downtown streets of Pueblo and out toward the foothills, where Cañon City is sprawled out against the mountainous backdrop. The stale donut is beginning to send me subtle messages from the pit of my stomach, but the clearly open spaces (absolutely no convenience stores as far as the eye can see) around me indicate I will have to wait for fifty or so miles before any gastronomic relief.

I drive into Cañon City and am immediately flanked by long rows of motels, fast food restaurants, and brightly colored gas stations on both sides of the road. I quickly notice that Cañon City is home to the Colorado Women's Correctional Facility. (Note to self: Talk nice to all the waitresses in town and leave extra large tips.) This town is also the gateway to the Royal Gorge—a stunning geologic wonder that will literally suck the breath out of you when seen for the first time—especially if, like me, you have a passionate and abiding respect for very high (and/or very deep) geologic wonders. However, my immediate destination is the Dinosaur Depot Museum, which is adjacent to the Royal Gorge Train Station. Dinosaur Depot has been lovingly turned into a small, but incredible, museum for dinosaur lovers of all persuasions.

Soon after I walk through the door, I meet Lois Oxford, who is both the Volunteer Coordinator and Lab Supervisor. A wide smile and an outgoing personality let me know that this will be both a rewarding and pleasant journey back in time. After a brief introduction, she leads me on a personal tour of the museum, which is crammed with dinosaur fossils of every size, shape, and description. The museum's space may be limited, but its displays are not.

One of the first displays that visitors (especially kids) notice is the *Allosaurus* skull greeting visitors in the main exhibit room. Lois tells me that most people assume it's a *T. rex* skull because it is similar in size and shape to that slightly more famous carnivore. However, as Lois points out, there are two ways to distinguish these creatures. For one, *Tyrannosaurus* was nearly twice as large as an *Allosaurus*.* But, even more significant is the fact that *Allosaurus* had three fingers on each hand, while *T. rex* only had two. Two fingers, three fingers—no matter, the razor-sharp claws on the ends of

*T. rex weighed in at about six tons, attained a height of approximately eighteen feet (to the head), and was about forty feet long. *Allosaurus*, on the other hand, came in at around one and a half tons, reached a height of nearly seven feet (at the hips), and had a body length of about twenty-five feet. You certainly don't have to be big to be remembered, but I suppose it doesn't hurt.

The Preparation Lab at Dinosaur Depot lets visitors get a first-hand look at scientists in action.

those fingers could do a job on any potential prey unfortunate enough to get a little too close.

On the right wall of the main exhibit area is the fossil of a complete *Stegosaurus*. Lois points to the informative sign and tells me, "We put the sign up there to let people know it's not a fish. People would often stop and stare at the fossil thinking it was something other than a dinosaur." The fossil is actually a replica of the only almost complete *Stegosaurus* (only the front legs and shoulder are missing) known to science—one that was prepared and worked on in the Dinosaur Depot lab.

It was June of 1992 when a group of paleontologists from the Denver Museum of Nature and Science was working a dinosaur site at Garden Park Fossil Area just outside Cañon City. As chance would have it, one of the workers was prospecting one evening up in a narrow canyon. Poking his rock hammer into an exposure on the rock face, he pulled out the neck vertebra of a *Stegosaurus* dinosaur.

The next day, a crew of diggers was dispatched to the site. Millimeter by millimeter and inch by inch, the neck vertebrae were unearthed. Then, the most incredible discovery of all—an apparently intact skull! (Dinosaur skulls are rare finds because their hollow and fragile nature is no match for intense and constant geological pressures over the millennia.) Using small probes, soft brushes, and dilute plastics, the fragile bone was slowly and most carefully exposed.

The excavation of the skeleton continued in August of that year. A complete and articulated tail (with three of the four tail spikes in place) was also uncovered. As the excavation continued, it was realized that this was an almost complete, and very large specimen. Due to its completeness, there was some degree of reluctance in dividing it up into pieces (a common practice in paleontology) for transport out of the isolated canyon. It was decided to contact nearby Fort Carson to see if they would be willing to donate the use of one of their Chinook helicopters to lift the completely jacketed *Stegosaurus* (with a total weight in excess of six and one-half tons) out of the canyon.

The excavation crew also contacted Colorado Quarries in Cañon City for some heavy machinery to dig out the complete skeleton. Meanwhile, volunteers worked feverishly to jacket the skeleton in layers of protective plaster. All that was left was for the Army to lift the payload out without banging into the narrow canyon walls. The entire crew watched (with the proverbial baited breath) as the helicopter pilot, using only verbal commands from the ground, successfully raised the payload and deposited it on a nearby flatbed truck. From there, it was transported to the Dinosaur Depot Museum in Cañon City for preparation. It eventually took more than four years of preparation work before the specimen was ready for public display in the museum.

Ever since the first specimen was discovered just north of Morrison, Colorado, *Stegosaurus* has been a prehistoric puzzle. It's name ("roofed lizard") comes from its most distinguishing feature—the double row of seventeen tall, triangular plates rising from its neck, back, and tail. O. C. Marsh, who originally named the creature, mistakenly believed that the plates overlaid each other much like the shingles on a roof.

To date, approximately eighty specimens have been recovered in North America, primarily throughout the Morrison Formation. However, most recently (2007), a partial specimen from Portugal has been unearthed. This new discovery may provide additional evidence in support of a prehistoric terrestrial connection between North America and Europe.

As I stare at the specimen on the wall of the museum, I am taken by the excessive mass of this creature. In fact, an average adult *Stegosaurus* reached a length of about twenty-five feet and weighed in at around five to five and one-half tons. This would have made it equivalent to a modern-day Minke Whale. It was also distinguished by an arched back that tapered to a tail (as long as its body) on one end and a seem-ingly under-sized head on the other. Its head was held low to the ground, an obvious advantage for a herbivorous dinosaur. It also possessed a toothless beak at the front of its mouth, which it used to tear away low-lying vegetation. With a lit-tle imagination, one could say that this creature looked like a small-headed elephant with severely shortened legs. It is speculated that it had a vora-cious appetite, feasting primarily on conifers, cy-cads, horsetails, ferns, and mosses. And, just like modern-day birds and crocodiles, it swallowed gas-troliths to aid in the internal processing of food.

Stegosaurus (From Wikimedia Creative Commons under the terms of the *GNU Free Documentation License*)

Lois shows me some gastroliths "that were in the stomach of a dinosaur, probably about 115 mil-lion years ago." When she passes these around to kids, they will often reply, "Ohhh, I don't want to hold these. I don't want to hold something that was inside the stomach of a dinosaur." "But," as she continues, "we'll tell them that when we dig up the big plant-eaters we'll look under the ribs in the area of the stomach and there are the gastroliths … and the little kids—they love it. And we'll pass them around. And, we'll ask them, 'how often do you get a chance to hold gastroliths?'" It's quite obvious that Lois and the other volunteers at the museum are keen on pro-viding visitors, particularly the youngest ones, with a wealth of "hands-on" experiences. "They learn so much more this way than just reading something," she states emphatically.

Scientists have been puzzled by the fact that *Stegosaurus* possessed a very small skull in proportion to the rest of its body. Analysis of the skull also suggests that they possessed an extremely small brain—about the size of a golf ball. Indeed, the brain was one of the smallest among all the dinosaurs* and was a factor that contributed to the mistaken and persistent belief that dinosaurs were dim-witted and unintelligent. Another erroneous assumption was that this diminutive brain was insufficient to control such a large creature. As most anatomy professors will tell you, brain size is only a rudimentary indicator of the intelligence of the animal to whom it belongs. That's primarily because there is a complex and interlocking set of factors that affect a creature's overall intelligence. There appears to be some degree of agreement, however, that higher ratios of brain to body mass (humans, for example) may increase the amount of brain mass available for high-level cognitive tasks (such as completing a 1040 form without precipitating an early-morning phone call from someone who begins the conversation with, "I'm from the government and I'd like to talk with you").

One of the ongoing conundrums of *Stegosaurus* research was the discovery of an enlarged region of the spinal column near the hip region. Initially, some scientists believed that this was a "second brain," something that controlled the creature's hind limbs. This theory has now been discounted and it is currently believed that the enlargement was not brain tissue, but a complex nerve center called the "sacral plexus." The sacral plexis was, quite possibly, a secondary control center for the creature's spinal cord.

Another enduring mystery associated with this beast pertains to the dermal plates along its backside. Although these plates arose from the surface of the skin, rather than from its skeleton, their function has never been clear. Original theories suggested that the plates were used primarily as defensive structures, protecting the animal from attacks by large predators. This idea has been largely discounted, yet modern-day paleontologists still

---

*While the overall weight of the *Stegosaurus* was in excess of five tons, its brain was a mere 2.8 ounces – an unbelievable ratio of brain weight to body weight of 1:57,142. Modern day creatures exhibit significantly higher ratios of brain weight to body weight as follows: fish – 1:5,000; reptiles: 1:1,500; birds – 1:220; most mammals – 1:180; and humans – 1:50. It would be appropriate to mention that the ratio of brain weight to the body weight for certain creatures (authors, for example) has yet to be determined.

can't agree on their function. One theory postulates that, because the plates had blood vessels running through them, they helped control the body temperature of the animals. Other researchers suggest that the plates were used to intimidate enemies by making the *Stegosaurs* look larger than it was. Still others suggest that they were used in some form of sexual display, or as a way of identifying members of the same species.

As I continue to examine the specimen on the wall, I'm curious about the placement of the plates. As Lois tells me, one of the enduring "... questions of the plates was whether they were alternating or straight-across from each other." This particular specimen convincingly proved that the plates occurred as two rows of alternating plates, one running down each side of the midline of the creature's back.*

Another mystery that has always been associated with *Stegosaurus*** is the function of its thagomizer (tail spikes). Speculation in the early part of the twentieth century postulated that these four spikes (O. C. Marsh originally thought that there were eight spikes) were used for display purposes only. However, paleontologist Robert Bakker provides some evidence (a tail more flexible than that of many other dinosaurs) that these spikes were used primarily as both defensive and offensive weapons. Ken Carpenter, a paleontologist who has done extensive field work at the Garden Park Fossil Area, offers additional evidence for this theory through an analysis of a punctured tail vertebra of *Allosaurus* into which a *Stegosaurus* tail spike fits perfectly.

When the 1992 specimen was recovered, two additional features about the spikes were noted. First, in opposition to some beliefs, it was discovered that the spikes came out from the sides of the tail, unlike old-fashioned models where the spikes would be arranged straight up and down. Second, it was noted that the bottom tail spike on this particular specimen was broken. The broken spike was immediately sent to Denver for a CAT scan, which determined that the spike had been broken when the creature was

---

*In the 1933 version of *King Kong*, the attacking *Stegosaurus* had its plates paired in a double row down its back. This was a popular interpretation in the nineteenth and twentieth centuries until the discovery of the specimen near Cañon City proved otherwise.

**Many paleontologists will tell you that the *Stegosaurus* is, quite simply, a most mysterious dinosaur ("A puzzle wrapped inside an enigma and surrounded by a riddle."). It has baffled scientists and perplexed the public ever since it was first discovered in the late 1800s. In short, it offers no easy answers. For all the easy answers in life, I frequently turn to the best-selling book by Mark Leyner and Billy Goldberg: *Why Do Men Have Nipples?*

alive—however, it never healed properly. As a result, a bone infection set in which eventually worked its way up the backbone of the creature.

As museum preparers were cleaning the specimen, they noted a series of brown markings near the front plate. These turned out to be pus pockets, indicating that the creature was seriously infected as a result of the broken spike. It is now believed that the animal died from that infection. When I asked Lois more about the animal's death, she tells me that the *Stegosaurus* probably "…went down to a pond and slid over on its side in the mud. That's why the fossil is in the laying position. It got covered up fairly quickly, which is why it's pretty much intact."

While the fossil replica is perched on the wall in the main room, the real bones are safely tucked away in a climate-controlled room in the back of the museum. "That's because if they were exposed to the air—because of that bone disease—they would just start to fall apart," Lois tells me. That exposure to air would undoubtedly cause the complete skeleton to essentially disintegrate in about ten years or so. While the public can see a very detailed and very well-articulated skeleton perched on the east wall of the museum, the actual bones are reserved for scientists to study in a more controlled environment.

There was another "*Stegosaurus* event" that took place years earlier and which cemented this prehistoric wonder firmly in the minds of every Coloradan. In 1980, a fourth grade class at McElwain Elementary School in Denver noted that Colorado did not have (at that time) an official state fossil. After considerable discussion, the students decided to push for *Stegosaurus* as the official state fossil (since it had been first discovered in the state). As an extended lesson on legislation, the students learned about and went through all the appropriate procedures for proposing a bill. They also spent considerable time lobbying for its approval. The students traveled all over Colorado to post displays (at other schools) and rally at various community events. Finally, in 1982, Governor Richard Lamm issued the order establishing the *Stegosaurus* as the Colorado State Fossil. Then in 1991, the state legislature passed another bill making it official. The lesson: Never underestimate the power of kids in love with a dinosaur!

As I conclude my tour of the museum, I'm introduced to Pat Monaco, who is one of the founding members of the museum and is currently on its board of directors. Pat will be my guide to nearby Skyline Drive (the location of several *Ankylosaurus* tracks) as well as the Garden Park Fossil Area (the location of the Cleveland Quarry and the Marsh Quarry) outside of town. A loquacious and vivacious woman, she tells me that she has always had "paleontology in my blood." Without wasting a moment, we are quickly out the door and headed west on US 50 (toward Royal Gorge). The road is flanked by rolling hills (draped in reds and crimsons) on the left and soaring cliffs on the right. Skyline Drive is about three and a half miles outside of town.

Shortly after we make a right turn onto Skyline Drive, we stop beside a deserted trading post. Pat tells me that the dinosaur tracks we are about to see were first discovered in the 1950s by a local teacher and his students. The teacher swore the kids to secrecy "because he didn't want anybody to deface them." Then, in the 1990s, a local paleontology student who was working in the area saw the tracks and came to the museum to report, "I think we have a trackway up there."

"And so, for about a year and a half we worked on exposing the tracks—there's about seventy of them exposed. There's probably more because this ridge goes for miles." Pat goes on to tell me, "We knew about the high school scenario because one of the students from the '50s came to the museum when we were working on the tracks and said, 'We knew about those things in the '50s, but we weren't supposed to tell anybody.'"

We head through a coffee-colored stone gateway that was originally built in the '20s and '30s. Emblazoned in the two stone columns flanking the road are the names of various states from around the country. Pat tells me that each of the names represent the home states of the prisoners who constructed the original archway more than eighty years ago.

Skyline Drive is a narrow one-way road that arcs up a single ridge. To say that the road is very curvy and very steep would certainly be a gross understatement. It winds and weaves upward in a twisting serpentine fashion

Skyline Drive as it soars off into the unknown.

(like an anaconda with a hangover) along the top of a precipitous hogback. After about a quarter mile, the sheer cliff on the left gives way to a massive drop-off—I'm guessing five hundred feet—that matches the one on my right-hand side. As I grip the steering wheel with an increased sense of determination, I feel as though I'm driving along the thin edge of a razor blade precariously perched on its edge. There is nothing but air and space on my right as well as on my left. I'm reminded that on several major bridges on the East Coast there are full-time employees (known as "escorts") who will drive any "bridge-a-phobic" motorists across those equally narrow and soaring expanses. Why not here?

We park in a small pullout on the right side of the road and walk back about a hundred yards to the dinosaur tracksite. The views in this area are just short of incredible, but it is the geology that offers the greatest spectacle. According to Peter Robinson of the University of Colorado Museum, "The Cañon City area is one of the very few places in the world where, due to the juxtaposition of sediments and geologic structures, 500 million years of fossils, from the earliest fish to Pleistocene camels, are exposed within one hour's travel."

Much of the vista surrounding this area was once the bottom of the Cretaceous Western Interior Seaway—a shallow sea that stretched from the Arctic Ocean down through the Gulf of Mexico. At the seaway's largest extent, Colorado was in the center of it, with shorelines in Utah and eastern Kansas. Many of the rocks were deposited when the area was at or below sea level. After the deposit of these sediments, the sides of the basin were raised by the uplift of the Rocky Mountains. This tilted all the rocks on their edges. Millions of years of wind and water erosion have shaped the entire valley in which Cañon City rests.

Pat points out one of several three-toed tracks embedded in the wall—except that there are only two toes left. She tells me that it's difficult to determine just exactly how many tracks there are because the tracks themselves are subject to the ravages of time and the ever-present effects of wind and water erosion. "We have no way of knowing … there could be God knows how many. We've identified seventy actual tracks … sometimes there are just toes left."

Tracks of *Ankylosaurus* dinosaurs are preserved in the rock face along Skyline Drive.

The tracks embedded in the wall before me are known as trace fossils. Trace fossils are not the actual remains of the animals, but are the result of their walking, burrowing, feeding, or being fed upon. The rock containing the tracks was laid down in an estuary just inland from the edge of the sea. An estuary is an area where a river enters a sea, and the fresh water of the river mingles with the salt water of the sea. From the tracks, it is evident that a small group of dinosaurs walked through the mud in a somewhat westerly direction. The tracks were then filled in by a flood of sand and plant debris, preserving them as casts of the actual footprints.

Since the tracks were made, the sea has come and gone. The Rocky Mountains were uplifted, pushing these formations up with them. Now the tracks are seen from underneath—looking at the bottom of their casts. There are handprints and footprints the size and pattern of which tells approximately how big the animals were that made them. Scientists have also identified the plant fossils found with the tracks, and they have studied the rocks to understand the environment in which these animals lived.

There is also some speculation that the tracks were left behind by a group of dinosaurs known as *Ankylosaurus*. These short-legged, squat herbivores remind one of a severely undersized *Triceratops*, but without the horns. What distinguishes these beasts is their heavy armor that appears as a shell on their backs, along with and a clubbed tail—made of two enlarged bone lumps—which may have been used for defensive purposes (think of a tortoise on steroids). Known as "fused reptiles," *Ankylosaurus* had broad, bony beaks for ripping out plant materials, and blunt, weak teeth that were deeply inset from the jaw. Although their exact diets are unknown, it is thought that they probably lived on low-lying plants such as club mosses, shrubby conifers, horsetails, and ferns. The tracks embedded in the wall along Skyline Drive may have been left by a small band of *Ankylosaurus* that walked through this estuary while browsing on plants or traveling along the edge of the sea to another feeding ground.

Ankylosaurus typically walked with a sprawling gait on broad, flat feet, each of which had four toes (some advanced forms of *Ankylosaurus* had three toes). They frequently squatted to protect their vulnerable bellies, thus presenting any approaching predator with an armor plating of fused bone, along with a host of spikes and lumps. They evolved during the Late Jurassic Period and became extinct about sixty-five million years ago. Unfortunately, specimens of this creature are rare—only a few bone fragments have been located in Colorado, Europe, and East Asia.

The final sign at the site reminds me that, "The tracks were left in place here in a public interpretive display to be enjoyed by all who cross Skyline Drive. To preserve them for the future, many still lie buried. Complete scientific data and casts of the visible tracks are kept at Dinosaur Depot Museum where they are available for research." I'm sure that last sentence was written for those who may have last-minute doubts about their ability to negotiate the remainder of this acrophobia-inducing single-lane road.

After leaving the tracksite, we are back along the razor-thin road that, according to my calculations, is about six feet wide. The ridge itself is approximately seven feet wide (which, if my figures are correct, means that I have a "comfort zone" of about six inches on either side. Hmmmm!). As we drive along I notice that we are right along a hogback ridge that splits through the valley and there's a jaw-gaping drop-off on my left of five hundred feet and an equally jaw-dropping precipice on my right of another five hundred feet. By now I have come to the conclusion that drivers should not be engaged in any excessive drinking, text-messaging, or sight-seeing (or all three together). This is definitely the time to keep your eyes on the road and your hands on the wheel. While the speed limit is posted at fifteen mph, I would think that most folks from out of the area would be creeping along this "goose-bumpy" road at about five mph.

Pat tells me that occasionally individuals who like to test the limits of human stupidity come up here on motorcycles, souped-up cars, and other motorized vehicles to challenge basic scientific principles such as "excessive speed + lack of adequate road = face-to-face meeting with large downhill boulders." As a former nurse, she has treated far too many broken bones and split skulls as a consequence of those daredevil engagements. An assortment of shattered automobiles has been winched up from the side of the hill as testament to some humans' inclination to propel one-ton vehicles into deep dark space. As we cling to this perilous roadway, I am reminded of the race scene in *Rebel Without a Cause* (1955) as James Dean and his arch nemesis each careen their car toward the edge of a seaside cliff to see who would "chicken out" first. Dean jumps, but his rival gets his jacket sleeve caught on the door handle of his car and he plummets to his death on the beach below. Unfortunately, a few generations later, that scene is repeated on Skyline Drive more times than Pat would care to see.

I can see Cañon City off to my left—well, not really, because I really have both eyes on the road. Let's just say that this is an exhilarating ride—one that could be used as a prototype for some daredevil roller coaster experience at a local amusement park. At the end of the ridge, we make a sharp hairpin turn to the left and begin descending downward along the back side of the ridge. Near the bottom of the (slightly wider) road, we stop, and Pat shows me some fragments of clam shells—oceans of clams—giant clams about the width of your outspread arms. She mentions that this part of the inland sea was thousands of feet deep at one time.

Back on the road, we make a quick right onto Fifth Street and then a left onto US 50. We're now back in Cañon City and headed toward the Garden Park Fossil Area. After about twenty minutes of driving, we arrive at the Cleveland/Delfs Quarry.

We walk over to a small observation platform that's perched next to the river. As we look across Fourmile Creek from the platform, we can see the remains of a quarry, which was excavated between 1954 and 1957. The person in charge of the excavation was one Edwin Delfs who, although an undergraduate student at Yale, was quickly sponsored by the Cleveland Museum of Natural History after he spotted some dinosaur bones protruding from the base of a cliff. It should be noted that Delfs subsequently went on to become an OB/GYN specialist because he came to the persistent and inescapable conclusion that there was not a lot of money to be made in a career devoted to the exhumation of million-year-old bones.

The excavation at the quarry resulted in the discovery of a new species of sauropod, *Haplocanthosaurus delfsi,* which is now on display at the Cleveland Museum of Natural History.* *Haplocanthosaurus* (meaning "simple spined lizard") lived during the Late Jurassic Period (161.2 to 145.5 million years ago). It is classified as a relatively small sauropod coming in at a weight of just over fourteen tons and a total length of forty-six feet. Since there is only one known specimen of *Haplocanthosaurus delfsi* (the one discovered here), very little is known about this creature, including the physiology of its head—an essential part of its anatomy that has never been recovered.

Pat informs me that just before the fiftieth anniversary of the dig, the museum wanted to have a commemorative ceremony with Edwin Delfs in attendance. Since Pat's deceased husband was a physician, she began contacting various medical directories to see if Dr. Delfs could be located. She soon discovered that he was working in California. She called him up and asked him if he would be interested in coming back and whether or not he had any artifacts from the dig. Arrangements were made for him to come back to the quarry and …

---

*As is often the case in paleontology, the first person to discover a previously unknown species frequently has the honor of having her or his name used as part of the plant or animal's name. Thus the "delfsi" at the end of this animal's name is in honor of Edwin Delfs. More recently, a newly discovered species of trapdoor spider located along the California coast was named for *Comedy Central* regular and faux talk show host Stephen Colbert—*Aptostichus stephencolberti.* I figure that if a TV personality can have an arachnid named after him, then there's hope for both the readers and writers of dinosaur books.

…he brought a 16mm film of the dig, along with pictures and all kinds of great stuff, which we have in our archives. He also related how, in 1954, he basically was given a van, tools, and dynamite and was told, "Okay take some students [they were mostly high school kids from Cleveland] and go out there for three summers and set up a dig." They stayed here and camped. One year they had a 100-year rain in Cripple Creek and the ranchers up-stream knew that the kids were working down here. So, they came down and said, "You'd better watch out with all this water coming." Well, we have pictures of brown surf coming down and the water was lapping at the quarry over there—they almost lost some of their [dinosaur] jackets. It was unbelievable. They'd never seen anything like it.

Also discovered near the excavation area was a dinosaur nesting site. Pieces of dinosaur eggshells have been located in the area. In addition, scientists have unearthed a dinosaur nesting site with egg fragments inside. Pat tells me that there is more—not just here, but further "…up the hill there's a whole nest site where four different dinosaur species of eggshell [have been] found."

Pat and I proceed up the road, and in less than a minute we are at the Garden Park Fossil Site. After parking my rental car, I notice a monument entitled "Garden Park Type Locality of Dinosaurs," which includes a plaque placed here in 1953 by local citizens. The plaque reads:

The first remains of several species of dinosaurs were found within a two-mile radius of the point in 1877 by Prof. O.C. Marsh of Yale University, and Prof. E.D. Cope of the Academy of Sciences of Philadelphia. The discovery of extinct reptiles in the Western Hemisphere received worldwide acclaim.

Below the inscription are illustrations of the various dinosaurs purported to have been unearthed in the Garden Park Fossil Area.

This particular plaque is interesting on several different levels. While I am certain that the good folks of Cañon City were well-intentioned in their desire to celebrate this paleontological wonderland and announce their pride with a likely expensive commemorative plaque, they perhaps should have checked their facts before casting this now permanent display. For, unfortunately, there are a few inaccuracies and scientific "boo-boo's" permanently inscribed in perpetuity.

Emblazed on the plaque is "Brontosaurus," along with an accompanying illustration. As you will recall from our discussion of dinosaur names in Chapter 5, *Brontosaurus* has officially ceased to exist from scientific nomenclature and has since been replaced with the more scientifically accurate *Apatosaurus*. The monument also indicates that a *Tyrannosaurus* was excavated at this site. Unfortunately, that's not quite right. It was an *Allosaurus* that was painstakingly recovered from these hills. I'm sure that to some untrained eyes the two creatures have somewhat similar physical features,

The good citizens of Cañon City erected a plaque at Garden Park with just a few scientific "boo-boos."

but the fact is, *Allosaurus* lived about eighty million years before *Tyrannosaurus* ever appeared in the paleontological record books. It would also be well to mention that the specimens attributed to Yale University have now been relocated to the National Museum of Natural History at the Smithsonian Institution in Washington, D.C.

The plaque also pays scant homage to one of the most contentious and fierce rivalries that ever took place in the wild Wild West—the infamous

"Bone Wars"—and two famous (or infamous, depending on your point of view) paleontologists of the late nineteenth century.

Edward Drinker Cope (1840–1897) had been fascinated with natural history ever since childhood. In the 1860s he was associated with the Smithsonian Institution, and after some work in Europe, he became curator of the Academy of Natural Sciences in Philadelphia. He eventually rose to become a professor of natural science at Haverford College (PA) and a professor of geology and paleontology at the University of Pennsylvania.

Othniel Charles Marsh (1831–1899) obtained his undergraduate degree at Yale and then studied in Europe for several years. He came back to become a professor of vertebrate paleontology at Yale and was closely involved in establishing the Peabody Museum of Natural History at the university. Later he was appointed as an honorary curator of the Department of Vertebrate Fossils at the Smithsonian.

Although the men had worked together for a brief period of time unearthing fossils in the Connecticut Valley, they soon developed an intense rivalry. During one incident, Marsh was accused of bribing local quarry officials to give him first rights to any recovered fossils. Then, in 1869, Cope described the fossil skeleton of a species of sea reptile—*Elasmosaurus*. Unfortunately, as Marsh pointed out, Cope had placed the head at the tail end of the skeleton. When this egregious error became public, whatever friendly relationship existed between Marsh and Cope quickly disappeared.

In the spring of 1877, Arthur Lakes, a teacher, discovered some dinosaur bones in an area near Morrison, Colorado. He sent a message and several bone samples to Marsh at Yale. Marsh, however, was busy with other matters and did not respond right away (oh, to have had modern-day email). After a period of time, Lakes sent another letter and an additional sample of bones to Cope in Philadelphia. Marsh then completed whatever project he was working on and proceeded to send Lakes $100, asking him to keep his discovery secret—not realizing that word was already out. Just to complicate things, Cope had not only heard of Lakes' discovery, but he was preparing an article for publication that would describe the bones. Then, to add potential insult to a definite injury, Lakes asked Cope to send his sample of bones to Marsh. One can only imagine the level of irritation, frustration, and really bad words that Cope expressed at this juncture in the story.

But it gets better! Ormel W. Lucas, another teacher and amateur paleontologist, was exploring the Garden Park area, also in the spring of 1877. There he discovered large dinosaur bones protruding from the mudstone. (These later turned out to be the remains of a *Camarasaurus* dinosaur.) Knowing that he was not equipped to unearth these bones, he sent a letter and some samples to … to … E. D. Cope. Quite naturally, Cope was most excited about this latest discovery. However, it wasn't long before O. C. Marsh heard about this discovery, which, as you might imagine, made him just a little unhappy—not just because he had not been contacted, but also because the *Camarasaurus* bones were larger and better preserved than the bones Lakes had discovered near Morrison.

Escalate! Escalate! Escalate! Now the feud got really interesting! During the summer of 1877, crews from both the Academy of Natural Sciences in Philadelphia (Cope's home base) and Yale's Peabody Museum (Marsh's home base) labored feverishly at the quarries at Garden Park and Morrison. Tons of dinosaur bones were extracted and shipped back to the East Coast—the competition was fierce and brutal. Excavations were sabotaged, sites were plundered, and misleading fossils from one site were planted at another. Teams would spy on each other, and at one point Marsh's crew opened up two sites near Cope's site because their spies felt that the bones there were of better quality. Cope's crew retaliated by hijacking an eastward bound train carrying some of Marsh's fossils.

Escalate! Escalate! Escalate! Sites were dynamited to prevent any further discoveries. Supplies of food and water were diverted or altogether destroyed. Quarries were vandalized regularly. Crews were armed with bowie knives, pistols, and rifles to protect their sites from poaching. It was frequently reported that one crew would take what it wanted from the other and destroy what was left.

According to Ken Carpenter of the Denver Museum of Nature and Science, "The result of this feud is that each man sought to name a new fossil species before the other and to discredit the work of the other." Carpenter goes on to state that, "… in their rush to name new dinosaurs the two men became careless. … A new species name might be given for fragmentary material or for different parts of a dinosaur already named. Today, such dubious names are not considered valid." Records indicate that between them, the two men coined more than a hundred and thirty new dinosaur names. These include (among others) *Triceratops*, *Stegosaurus*, *Camarasaurus*, *Coelophysis*, *Apatosaurus*, and *Allosaurus*.

Despite all the animosity and range warfare that existed in and around the Garden Park area during the "Bone Wars" of the 1880s and 1890s, some good did come out of all this commotion. The need to remove the bones and get them back East as quickly as possible resulted in the creation (often on the spot) of several new field methods. One of the methods involved leaving partially exposed bones buried in the rocks in which they were discovered. Then, that rock mass would be cut up into enormous blocks and jacketed (covered with plaster) for shipment on eastbound trains. When the bones arrived at the eastern museums, the plaster was removed and the fossils extracted, studied, and put out for display. Interestingly, these same methods are still being used today by paleontologists around the world.

That the Cope and Marsh rivalry had a tremendous impact on paleontology at the end of the nineteenth century is a given. Just as significant was the fact that dinosaurs became an integral and persistent element of popular culture. Newspapers and magazines kept the public aware of paleontological developments in the West—including all the new examples of "Terrible Lizards" that would eventually find their way into prestigious eastern museums and scientific circles. Although it was bitter and vitriolic, the feud between Cope and Marsh cemented "dinosauria" in the public consciousness—a cultural phenomena that has long persisted.

As we begin our journey along the trail, Pat points out a massive river channel that used to traverse this area. The course of the river can be viewed from the cliffs above, where one can actually see marks on the ancient rocks indicating the river's direction. The dinosaurs discovered here were all washed into an oxbow in the river. In fact, the conditions here 150 million years ago were excellent for preserving the bones of dinosaurs. The climate was warm and dry with occasional heavy rains and flash floods. In such an environment, dead animals did not immediately decay and fall apart. Some carcasses, not eaten or carried off, were buried and preserved by thick layers of mud carried by the enormous river—one often swollen by heavy rainfalls.

In most cases, the bones of deceased animals are scattered after death, washed away by streams or carried off by other animals that fed on them. Yet, in an amazing sequence of geological luck and prehistoric circumstance, the bones in Garden Park were nearly complete skeletons of huge dinosaurs. Finding skeletons that are nearly complete, with bones arranged as they were when the animals were alive, is, as you might imagine, an enormous aid to paleontologists. Those articulated skeletons answer many questions about what the dinosaur really looked like and how they behaved when alive.

After a short walk we cross over a wooden bridge. I wonder out loud, "Why would there be a wooden bridge over a very arid expanse of landscape?" Pat explains that, "… the bridge was put here because there's a couple of anthills scattered around here that have eggshells on them." She goes on to explain that even though there are quarries for the eggshells about a half a mile away, it is known that this species of ant doesn't travel that far. "So the question is, 'Okay, where are they getting those?'" That suggests that there may be additional dinosaur egg sites close by.

As I later learn, when a colony of ants begins to build its underground kingdom, they pull debris (which may include dinosaur eggshells and fossil bits) from deep underground. In fact, it is possible to locate potential dinosaur nesting sites (such as the one at Cleveland/Delfs Quarry) and/or larger fossils by carefully observing the tunnel-building behavior of ants. The wooden bridges (there are three) were erected in order to protect the sites from trampling and to give the ants sufficient opportunity to build their nests and reveal the nests of other, considerably older and quite deceased, creatures.

Just before leaving me on my own, Pat mentions that there is an area of very hard limestone about eight miles away from the Marsh Quarry. This particular location is known worldwide as a premier rock climbing area.

But, as Pat explains, "What they're actually climbing on is old coral reefs. The climbers will often find the entire half of a coral head. They will then ask, 'What's this stuff in the rock?' If they ask that question of someone at the museum we'll reply, 'Well, it's a lot of ocean that you're climbing on!'"

The day has now turned quite pleasant. There's a gentle breeze blowing through the canyon and the traditional crisp blue air of Colorado greets me at every turn. I'm headed in a northerly direction up the canyon along an old wagon road that once connected small quarries on the west side of the gully with the main road (now Field Road) that lead into Cañon City. I can barely see the main wagon road on the other side of the canyon. This was the primary route for hundreds of boxes of dinosaur bones that were transported to the train station in Cañon City (very close to the Dinosaur Depot Museum) for eventual shipment to O. C. Marsh at Yale.*

As I walk up the trail, I notice that the landscape is composed primarily of green mudstone with various layers of sandstone and limestone. On top of the grayish cliff across from me is what used to be the Marsh Quarry. A historic photograph in the "Self-Guided Tour of the Garden Park Fossil Area" indicates that the quarry was a collection of ramshackle huts, hastily constructed sheds, and at least one log building. I can imagine a concentration of crude sleeping tents nearby along with a small area designated as a kitchen. I can also imagine that this area was humming with activity (and a requisite number of armed guards) as fossil excavations proceeded at a feverish clip. As a note on interpretive sign #3 reminds me, I can also "imagine the shouts of amazement as the field crews excavated huge dinosaur bones" from those same precipitous cliffs.

That same interpretive sign informs me that, "The Marsh Quarry was one of the first sites where excavators used a grid map to record the locations of their discoveries. The Marsh Quarry map … is preserved at the Smithsonian Institution."

At this point in my journey the trail is getting a little strenuous. I begin to climb over a jumble of rocks and notice that my breathing is just slightly labored. There are a few sharp ascents as the trail climbs up the west wall across from Marsh's Quarry. But, hey, for a guy who just inched his way past his sixth decade—not too bad!

*During its heyday, 270 crates containing the bones of over sixty-five dinosaurs were excavated from the Marsh Quarry.

As I stand at the terminus of the trail, it's difficult to imagine that everything before me was once an enormous and very wide floodplain. Folks who know about these things (might one be inclined to identify them as "floodplainologists"?) will say that this area—at least 150 million years ago—had a subtropical climate with alternating wet and dry seasons, although for most of the time there was an abundant supply of water. What is now a dry rocky expanse known as the Marsh Quarry was then a wide and powerful stream. Over time, sand deposited by the stream hardened into a sandstone layer. Now, those same experts will point to evidence (which I'm unable to see right now) that over many hundreds of thousands of years the stream shifted its course—four times to be exact. (Here's another one of those facets of scientific study that is so far beyond my level of scientific comprehension that I'm truly left in the paleontological dust. How do they know it's exactly four and not five or sixty-six? Dunno!). The swiftly flowing water created a deep pool at a bend in the stream near where the old channel crossed the new channel. Across from me, at the base of the sandstone layer, is a pronounced bulge. That bulge represents the deep pool in the ancient stream.

The "Bone Wars" are long over, but the Marsh Quarry is still an impressive sight.

Now (assuming we're still talking to those same flood plain experts) this is where things get interesting. That's simply because we're not exactly sure how the dinosaur bones got to be where they are. One theory holds that floods moved some dinosaur bones from upstream into the pool where they were covered by layers of sediment. The other theory holds that during a severe drought dinosaurs came to drink from the pool. Some died and their skeletons were preserved almost intact. When the drought ended floods covered the bones with sand. This theory is supported by the fact that at least three almost complete dinosaur skeletons (i.e. *Allosaurus, Stegosaurus, Ceratosaurus*) were located in what was once this ancient pool. Of course, you could say that both theories were working together to create the concentration of both disarticulated bones and complete skeletons.

I imagine that this may have been quite the foreboding place when Marsh was here more than one hundred years ago. Steep canyons, tumbles of rock spilling down the face of cliffs, and various geologic formations in tans and siennas made for an austere landscape. The hills are punctuated by patches of juniper bushes, thin-line concentrations of sandstone, and the requisite and solitary stands of cacti. This is the palette of a geological artist—one who is able to combine hues and tints and shades with un-replicable geometric forms to create a sculpture that is both timeless and solitary. Yet it is just as isolated and remote today as it was then—a testament to the plodding and pedestrian pace of geology.

I begin my slow and careful descent back down the hill. I'm just a few yards along the trail when I encounter a couple in their mid-twenties on their way up. "Pretty impressive sight," I say to them. "Yeah," he says breathlessly. As I step aside to let them pass I hear him mumble to her, "I guess I shouldn't have had that cigarette for breakfast."

NEED TO KNOW ABOUT **Skyline Drive & Garden Park Fossil Area**

DIRECTIONS Dinosaur Depot Museum: 330 Royal Gorge Blvd. (also known as US 50). It is situated between 4th St. and S. 3rd St. on the west end of Cañon City. Skyline Drive: From the corner in front of the Dinosaur Depot Museum, turn left onto US 50 (heading west toward Royal Gorge). Travel about 3.4 miles and turn right just after the Razor Ridge Trading Post (closed). The road is one-way and leads through a stone archway. Proceed up Skyline Drive to the first turnout, which is on the right side of the road. Get out of your car and walk back about a hundred yards to the dinosaur tracksite. After viewing the tracksite, get back into your car and continue along the top of the ridge (the road is still one-way). Proceed along the back of the hogback and through two switchbacks. At the end of the road, turn right onto Fifth Street and proceed to US 50 (Royal Gorge Boulevard). Turn right and the Dinosaur Depot Museum will be the first left turn (on Fourth Street).

Garden Park Fossil Area: Head east on US 50 from the Dinosaur Depot Museum in Cañon City. Proceed to the fourth traffic light (there is a Burger King on the left). Turn left (north) on Raynolds Avenue and follow Raynolds Avenue as it jogs to the left one block to Field Avenue. Turn right (north) on Field Avenue and follow it for about six and one-quarter miles (after about three miles the road begins to parallel Fourmile Creek). The Cleveland Quarry will be on your right (small parking area with a restroom) just past mile marker 5. The Marsh Quarry site will be an additional quarter mile up the road and on your left. It has a generous parking area.

CONTACT INFORMATION Be sure to obtain a copy of the "Self-Guided Tour of the Skyline Drive Dinosaur Tracks" ($1.00) and/or the "Self-Guided Tour of the Garden Park Fossil Area" ($2.00) from: Dinosaur Depot Museum, 330 Royal Gorge Blvd., Cañon City, CO 81212, (719) 269-7150, www.dinosaurdepot.com

FEES None.

HOURS Dawn to dusk. Skyline Drive is not a road you want to travel at night. In fact, driving this road after the sun goes down is only for the extremely stupid or moderately insane. When driving to Garden Park, please note that all the land prior to crossing the cattle guard (on Field Avenue) is private land. Please respect all fences and signs. The lands on the other side of the cattle guard are public lands managed by the United States Department of the Interior, Bureau of Land Management.

BEST TIME TO VISIT Any time of the year is good.

CAMPING/LODGING There are about fifteen motels, hotels, and inns in the Cañon City area, along with about five different campgrounds. Most of these facilities cater to folks coming to visit the Royal Gorge, so you will find accommodations in all price ranges. Check out www.canoncitycolorado.com for the latest listings. For a special treat, book a room at the Quality Inn (3075 East Highway 50). Ask for Room 101 ("John Wayne Slept Here") or Room 122 ("John Belushi Slept Here").

continued next page

SERVICES There are no rest rooms or water available on Skyline Drive. At the Garden Park Fossil Area, there is a rest room, exhibits, and a picnic area at the Cleveland/Delfs Quarry. However, there are no services at the Marsh Quarry.

ACCESS Skyline Drive is most appropriate for physically and visually challenged individuals, as is the Cleveland/Delfs Quarry at the Garden Park Fossil Area. On the other hand, the Marsh Quarry is a slightly strenuous trail. The first part of the trail is relatively flat; however, the second half is somewhat steep as it approaches the quarry overlook.

DIFFICULTY RATING Skyline Drive: Easy. Cleveland/Delfs Quarry: Easy. Marsh Quarry: Slightly strenuous. The trail at the Marsh Quarry is approximately one-half mile round trip and will take about forty-five minutes (including reading the interpretive signs) to complete (smokers will want to allow lots of additional time to catch their breath at the top of the trail).

NOTES As noted in this chapter, Skyline Drive is not a road for wimps. If you have acrophobia (fear of heights) it might be a good idea to stay back in town and hyperventilate while the rest of your group tours this impressive site. If you also suffer from "who-the-hell-designed-this-stupid-road?-a-phobia" (fear of driving roads with 500-foot drop-offs on both sides and absolutely no guard rails), then you will definitely want to spend the day floating in the hotel pool with some liquid libations.

On the other hand, the Garden Park Fossil Area is a considerably less perilous step back into time. Here you will get a sense of what it might have been like for early paleontologists to live and work in a remote area for months at a time. The ruggedness of the terrain and its distance from any form of civilization demanded individuals to be both hardy and self-sufficient. This was not a place for folks demanding creature comforts.

There are no dinosaur fossils to see at the Garden Park Fossil Area, but this site overflows with historical and prehistoric significance. It's one of those places you really can't afford to pass up if you want a sense of the complete paleontological picture in Colorado. I like to walk the trail at the Marsh Quarry and imagine myself back more than a hundred years ago coaxing scattered bones out of the landscape or reading the geological clues hidden in the cliffs and dry washes.

To truly appreciate both Skyline Drive and the Garden Park Fossil Area, a visit to the Dinosaur Depot Museum beforehand is a must. Not only will the background and history of the area be shared with you, but you'll also view a few of the critters (or their remains) that have made these sites some of the most intriguing in Colorado. Besides, the folks at the museum are just plain nice—they know their dinosaurs and they are eager to help you get to know them, too.

CHAPTER 9

Stepping Back in Time

DINOSAUR RIDGE

In all my reading, in all my research, and in all my travels I can't recall that I've ever met a *Stegosaurus* festooned in a panache of red, green, yellow, blue, purple, and pink. Oh, sure, there was that time back in college when I "accidentally" walked into someone's dorm room that had a distinct cloud of ... ah, well, never mind. But, hey, other than that, I've never seen a multicolored dinosaur ... that is, until I journeyed to Dinosaur Ridge and saw their two "official greeters" (the other *Stegosaurus* was more patriotic in nature: red, white, and blue, with an "Uncle Sam" hat on its head) at the front of the visitor's center.*

Now, I certainly realize that multicolored dinosaurs greeting you at the entrance to a world-class dinosaur site may seem a little ... shall we say, odd. But, as I've quickly learned during my travels—always expect the unexpected and you'll never be surprised. So, while I wasn't anticipating a pair of multi-hued herbivores meeting me head-on at the start of this particular paleontological

*These "greeters" should not be confused with the ones you might encounter at your local Wal-Mart. These had multicolored bodies as opposed to multicolored uniforms (or hair).

excursion, they were definitely considerate and polite (traits not often accorded certain types of public employees who, shall we say, sometimes exhibit decidedly prehistoric attitudes).

The town of Morrison is about thirty minutes from downtown Denver, but eons away in terms of geological history. According to the town's official website, "… Morrison's location on the west side of the Hogback rock formation provides separation from our metropolitan neighbors and makes it feel like a remote mountain town. That's why we call Morrison 'The Nearest Faraway Place.'"

Most locals and visitors will know Morrison for its location at the base of the breathtaking and geologically formed open-air amphitheatre known as Red Rocks Park and Amphitheatre. The design of the amphitheatre consists of two, 300-foot monoliths—Ship Rock and Creation Rock*—that provide acoustic perfection for an amazing diversity of performances. Some of those performers include artists such as the Foo Fighters, Earth, Wind & Fire, B.B. King, Etta James, ZZ Top, Tom Petty and the Heartbreakers, and the Dave Matthews Band. In the summer, these are hills that are truly "alive with the sound of music."

Just along the eastern edge of Red Rocks Park lies County Road 93, a north/south byway that extends from Morrison up past I-70 and into the town of Golden. Just to the other side of that road is 150 million years of geological history that spans the "Age of Dinosaurs," and allows one to walk the same routes as did herds of prehistoric beasts.

Dinosaur Ridge is a hogback. Hogbacks are geological formations that are shaped by the erosion of sedimentary rocks, as well as by the uplift that results from mountain-building processes. Sedimentary rocks are formed when materials such as mud or sand are deposited in layers at the bottom of shallow seas or other large bodies of water. The older sediments, or layers, are underneath the younger sedimentary layers. Eventually, over many millions of years, these sediments compact and harden into rock.

However, some rocks, such as mudstone and shale, are more susceptible to erosion than are hard rocks, such as sandstone. Wind and water act as erosive agents, wearing away softer layers of rocks and leaving behind

*Both of these rock formations are taller than Niagara Falls, and the Red Rocks Amphitheatre was once listed as one of the Seven Wonders of the World.

harder layers. Those harder layers are often left in the sharp relief of a ridge—what geologists call a hogback.*

The rock is also influenced by forces within the earth that fracture and displace some of the rock layers. At Dinosaur Ridge, the layers of rock on the western side have been uplifted, causing them to tilt or tip toward the east. Thus, the rock that lies on the western side of this hogback is considerably less resistant than the rocks composing the eastern side. The younger rock on the east side of the ridge was laid down during the Cretaceous Period (145.5–65.5 million years ago). The west side of the ridge represents rock that was deposited during the Late Jurassic Period (161.2–145.5 million years ago). As you might imagine, the fossils represented by each side of this hogback are decidedly different and decidedly unique.

Imagine two different colored blocks of clay—one on top of the other (for our purposes let's assume that the top slab of clay is red and the bottom is green). Now, imagine that it is millions of years ago. The red slab simulates a hard layer of sandstone and the green slab simulates a soft layer of shale. Both of these layers (among others) were laid down over the course of millions of years. Now, about sixty-five to seventy million years ago, the Rocky Mountains began their slow and deliberate rise. This tectonic uplift—which was often unevenly spaced—caused the layers of the earth (the two clay slabs) to tilt. The tilt, or inclination, in this area of the Rockies reached an angle of approximately forty degrees.

Now, take your two blocks of clay and tilt them at an angle. What you have created is a simulated mountain range. Although your two blocks may only measure several inches in length, the comparable Rocky Mountain uplift and the Dakota hogback—as it is named—extend for hundreds of miles in a north-south direction along the Front Range of Colorado. It represents a significant era of both Colorado geological history as well as the incredible history of this region of the world.

The history of Dinosaur Ridge, while quite recent, is no less fascinating. In 1877, our friend Arthur Lakes (who we met in the previous chapter), a local teacher and minister from the nearby town of Golden, began digging around Morrison. Although Lakes was an amateur, he had been

*Which in no way should be confused—physiologically, geologically, psychologically, or gastronomically—with the distinctive porcine creature (Razorback) that serves as the mascot for the University of Arkansas.

trained in natural history while a student at Oxford University. In March of that year, he was poking around a rocky slope just east of what would eventually become Red Rocks Park. Although he was searching for plant fossils, it wasn't long before he began to unearth some large fossilized dinosaur vertebra and a front leg bone of an *Apatosaurus* dinosaur.

Lakes knew that professional paleontologists would be quite interested in these discoveries (let me rephrase—they would be ECSTATIC!!). He sent a letter along with sketches of his discovery to O. C. Marsh of Yale University (whom you will no doubt remember from the previous chapter as one of the principle characters in the infamous "Bone Wars" of the late nineteenth century). Professor Marsh did not reply. Lakes sends a second, third, and fourth letter to the noted, and obviously quite busy, scientist. Frustrated by the non-responsiveness of the eminent paleontologist, in May of that year he packed up more than one ton of dinosaur bones and had them shipped off to Marsh (quite a lovely gift, you must admit).

But, as they say, now the plot thickens just a little. For, you see, Lakes had also contacted E. D. Cope, to whom he also sent missives and bones. Marsh was, as you might imagine, not a happy camper when he received *that* news. He quickly dispatched his friend Benjamin Mudge to Golden, Colorado, to verify the discoveries that Lakes was making. Mudge's report was both complimentary and flattering. It verified everything Lakes had uncovered in the area.

In short order, Lakes was employed by Marsh to work the area south of Golden and just north of Morrison. As you'll recall from the previous chapter, the discovery of these and other dinosaur bones sparked a fierce rivalry that resulted in the excavation of trainload after trainload of dinosaur bones and their eventual shipment back to the museums of the East Coast. Interestingly, several of the still-encased fossils remain in the vaults of several universities—still waiting to be excised from their stony tombs.

The bones that Lakes recovered (including *Apatosaurus*, *Diplodocus*, *Stegosaurus*, and *Allosaurus*) were locked in various sandstone layers. Each of those layers represents several ancient river channels. After the animals died, their bones were washed into the rivers and sent downstream to be deposited and buried under several layers of sediment. Eventually those bones were fossilized and preserved for millions of years. In time, Lakes was to discover and excavate over ten different quarry sites (just five of the quarries contained dinosaur bones) in close proximity to Morrison. Although these sites were excavated for only three years, the discovery of those bones fueled a frenzy of paleontological exploration across the West—sometimes known as the "Golden Age" of dinosaur exploration in the nineteenth century.

Fast forward now to the year 1937. The city and county of Denver was beginning to build the aptly named Alameda Parkway as the main route to Red Rocks Park. During the construction process, heavy machinery began cutting a trail along the eastern side of the hogback. As dirt was being removed, a series of dinosaur footprints were revealed on top of a sandstone layer in 100-million-year-old rocks. This sandstone layer was part of an ancient beach that had been, over millions of years, uplifted by the tectonic and geological forces that were creating the Rocky Mountains. The layer, as part of the Dakota Hogback, was eventually tilted to its present-day angle of approximately forty degrees.

Shortly thereafter, Harvey Markman, Curator of Geology at the Denver Museum of Natural History (now the Denver Museum of Nature and Science) documented the discovery. However, for many years geologists and members of the public observed them without studying them in any significant detail. Then, in 1983, the area now known as Dinosaur Ridge was designated as a national natural landmark to protect its fossil bones and tracks. In 1986, Dr. Martin Lockley (from Chapter 7), a geology professor at the University of Colorado at Denver, began an intensive study of the tracks.

In 1987, the National Science Foundation funded considerable research on the tracks by the University of Colorado–Denver Dinosaur Trackers Group. Since then, the group has been able to demonstrate that the creatures that made these tracks represent a variety of both carnivorous and herbivorous dinosaurs that walked through this area approximately 110 million years ago. In 1991, the site was placed on the state register of historical places, and in 1994 the name "Dinosaur Ridge" was officially approved by the U.S. Board of Geographical Names. It should also be noted that in 1992 the Scientific and Cultural Facilities District funded excavations that uncovered many new tracks along the ridge.

As you may also recall from Chapter 7, research has uncovered extensive track-bearing beds that can be traced along much of Colorado's Front Range. This strata represents the shoreline sediments of an ancient seaway along which large populations of dinosaurs traveled or migrated during the Cretaceous Period. Alameda Parkway was a most fortuitous name for the automobile route constructed around the hogback in the 1930s. That's because many of these tracks found in these same rock layers to the north and several hundred miles to the south indicate large populations of dinosaurs traveling or migrating along the shores of the Western Interior Seaway. *Alameda* means "promenade" in Spanish—so this well-traveled route is appropriately known as the "Dinosaur Promenade" or, using modern nomenclature, "Dinosaur Freeway."

I am driving in from the south—meandering my way up I-25 as it joyfully slips and slides over the wide expanse of land that sweeps up from Colorado Springs. I make my way past the foreboding and iconic majesty of Castle Rock and become part of the metallic serpent known as Denver commuter traffic. I had, in a bit of tourist naiveté, thought that an early morning exit from my hotel room in Cañon City would afford me a leisurely drive up the Front Range, Apparently, I have not properly considered the hordes of text-messaging travelers heading for their high-rise offices in the bowels of the mile-high metropolis.

Traffic slows perceptibly as our carbon-spewing parade approaches the intersection with highway C-470. "Remember," I keep telling myself, "to take the turnoff headed west, rather than the one headed east, or I will be forced to frantically search under the seat for some (hopefully) loose change to pay the required toll." Toll-east; no toll-west.

I make the right choice and am now part of another convoy of SUVs, convertibles, and noxious eighteen-wheelers headed toward the snow-capped Rocky Mountains poking up from the landscape. The mountains in the immediate foreground are covered with dark blankets of green, and those in the background are ice cream cones of lingering winter snow still left on their peaks. There is a tinge of gray in the sky, but I suspect that it will be long gone by the time I become one with the creatures and their remains at Dinosaur Ridge.

Dinosaur Ridge Visitor's Center is right off C-470. The roar of traffic going by is constant—an interesting backdrop considering the "ancientness" of the territory and the modes of transportation being used when the beds of sandstone, mudstone, and shale on which I now park my car were first being laid down. My two *Stegosaurus* friends greet me in their Technicolor coats of weather-resistant paint.

This particular site, I soon learn, is one of several designated natural areas in Colorado. Officially designated in 2002 as the Dakota Hogback Dinosaur Ridge Natural Area, its claim to fame is the incredible diversity of wildlife that currently exists, as well as that which existed long ago. Here visitors can find dinosaur footprints, fossils, tallgrass communities, rare plants, migratory bird pathways, and some of the most diverse geologic history of the state. The intent of Colorado's natural program is to identify and protect the very best natural areas in the state. The natural areas system recognizes and conserves the most unique and significant biological, geological, or paleontological sites in the state.

In 2007, the Colorado natural areas program obtained funding from the Colorado lottery to assist the "Friends of Dinosaur Ridge" (a coalition of scientists, volunteers, community members, and staff) with protection of this world-class site. Since the tracks were first exposed during the road excavation in 1937, rock slabs have been slowly sliding and some are on the verge of collapse or degradation.

Shortly after my arrival at the visitor's center, I meet Tom Moklestad, who is the Education and Operation Director for Dinosaur Ridge. A personable and easy-going man, Tom is as passionate about this site as he is about his responsibilities to the public.

"Dinosaur Ridge, first of all, is one of the most accessible dinosaur localities in the United States," Tom tells me. "It's on the fringe of a major metropolitan area. We have about 100,000 people visit a year, along with about 10,000 school students. The historical significance is that this is where the so-called Jurassic giants were first found."

As we chat, Tom leads me over to the newest addition to Dinosaur Ridge—the Dinosaur Ridge Exhibit Hall, which features displays, murals, and other exhibits that provide visitors with a brief overview of this area in prehistoric times, as well as the creatures that inhabited this region. The murals depicting ancient life were drawn by local artist Mike Skrepnick. They offer visitors a richly detailed and multi-colored perspective about the ancient environment.

In addition, there are plenty of hands-on exhibits for the kids, including my favorite, the "Goldilocks Experiments." Here, youngsters can press small wooden dinosaur feet into several types of materials, including rock (too hard), foam padding (too soft), and "foam core" (just right). This simple activity helps kids understand that the dinosaur tracks they will see on the ridge were the result of just the right conditions at just the right time. In other words, the sediments that the dinosaurs walked on had to be a certain consistency in order for the track to be preserved. The environmental conditions had to be perfect as well. Thus, the fact that these tracks are now available for viewing millions of years after they were made is the result of lots of prehistoric luck and tons of geological circumstance.

Triceratops (courtesy Dick Hodgman)

As I make my way past the displays, Tom provides additional information on the sections detailing the environmental conditions of the Early Cretaceous to Late Cretaceous Periods represented along the ridge. He tells me that this particular region is significant, not only because it has revealed the tracks of dinosaurs such as *Triceratops*, theropods, and *Champosaurs*, but that it is "… one of the few places in the world with both dinosaur and mammal tracks together."

The Exhibit Hall also houses a children's video area, where groups of kids can watch educational films (as part of a field trip or group excursion). One wall displays various newspaper accounts of dinosaur discoveries in the area, including one made by a local child. Tom points out the casting lab just to the side of the Exhibit Hall. Here, he tells me, "People can make their own dinosaur casts." Tom offers me a quick tour of the upstairs offices and classroom area, where teachers come to earn college credit through the Colorado School of Mines. It is apparent that Dinosaur Ridge is as much an educational facility as it is a repository for the trace fossils of long-ago dinosaurs.

I'm now setting out on a walk from the visitor's center. It's another beautiful day with temperatures in the mid-seventies. As I'm walking along the side of Alameda Parkway approaching Dinosaur Ridge, I notice several signs along the asphalt path that parallels the road. These interpretive signs provide visitors with information about life in the Cretaceous (145–66 million years ago), Jurassic (208–145 million years ago), Triassic (245–208 million years ago), and the Permian (290–245 million years ago) Periods. Additional information about what the supercontinents looked like, what Colorado was experiencing during those periods, and the representative dinosaurs that existed during each of those eras is also shared.

As I walk past N. Rooney Road on my right, I come to another interpretive sign—this one introducing pedestrians to the Dinosaur Ridge Trail. Along with the usual information about the educational value of the trail and some of the unique natural resources visitors will encounter, I'm pleased to see that the Friends of Dinosaur Ridge, the volunteer group that maintains this site, has not lost their sense of humor. There, emblazoned on an interpretive sign, is a strong discouragement about removing any fossils from this site. Then, just below that warning is the following:

> *Please be careful—the dinosaurs have gone, but rattlesnakes and falling rocks are still here. Enjoy this trip back in time and leave only footprints and take only pictures. The next generation will thank you.*

Falling rocks and rattlesnakes ... Hmmmm, I'm not sure whether I should be looking up or looking down.

Soon after I begin the ascent up the east side of Dinosaur Ridge, I arrive at an interpretive sign for the "Western Interior Seaway." Here, visitors get a short history lesson about how, during Cretaceous times (about 100 million years ago), this area would have been at the bottom of a large inland sea. Here in this formation, paleontologists have located an enormous variety of fossils, including ammonites, clam-like mollusks, fish, marine crocodiles, and other small reptiles. I'm quickly reminded that even though most visitors are here for the dinosaurs, many other varieties of animals existed in this era as well.

I continue my climb up the hill. I'm able to maintain a reasonable pace—the ascent at this point is not very strenuous and can be easily traversed by people of all ages. In short order, I come upon the highlight of Dinosaur Ridge—the dinosaur tracks. Enclosed by a protective chain-link fence and cast into the side of a forty-five-degree slope are 335 tracks made by at least thirty-seven different animals that passed this way millions of years ago. These tracks are no less impressive than the 1,300 I saw embedded in the limestone layers along the edge of the Purgatory River (Chapter 7). They are just as remarkable and just as awe-inspiring.

Sauropod tracks meander along an ancient seaway.

As these tracks have been studied by paleontologists over the years, they have revealed that two very different types of dinosaurs passed this way. The most common kind left large, broad three-toed tracks of its hind feet and the smaller crescent-shaped tracks of its front feet. It was probably an ornithopod like *Iguanodon* or something similar. This dinosaur could walk on either two legs or four legs. There is speculation by some scientists that young *Iguanodons* were primarily bipedal (two-footed) and that as they aged and became heavier they tended to become more quadrupedal (four-footed).* Furthermore, it has been estimated that the younger *Iguanodons*, running on only two legs, could reach a maximum speed of nearly fifteen mph.** Extensive examination of these tracks indicated that ornithopod dinosaurs traveled in herds or social groups.

The larger tracks also show that there were differences in size among the dinosaurs. It may be assumed that the larger tracks represent adults, while the smaller tracks represent juveniles. Track size may also be an indication of sex. But, what's even more interesting is the undeniable fact that individuals of the same size tended to congregate and/or travel together (something I was able to see at the Purgatoire tracksite, too). That is, the dinosaurs that made these tracks may have been social creatures that tended to associate with others of the same size and stature (as modern-day cows tend to associate with each other in herds—although their tracks are considerably less interesting … at least to humans). It has been estimated that the *Iguanodons* at this site ranged in size from youngsters ten feet long to adults twenty to thirty feet long.

The term *Iguanodon* (meaning "Iguana tooth") is comprised of many named species that lived from the Late Jurassic to the Late Cretaceous Periods. It was the second dinosaur officially and formally named (*Megalosaurus* was the first), shortly after the first specimen was unearthed in

*Humans, on the other hand, start off quadrupedal (hands and knees), then become bipedal (two-footed), and finally end up as tripedal (two slow feet and a hand-carved wooden cane).

**By comparison an elephant can reach a top speed of 25 mph, a human (100 meter dash) 27 mph, a domestic cat 30 mph, a quarter horse 47 mph, a cheetah 70 mph, and the world's fastest animal, the peregrine falcon, over 200 mph. Those animals not known for their velocity include the domestic pig 11 mph, the chicken 9 mph, the giant tortoise .17 mph, the three-toed sloth .15 mph, and, at the very end of the swiftness scale, the garden snail .03 mph.

The author poses beside a line of tracks at Dinosaur Ridge.

Sussex, England, in 1822. Our knowledge of this dinosaur has continually changed over the years as new information has been obtained from the wide variety of fossils uncovered since the early nineteenth century. For example, it was originally thought that these creatures had long, prehensile tongues similar in appearance to those of giraffes (undeniably one of the animal kingdom's most disgusting-looking tongues). However, recent investigations have shown this to be a serious error, and that, instead, they had short, muscular tongues used to move food around in their mouths.

Iguanodons were herbivorous creatures, although the proverbial "jury is still out" on exactly what they ate. Some scientists speculate that they existed on a diet of medium-height plants, while others speculate that its low-browsing habits would have made shorter plants the predominant food source. Whatever the case, it is believed that it was a migratory creature that kept on the move searching for fresh vegetation. Considerable research is still needed before definitive conclusions can be made about these creatures.

Tom has been kind enough to give me a key to the locked enclosure—an access not normally available to the general public. I carefully unlock the gate and walk into an area that is almost surrealistic in its appearance. Before me lies a slope of prehistoric prints in what appeared to be a haphazard and random array. I stand transfixed (just as I had at the Purgatoire River) by not only the accumulation of tracks, but their detail and proximity. Here are the trace fossils of animals that walked the very ground I am now standing on—animals that lived millions of years before I was even a gleam in my father's eye. If ever there has been a time when I felt as though I was "walking with dinosaurs," then this is it. Each track, each print, not only makes an impression on the shale and sandstone, but an equal impression on my consciousness. Goose bumps run up and down my arms as I stand firmly rooted to this geological and paleontological spot in time.

I slowly move around the enclosed area, taking several photographs of the tracks. As I am shooting one series of photos, a mother and her four young children come up to the fence and gaze at the tracks. One of the young girls, approximately five years old, asks me, "What are you doing?" I reply that I am taking photographs for a book. Then, I ask her what she is doing, and she responds, "We're looking at footprints." Her mother adds, "… really old footprints." The young girl quickly corrects her mother by adding, "Yeah, but they're from real dinosaurs."

Wanting to get a perspective of the size of the various tracks I am observing, I carefully place one of my shoes next to several selected *Iguanodon* tracks before snapping off another series of shots. I wear a size ten shoe, which is about eleven and a half inches in length, and I am surprised to see that the tracks I am photographing are about sixteen inches in length, suggesting that the creatures that made them were relatively large in stature. Depending on the species, *Iguanodons* may have weighed upwards of three and a half tons and achieved lengths of up to forty-two feet.

Sprinkled across the slope is a scattering of smaller tracks, most of which appear to be isolated individuals who may have also wandered along the edge of the ancient seaway. Each of these tracks is about nine inches

The author's shoe (size 10) inside a (size 86) sauropod track.

long and is made by small *ornithopods*—dinosaurs that were about the size of modern-day ostriches or emus.

These dinosaurs lived during the Late Cretaceous Period throughout what is now the western United States and up into Canada. Although small (twelve feet long, seven feet high, and weighing a few hundred pounds) in comparison to the larger herbivores that also walked these prehistoric beaches, ornithopods were carnivorous—although, once again, it is uncertain what they fed on.

Ornithopods walked on their hind feet, each of which had three slender toes tipped with pointed claws. Their legs were well suited for running (a most handy feature—particularly when chasing down a potential dinner). An analysis of the tracks at this site, however, indicate that the creatures who traveled through here were ambling along at a speed of approximately five miles per hour, which given their size seems to indicate that they were walking rather than running. Unlike the *Iguanodon*, it doesn't appear these creatures traveled in packs or herds.

I note that the larger trackways seem to be running perpendicular to the smaller ones. This lends further weight to the idea that large dinosaurs tended to stay with large dinosaurs and small dinosaurs tended to stay with other small dinosaurs. Whether this pattern is the result of the relative age of the dinosaurs that left each set (small tracks—young dinosaurs; large tracks—older dinosaurs) or of sexual dimorphism (males—large tracks; females—small tracks) is unclear. What is known, however, is the total number of track makers (at least seventy-eight), their approximate sizes, and their respective direction(s) of travel.

After spending nearly thirty minutes at the tracksite, I exit through the gate, making sure to carefully re-lock it. As I again ascend up the hill, I can't help but look back one more time at the tracks. I am still taken with how well these tracks have been cemented in both rock and time. They are trace fossils that have preserved a living piece of prehistoric history and have also revealed the answers to several long-standing paleontological questions. They are as impressive in their display as they are in their stories.

The next interpretive sign along Alameda Parkway describes a concentration of quite different trace fossils in the cliff face before me. Here are the burrows and trails of thousands of invertebrates—primarily worms and shrimp—that inhabited this inter-tidal area about 100 million years ago. Not only were these prehistoric times known for the enormous creatures that walked along the edges of the shallow sea, it was also full of considerably smaller creatures that made their home groveling and squirming through the sediments of a Cretaceous inland sea.

My journey up the mountain takes me past several other interpretive signs describing both ancient and present-day geological features. These include a description of the unique ecology of the area, ripple marks of the ancient sea frozen into the side of a rock face, a description of coal and clay mining as well as oil and gas reserves in the Denver Basin, an overview of the Cretaceous Period, a "Geologic Puzzle" that some have interpreted as a dinosaur egg (it's not!), layers of volcanic ash, a geologic overview of the Red Rocks area, and a series of fault lines that course through the hogback.

After about thirty minutes, I arrive at the "Brontosaurus Bulges"* on the western side of the ridge. This section of the road has actually moved me back in time—from the Cretaceous Period to the Jurassic. During this time, mudstone, claystone, and shale were deposited in swamps and floodplains. Enormous *Apatosaurs* (or, if you prefer, *Brontosaurs*) waded through these ancient mudflats. Their footprints—up to three feet in diameter and a foot deep—filled up with sandy mud. That mud, over time, solidified and was transformed into rock. When Alameda Parkway was being constructed, those large footprints were revealed as bulges in the cliff side.

The downward bulges are viewed in cross section. As the dinosaurs walked on the soft muddy ground, their feet pushed down and distorted the layers below. The size of the tracks suggest a particularly large animal, and *Apatosaurus* is the only one—in terms of its size and where its fossils have been discovered—that could have made these tracks more than 150 million years ago.

*I suppose that the alliteration in "Brontosaur Bulges" was deemed more "user friendly" than would have been the case with the more scientifically accurate "Apatosaurus Bulges." I checked all the dictionaries I could and, unfortunately, could not locate any alliterative "footprint words" for Apatosaurus. Other prehistoric beasts do not present that conundrum. To wit: Tyrannosaurus Tracks, Protoceratops Paw Prints, Dilophosaurus Dents, Iguanodon Imprints, Maiasaura Marks, and Fruitafossor Footprints.

"Brontosaur Bulges" provide visitors to Dinosaur Ridge with a sense of the size of these enormous creatures.

I'm nearing the end of my journey when I arrive at the Dinosaur Bone Quarry. It was here that Arthur Lakes made his monumental discovery in 1877. Most of the bones embedded in these boulders are a disjointed array of ribs, limbs, vertebrae, skull fragments, and pelvic bones. They are jumbled together much like the contents of a child's toy box (or the contents of my attic). This indicates that they were probably transported here by an ancient stream or river from their original resting place. The bones may have been pulled apart by various forces of nature, including weather, floods, or even animal scavengers. Complete skeletons are virtually nonexistent.

The interpretive sign informs me that the dark brown fossilized bones in the boulders form part of the skeleton of a medium-sized sauropod such as a *Camarasaurus*. There are other bones that have a honeycombed texture that makes them appear lighter in color. These are part of an unknown sauropod backbone. The large cylindrical bones in a nearby boulder are portions of various dinosaur leg bones.

I retrace my way back along the road, up over the ridge, and down the back side to the visitor's center. The vistas of the greater Denver area are spectacular and serve as a backdrop to the ancient areas I have been exploring for the past one and a half hours. Gas guzzling cars and carbon-emitting tractor-trailers speed below me on C-470 as I make my way past Jurassic and Cretaceous fossils that have existed since long before the invention of the internal combustion engine (which, in an ironic twist of fate, uses fossil fuels to power its way along asphalt highways and concrete roads).

I've now returned to the visitor's center, where, once again, I am interviewing Tom Moklestad. Since I have just completed a breathtaking two-mile hike up and over the ridge and back again, I'm now wondering about the best way for people to see this incredible site. Tom confirms what I already suspect—the best way is to "… hike along our interpretive trail, which is beside the road—where we have twenty interpretive signs for people to read." The hike offers visitors an up close and personal look at tracks and bulges and geological formations that they might miss from inside an enclosed vehicle. On the other hand, the shuttle bus might be the transportation of choice, particularly for the "I promise to quit smoking tomorrow. No really, I promise" crowd.

I also ask Tom about the nearby Morrison Natural History Museum and how Dinosaur Ridge complements their mission ("Come explore the history of discovery …"). "I think [visitors] should visit both," he says. "We are an outdoor museum. Our mission is preservation of what's here and also education to the general public. The museum is more of an indoor museum. But, they … have some active research projects going. … Much of what they do is related to what's on Dinosaur Ridge. In some way I wish we were together, so [visitors] could do it in one stop, but they're not that far away."

I ask Tom what he would like Dinosaur Ridge visitors to remember after their journey through time. With a decided note of pride in his voice he states, "I would hope they would leave with some notion, some idea of the kinds of things that scientists, particularly geologists and paleontologists, look at and deal with when they try to figure out the history of the earth." He emphatically punctuates that statement when he states that, "Our mission is education and preservation and the corollary to that … would be to come out here and find out that science is fun."

I couldn't agree more.

After leaving Dinosaur Ridge, I head down CO 26 to the town of Morrison. I swing a right onto Morrison Road (CO 74) and then a quick left onto CO 8. After about half a mile, the Morrison Natural History Museum pops up on my right. The building reminds me of a Swiss chalet—with a somewhat western theme about it.

As I enter the museum, I'm greeted by Chelsea Hutson, a perky and enthusiastic member of the museum staff who helps schedule tours, runs the gift shop, trains volunteers, and "keeps everything functioning." She's a student at the local community college where she studies paleontology, and she's been "a dinosaur lover ever since I could talk." She is quick to point out that for her this is more than a job because "every day I'm learning something new."

I ask Chelsea about some of the typical questions people have when they visit the museum, as she's been trying to put together a compendium

Yes, you can pet the *T. rex* at the Morrison Natural History Museum!

of some of the more "popular" questions. She tells me that adults seems to be more focused about the kinds of dinosaurs found throughout Colorado, those that have been found around the town of Morrison, and what kinds of species are featured in this little, but exhibit-rich, museum.

Kids, on the other hand, have more important questions to ask such as, "Can I pet the *T. rex*?" Looming in his own alcove across from the front door is a *T. rex* skull with its appropriate signage. Kids (and certain authors) can walk right up to the skull and pet it as much as they want. It's a great way for youngsters to get a "hands-on" experience with an actual fossil. One can only imagine how many parents have taken photographs of their children with their heads inside the head of this monster. If you received a Christmas card with a child's head being chomped on by a sixty-five-million-year-old skull belonging to a former predatory carnivore—now, at least, you'll know where the photo was taken.

Chelsea tells me that kids are also interested in how the paleo lab on the premises works, and especially how fossils are formed. One thing that becomes immediately apparent is that the museum takes its educational mission seriously and helps to provide all its visitors with the most up-to-date and accurate information. For example, when kids see the *Triceratops* skull (perched across from the *T. rex* skull) they want to know, "Is he full-grown?" The staff assures kids that it is, indeed, full-grown, prompting them to stand alongside it for another set of potential holiday greeting cards to be sent to long-lost relatives.

Given that the museum is so close to Dinosaur Ridge, I wondered about the relationship between the two sites—one outdoors, one inside. Chelsea assures me that the relationship is a positive one. "We're definitely friends. We love working with Dinosaur Ridge." She informs me that they have an ongoing partnership over the summer months as well as over the academic year when school tours like to visit both sites on the same day. There are advantages to both sites, each offering slightly different perspectives of prehistoric life. Chelsea explains it best when she states, "Dinosaur Ridge is really good about dinosaurs on the outside. We're really good about dinosaurs on the inside."

The museum also has an active research program in the local area. Recently, researchers have re-discovered one of Arthur Lake's original ten quarries. There, three *Apatosaurus* skeletons were unearthed—buried one on top of the other. This is the only place in the world where this has occurred. In another of Lakes' quarries, museum researchers uncovered ten *Stegosaurus* hatchling tracks—again, the first ever discovered. One of the quarry rocks revealed the prints of four or five baby *Stegosauri* all headed in the same direction. Another first for the museum staff was the recent discovery of the tracks of a baby *Apatosaurus*. Some of these new finds will inevitably become part of the museum's permanent displays.

Deciding to eschew the "Help-help-my-head-is-inside-a-*T. rex*-skull!" photo opp, I decide to take a self-guided tour through this amazing world. In short order, I come across the left forelimb of an *Apatosaurus*, the fully formed footprint of a *Stegosaurus*, the right hind-limb of an *Allosaurus*, and the right hind-foot toes of an *Apatosaurus*. Each of these individual exhibits encourages visitors to get "up close and personal" with the fossils. Touching is encouraged—an opportunity that balances well with the trace fossils those same visitors can discover over at Dinosaur Ridge.

Just before I head out the door, I ask Chelsea what she would like to have people walk away with after visiting the museum. She reminds me that as a museum their principal mission is to provide visitors of any age with an educational experience. "This is a museum not just for kids, but also for adults," she states emphatically. "We want everyone—young and old—to have a great experience."

I ask her for one final quote.

"This is just such a magical place to come and experience and explore and educate. It's almost like a little kid's fantasy—who wouldn't want to come here?"

I walk over and give the *T. rex* one more pat on the head.

NEED TO KNOW ABOUT **Dinosaur Ridge**

DIRECTIONS Dinosaur Ridge is located ten miles west of downtown Denver near Red Rocks Park. From the Denver International Airport (DIA), take I-70 west. Turn south on Colorado C-470 and exit at the Alameda Parkway (west). The road swings around to the right, and the entrance into the visitor's center (right turn) is a quarter-mile down the road.

From Colorado Springs and other points south, head north on I-25. At Exit 194, head west on Colorado C-470 (turn east on C-470, and you'll have to pay a toll). Head west for about twenty-one miles and exit at the Alameda Parkway (west). At the top of the ramp, make a left-hand turn (you'll go back over C-470). The entrance into the visitor's center is a quarter-mile down the road on your right-hand side.

CONTACT INFORMATION Dinosaur Ridge, 16831 W. Alameda Pkwy, Morrison, CO 80465, (303) 697-3466; http://www.dinoridge.org

FEES There is no charge to visit the visitor's center or to view the fossil sites on the ridge. Guided tours of Dinosaur Ridge can be arranged by calling (303) 697-3466. The Dinosaur Ridge Exhibit Hall has a $1.00 entrance fee.

HOURS Sun-up to sun-down, seven days a week.
The Visitor Center and Gift Shop has the following hours:
May through October
Monday–Saturday: 9:00 a.m. to 5:00 p.m.; Sunday: 11:00 a.m. to 5:00 p.m.
November through April
Monday–Saturday: 9:00 a.m. to 4:00 p.m.; Sunday: 11:00 a.m. to 4:00 p.m.

BEST TIME TO VISIT Dinosaur Ridge is open for drop-in visitation every day of the year. I recommend visiting in spring, summer, or fall (tramping up and down the ridge in the middle of winter tends to create whiney kids and equally whiney adults).

Be sure to check out Dinosaur Discovery days, which are scheduled for the first Saturday of the month during the summer. These are wonderful opportunities for guided tours of the entire ridge. Dinosaur Ridge's website (www.dinoridge.org) is comprehensive, thorough, and informative, and should be consulted in advance of any visit.

CAMPING/LODGING There are hundreds of lodging facilities in the greater Denver area. If you want something a little closer to Dinosaur Ridge, check out lodging in the city of Golden (lots) or in the town of Morrison (two B&Bs—Horton House and the Cliff House Lodge).

SERVICES There is an enclosed pit toilet available. During the summer months, the snack bar—Stegosaurus Snack Shack—is open. Candy, soda, water, ice cream, and popcorn are available both before and after your visit. Don't forget to visit the souvenir store for the requisite toys, jewelry, posters, postcards, magnets, fossils, shoes, replicas, and other artifacts of any dinosaur expedition.

ACCESS The Alameda Parkway up and over the ridge is closed to vehicular traffic. As a result, the ridge itself can only be visited on foot, by bicycle, or by riding the Vanosaurus, which loops the ridge approximately every half-hour. There is a charge of $3.00/person for riding the van. Special accommodations can be made for handicap access to the ridge. Inquire at the visitor's center.

DIFFICULTY RATING Easy if riding in the Vanosaurus, to moderately strenuous if using foot power.

NOTES This is another site I have visited several times. The folks who run Dinosaur Ridge are friendly and care deeply about their exhibits and the people who visit them. They are ready and eager to explain anything about the site or answer questions, and they'll even take your photograph next to the red, white, and blue *Stegosaurus* (with an "Uncle Sam" hat perched on its head) that greets folks on their way into the visitor's center.

This is truly a place to bring the whole family. There is lots to keep kids interested and plenty of information to capture the attention of adults. Although I have not taken it, I would definitely suggest the guided tour, which will help you locate (and understand) various stopping points along the road. If you don't take the guided tour, I would recommend that you get a copy of "A Field Guide to Dinosaur Ridge" (approx. $8.00) by Martin Lockley, or "Dinosaur Ridge: Geologic Yardstick & Self-Guided Tour" (approx. $2.00), available at the visitor's center. Both will describe and explain the various sites as you walk (or bike) the road.

Combine a visit to Dinosaur Ridge with a trip to the Morrison Natural History Museum (501 Colorado Highway 8, Morrison, CO, 303-697-1873; www.mnhm.org) and you'll have a well-rounded journey into and through the prehistoric life that existed in this part of the world. It makes for a complete day and a complete family adventure.

NEED TO KNOW ABOUT **Morrison Natural History Museum**

DIRECTIONS   From Denver International Airport, take I-70 west to the Colorado Springs exit (C-470 East). Travel on C-470 East to the Morrison Exit and turn right. Proceed through the town of Morrison on Morrison Road (CO 8). Turn left at the third stoplight and travel for half a mile. The museum is on the right side of the highway.

From Colorado Springs, take I-25 north to Denver. Head west on C-470 (Exit 194). Travel for approximately twenty-one miles to the Morrison Exit (CO 8). Turn left and proceed through the town of Morrison on Morrison Road (CO 8). Turn left at the third stoplight and travel for half a mile. The museum is on the right side of the highway.

CONTACT INFORMATION   Contact the Morrison Natural History Museum for updated information on tours, hours, and fees.
Morrison Natural History Museum, 501 Colorado Highway 8, P.O. Box 564, Morrison, CO 80465; (303) 697-1873; www.mnhm.org

FEES   Adult (age 13–64): $5.00; Senior (65+): $4.00; Youth (age 2–12): $4.00; Child (age 0–1): Free

HOURS   March through October:
Monday–Saturday 10:00–5:00 p.m.; Sunday 10:00–6:00 p.m.
November through February:
Monday–Saturday 10:00–4:00 p.m.; Sunday 10:00–5:00 p.m.

BEST TIME TO VISIT   Any time during the year.

CAMPING/LODGING   There are hundreds of lodging facilities in the greater Denver area. If you want something a little closer to the museum, check out the two B&Bs in Morrison—Horton House (http://horton housebnb.com) and the Cliff House Lodge (http://www.cliffhouse lodge.net).

SERVICES   There is a rest room in the museum. In addition, they have a small gift shop with a good assortment of dino-items including books, models, toys, games, etc.

ACCESS   The building is handicapped accessible.

DIFFICULTY RATING   N/A

NOTES   This is just a delightful little museum. I've visited on several occasions and always come away with new tidbits of information. The staff is very friendly, helpful, and will answer almost any question you pose (even "Can I pet the T. rex?"). There's plenty to inform the adults and lots to keep the kids engaged. This is a true "hands-on" museum where all the displays are right out in front for all to see and touch. Unlike larger museums, the exhibits here are not barricaded behind long ropes or secreted under panes of unbreakable glass. If you want to get close to the left fore-limb or right hind-limb of an *Apatosaurus*, you can do that without incurring the wrath of a uniformed security guard in this distinctive and awe-inspiring museum.

Combine a trip to the Morrison Natural History Museum with one to Dinosaur Ridge, and you'll create an unforgettable experience. It will be a day complete with information, real dinosaur fossils, and an incredible variety of prehistoric trace fossils found in few other places in the world. The museum truly complements a visit to Dinosaur Ridge and Triceratops Trail. This is an experience the whole family will be talking about for years.

CHAPTER 10

Over the Ridge and Down the Trail

TRICERATOPS TRAIL

In Stephen Spielberg's original *Jurassic Park*, there is a classic scene in which three adults and two kids are taking their first venture through the "prehistoric Disneyland." Frustrated by the inability of the computerized vehicles to keep moving along the track, the five individuals scramble out of a tour car and into the brush. There, they discover a lone *Triceratops* prone on the ground and in extreme agony. The character played by Laura Dern is certain that the creature has eaten some type of poisonous plant life and makes the classic statement, "There's only one way to be positive—I need to see the dinosaur's droppings." After a short search, the telltale pile of poop is located (along with the appropriate comment by the Jeff Goldblum character: "That is one big pile of crap!"). Dern's character proceeds to plunge her hands and arms into the mountain of poop (although it is unclear at this point what she might be searching for). After sifting through the crap she stalks back to the car (and presumably some hygienic cleansing). Goldblum's character shouts at her (truly one of the best movie lines of all time): "You will remember to wash your hands before you eat anything!"*

This scene from *Jurassic Park* was playing in the back of my mind as I drove to Triceratops Trail. I wanted to check out some prehistoric footprints preserved in the clay pits that were mined in this area from the 1870s until the 1990s. The trail is located at the Parfet Prehistoric Preserve and is maintained by the Friends of Dinosaur Ridge (see the previous chapter). This half-mile trail is about five minutes from Dinosaur Ridge and preserves footprints left by dinosaurs during the Late Cretaceous Period (99.6 to 65.5 million years ago) as they slogged through the marshy environment. I was also hoping to grab a bite to eat for lunch on my way to the trail, but the *Jurassic Park* scene kept replaying in my mind, seriously dampening any hunger pangs.

After a short drive, I turn off a side road and rumble down a dirt road to a very small parking area that flanks US 6, the main thoroughfare connecting Golden with Denver. The parking area is tucked between a scattering of apartment buildings near the campus of the Colorado School of Mines. I suspect that the apartments are inhabited by colonies of graduate students,

Triceratops (courtesy Dick Hodgman)

given the somewhat fossilized condition of the cars parked around the perimeter. I slide out of my air-conditioned vehicle and into a warm summer day. The temperature is in the mid seventies, and there are rows of white-washed mountains off in the distance beyond the valley. The vista for dozens of miles in front of me is crisp and clear—Golden has never looked better. Cars whiz by me on US 6 as I saunter down a concrete pathway. It's about a fifth of a mile from the parking area to the trailhead for Triceratops Trail.

---

*I've never quite figured out why the manufacturers of certain brands of hand soap haven't used that scene as part of their TV advertising campaigns. Perhaps it's too close to reality for most parents of nine- and ten-year-old boys.

IT IS THE LATE CRETACEOUS PERIOD—
ninety-nine to sixty-five million years ago.
During this time, sea levels were dropping
around the world. The continents had broken away from the su-
percontinent of Pangaea. North America and South America had
separated from each other, and Africa had distanced itself from South
America. The continents would still continue to shift, moving inch by
inch over millions of years.

Much of the land was covered by shallow seas. The Western Interior Seaway divided the continent of North America in two. It was a
broad shallow sea that bisected the middle of the continent from north
to south. It covered what would eventually become the Rocky Mountain states and the fertile Midwestern plains.

Worldwide temperatures rarely dipped below freezing and there
was more seasonal variation in the overall climate at this time than
earlier in the earth's history. There was an abundance of flowering
plants scattered across the landscape—a wide variety of species that
choked waterways and filled flood plains with an array of colors. There
was no grass—grass had yet to evolve. Palm trees grew in warmer climates and wide forests of willows and oaks could be found on plains
and mountainsides. Groves of flowering trees were scattered across the
landscape, and clumps of broad-leafed ferns and ground-hugging
shrubs were everywhere.

A wide variety of creatures lived in this environment. Small mammals scurried through the underbrush or in and out of tiny burrows.
The first primates began to appear, and the first bees and ants made
their appearance. Modern-looking birds appeared and became more
common. It was also the time of the greatest diversity of dinosaurs.

This is near the end of the Age of Dinosaurs. More than half of
all known dinosaurs came from the last eighty million years (one hundred forty-five to sixty-five million years ago) of this era. The dinosaurs
were widespread and numerous, and included the meat-eating Tyrannosaurus, the three-horned Triceratops and the armored Ankylosaurus.

continued next page

continued from previous page

Some of the most unusual, the duck-billed dinosaurs, appeared during this time. These ancient creatures were named for their spoon-shaped bills that allowed them to graze on a wide variety of vegetation. Their teeth enabled them to eat both stems and leaves. At thirty feet long and with a weight of three tons, they would need to chew and eat a lot of vegetation each day just to stay alive.

Clutched in my hands is "A Guide to Triceratops Trail at Parfet Prehistoric Preserve," which I obtained at the visitor's center at Dinosaur Ridge (see "Need to Know" at the end of this chapter). This booklet is essential for both a scientific interpretation of the area and necessary diagrams and photographs of each of the six interpretive stops along the way. The guide is careful to point out that the area is rich in trace fossils—footprints, impressions, and natural casts—rather than body fossils such as teeth and bones.

Just beyond the trailhead is a split-rail fence that runs along the bike path fronting US 6. Stop #1 on the trail describes an elongated trench that was mined for clay for nearly 120 years (1870s–1990s). As clay was removed from the pits, a variety of trace fossils were revealed, indicating the prehistoric significance of this region.

After a very short walk, I find myself at the second of the six informational signs. I'm now perched at the brink of an enormous clay pit, and at the bottom are some of the most incredible dinosaur footprints I've ever seen. As I walk down the short winding trail into the pit, I am amazed to discover a scene unlike any other I have witnessed—three-dimensional tracks of Late Cretaceous dinosaurs preserved in the hard clay wall of the pit. These footprints are nothing short of spectacular, and when I stop and observe them closely, I get a true sense of the enormity of these ancient beasts.

Embedded in the side of the wall are two distinct dinosaur footprints. Some scientists have interpreted these to be the trace fossils of *T. rex*, while others have described them as prints of a hadrosaur. The lack of agreement is due to some damage to the toes of the tracks, making it somewhat diffi-

This may or may not be the footprint of a *T. rex*.

The tracks at Triceratops Trail are kept safely preserved inside a locked cage.

cult to identify the original track-makers. In order to get a sense of their size, I use my hand as a crude measuring tool (there is a large protective cage around the tracks preventing visitors from touching them). The larger track is approximately three hands across and three and a half hands in length. When I get home I measure the length of my hand—it's eight inches long. Thus, the large track is approximately two feet across and twenty-eight inches in length.

I was curious whether there was a relationship between the length of a single dinosaur track and its overall body weight. According to several scientists in the U.S. and Australia, there is a distinct (if very rough) correlation between the length of a track and an individual's weight. We know, for example, that the maximum length of an adult dinosaur track (so far discovered) is thirty-nine inches and that the maximum weight (again, an approximation) for an adult dinosaur is about fifty tons. Using those figures as extremes, scientists can estimate (through a complex mathematical formula that is well beyond my level of comprehension) that a creature with a twenty-eight inch footprint probably has an estimated weight of six to ten tons. It's interesting to note that your average *Tyrannosaurus rex**weighs in at about six to seven tons (remember Sue from Chapter 7?).

Also embedded in the wall of the clay pit are several tracks of hadrosaurs. In fact, the first dinosaur discovered, excavated, described, and named in North America (see the Introduction) was the *Hadrosaurus* unearthed in 1858 from an abandoned quarry in Haddonfield, New Jersey. As you'll remember from the Introduction, the *Hadrosaurus* was officially adopted by New Jersey as its official state fossil in 1991. However, that particular skeleton was (since 1868), and still is, displayed at the Philadelphia Academy of Natural Sciences (truly a reprehensible and egregious example of interstate thievery).

Hadrosaurs (meaning "bulky lizard") are also known as duckbills. That's because the front of the mouth is wide and flat (and frequently toothless)—much like that of a modern-day duck. It is believed that hadrosaurs arose during the Late Jurassic and Early Cretaceous (161.2–99.6 million years ago).

---

*Just to prove that scientists suffer from periodic bouts of forgetfulness just like you and me, consider that the first fossil evidence of *T. rex* was a tooth discovered by Arthur Lakes in 1874 at South Table Mountain, about a mile from Triceratops Trail. Somehow this paleontological treasure was misplaced and presumed "lost" for 125 years. Remarkably, it was recently rediscovered lying in a drawer at the Peabody Museum of Natural History at Yale University.

They were a geographically diverse group of dinosaurs, with specimens uncovered throughout North and South America, Asia, Europe, and even Antarctica. They were equally diverse in both size and shape. Some hadrosaurs were large and sturdy, while others tended to be small and squat. Some species of hadrosaurs had elaborate crests, tubes, or plates of bone on the top of their skulls. Recent computer simulations at Sandia National Laboratories and the New Mexico Museum of Natural History confirm that various species of hadrosaurs (i.e. *Parasaurolophus*) used their distinctive crests to amplify their trumpeting calls. These calls were most likely made as part of a courtship ritual or as a means of inter-species communication.

One of the most distinctive and best-studied hadrosaur is *Edmontosaurus*. This particular dinosaur weighed in excess of four tons and achieved a length of over thirty feet. Originally discovered in Alberta, Canada, fossils have also produced skin imprints showing that the dermis of some dinosaurs was both leathery and scaly. Another hadrosaur, *Maiasaura*, whose name means "good mother reptile" has been described by paleontologist Jack Horner (who was, incidentally, the prototype for the paleontologist in the first *Jurassic Park* movie) as one of the few dinosaurs that guarded and cared for their eggs and, most likely, their hatched offspring as well.

Since there were so many different types of hadrosaurs throughout North America, it's difficult to determine which type left its footprints in this prehistoric soil. There is some evidence (and speculation) that the hadrosaurs in this area traveled in herds and may have exhibited rudimentary social tendencies.

I am intrigued to discover the track of a theropod (meaning "beast-footed") on another portion of the wall. Theropods were an equally diverse group of two-footed dinosaurs that lived during the Triassic Period (251.0–199.6 million years ago). This group of dinosaurs includes some of the largest carnivores to ever have walked the earth (i.e. *Tyrannosaurus rex*, *Allosaurus*, and *Ceratosaurus*), as well as many smaller specimens (i.e. *Oviraptor*, *Dromaeosaur*). Recent studies have provided evidence indicating that birds are actually the descendants of small non-flying theropods. The track embedded in the clay wall before me shows a distinctive hallux (or toe) on the side of its foot. In many modern-day birds, the hallux is used for grasping and perching. Although the thought of a one- or two-ton dinosaur perching on the branch outside my office window is difficult to imagine, suffice it to say that (thanks to studies of theropods) dinosaurs are not really extinct—their ancestors squabble and squawk around the bird feeder in my backyard all the time.

I climb up the pathway out of the clay pit and continue along the trail. I pass by two more interpretive signs that identify the clay mining pits of the early 1900s (Stop #3)and describe the geologic features of this former ancient seaway (Stop #4). I arrive at Stop #5, which marks a set of *Triceratops* tracks clearly embedded in a clay wall.

Gather any group of kids together and ask them to make a list of their all-time favorite dinosaurs and it is certain that *Triceratops* will be on almost every one of those lists. Perhaps it's because of its three distinctive horns. Or perhaps it's because of its supposedly bad temper. Or, perhaps it's because it just looks ugly and mean—like a rhinoceros with an attitude. Whatever the reason, kids (and adults) have been fascinated with this Late Cretaceous creature ever since the first one was discovered in 1887.

The discovery of *Triceratops* got off to a rocky start, paleontologically speaking. When the first *Triceratops* came to light* (in actuality it was just a skull roof with the bony cores of two brow horns), our friend O. C. Marsh concluded that it represented not a dinosaur from the end of the Cretaceous Period, but a long-horned bison from the Pliocene Epoch (5.3–1.8 million years ago). Marsh gave this new discovery the name *Bison alticornis*. However, when a more complete skull was unearthed in Wyoming in 1888, Marsh concluded that his original ideas were erroneous and the *Bison alticornis* passed into a paleontological black hole from which it has never returned.** The "new" creature was given the name *Triceratops* ("three horned face") in deference to the two long facial horns (up to three feet in length) and a somewhat shorter nose horn.

 *In 1887, the first *Triceratops* bones were discovered at a site near what is now Thirteenth Avenue and Federal Boulevard in Denver.

**It is not unusual for paleontologists to change their mind from time to time. As new evidence is unearthed, old theories and ideas are altered, changed, or even eliminated. Paleontology is a constantly evolving science—one that is seldom, if ever, stagnant. Karl Popper, a philosopher of science, has written that "science proceeds not by proofs, but by disproofs."

A *triceratops* track is preserved for the ages.

Triceratops lived during the Late Cretaceous Period (99.6–65.5 million years ago) throughout what is now North America. Fossils have been discovered as far north as Saskatchewan and Alberta, and as far south as Wyoming and Colorado. A *Triceratops* reached a weight of six to twelve tons, a length of twenty-six to twenty-nine feet, and a height of about nine-and-a-half to ten feet. This beast would be equivalent to two modern-day black rhinoceroses packed into a single creature.

Quite obviously, the *Triceratops* most distinctive feature was its skull, which could be almost a third of the length of the entire animal (approximately seven feet). By comparison, our skull is about one-eighth of our height (thus a six-foot adult human would have, on average, a skull that was nine inches from top to bottom). Recent studies of the skull case have indicated that the *Triceratops* brain was about the same size as a closed human fist. This seems to point to the fact that this beast was not the sharpest knife in the drawer—paleontologically speaking—lending support to the theory (proffered by some scientists) that there may be little correlation between brain size and body size.*

To the rear of the *Triceratops* skull was an impressive bony frill. This frill could often extend to nearly seven feet in length. There is much disagreement and lots of theories about its function. There's one camp of scientists who believe that the frill helped protect the dinosaur's vulnerable neck area against any would-be predators. Unfortunately, this contention is not borne out due to discoveries in which *Tyrannosaurus* bite marks have been detected on frill remains. It seems the frill may not have been a successful deterrent against some predators. Other scientists postulate that the frill helped this enormous beast regulate its body temperature. And yet another contingent of scientists believe that it may have been used in mating displays or in helping the *Triceratops* identify members of its own species.

There has also been considerable disagreement among paleontologists as to the function of the three horns. Early speculation was that the horns were used for defensive purposes against any would-be attackers. However, current theories postulate that the horns were most likely used in courtship and dominance displays—similar, in many respects, to the way in which reindeer and other ungulates use their antlers. Despite cartoons, children's books, and movies illustrating *Triceratops* in mortal battle with its (supposed) arch enemy—the *Tyrannosaurus*—there is little evidence to support the contention that *Triceratops* used its horns as primary weapons.

What makes the skull of a *Triceratops* even more unique among dinosaurs is its tendency to resist the pressures (literally) of decomposition. In most paleontological digs, the skull is often the most difficult to locate, if at all. That's simply because dinosaur skulls, for the most part, were fragile (due to their composition and all the cranial cavities and openings) and tended to break apart easily during the fossilization process. Not surprisingly, incredible and sustained geological pressures are constantly exerted on buried dinosaur bones over the millennia. As a result, while the vertebrae (which are more resistant to geological pressures) of a long-ago dinosaur may be found intact, the skull is often smashed or absent. However, due to

---

*The animal with the largest brain (about thirty pounds) is the Sperm Whale. The animal with the largest brain in proportion to its body is the dolphin. Incidentally, an average human brain weighs about three pounds—with the possible exception of those belonging to the idiots who persist in tailgating you at 85 mph on I-70.

its uniquely thick skull, scientists have been able to discover many *Triceratops* skulls throughout the West. Barnum Brown, a well-known paleontologist of the early twentieth century, claimed to have seen over five hundred *Triceratops* skulls in the field.

In spite of its fearsome appearance, this Cretaceous tank was an herbivore. It browsed primarily on a range of low-growing plants, which may have included ferns, cycads, and grasses. Its jaws ended in a deep, narrow beak that may have been used to grasp and pluck fibrous plants extant during those times. What is less known is that *Triceratops* had between 432 and 800 teeth in its mouth, arranged in batteries and stacked in rows three to five deep.* Like modern-day sharks, which continually shed and replace their teeth, tooth replacement for the *Triceratops* was continuous and occurred throughout the life of the individual. Given its enormous size, it is likely that it required great quantities of plant material each day in order to maintain its bulk.

Triceratops and the greater Denver area are closely associated. That's because several tracks of *Triceratops* (or a closely related dinosaur) were first discovered in this area. There has been some speculation that the tracks at Triceratops Trail were formed when the animals stepped in a wet, sandy streambed. They then pressed through to a layer of clay, leaving an impression of the tracks, and forming a mold of the footprint. It is likely that these molds filled with more sand—preserving the tracks as casts, or negative footprints. As the Rocky Mountains began to rise near the end of the Cretaceous Period, the once horizontal layers containing the tracks were tilted to a nearly vertical plane, where they can be seen today.

Of significant interest to scientists, the *Triceratops* tracks at Triceratops Trail helped dispel one of the great myths about these beasts. For many years it was believed that *Triceratops* had legs that were sprawled at angles from the thorax—much like modern-day alligators and crocodiles. This sprawling posture was proposed as a way for the creature to bear the enor-

*If you are interested in winning some bar bets you may wish to take notice of the following anatomical measurements of adult humans: 1) The eyes are in the exact middle of the head — between the top of the head and the tip of the chin. 2) The distance around a closed fist — over the knuckles — and the length of a foot (from the end of the heel to the end of the big toe) are equal. 3) The distance from the wrist to the elbow and the length of a foot (see #2) are equal. 4) The width of the mouth (from corner to corner) is the same as the distance between the middle of one eyeball to the middle of the other eyeball.

mous weight of its bony head and the great mass of its body. Illustrations and paintings in the early twentieth century capitalized on this theory and presented the public with the "sprawling model." However, close examination of various *Triceratops* trackways (e.g. horizontal spacing between footprints on one side versus those on the other side, and vertical distance between footprints on the left and on the right) demonstrate that this animal walked with an upright posture like modern-day rhinoceroses and hippopotamuses.

Stop #6 is just down the rock face and reveals a series of animal and plant impressions embedded in a vertical rock face beside the Fossil Trace Golf Course in Golden. Here is evidence of plant life that lived during the time of *Triceratops*. Most notable is a series of palm leaf impressions that are indicative of the semi-tropical environment that existed about sixty-eight million years ago (yes, there was a plethora of palm trees throughout what is now Colorado). Included with the palm leaf impressions are those of several varieties of deciduous trees, such as willow and sycamore. At least two bird footprints are also revealed in the rock wall. A large footprint is that of a crane-like bird, while the smaller one is similar to that of a modern-day plover. Interestingly, such tracks—particularly in this hardened prehistoric mud—are quite rare in North America.

I'm now at the end of the trail. I pause for a few moments to watch a foursome of golfers just beyond the fence hole out and climb into their carts for the next tee. I'm certain there are unique parallels between the set of *Triceratops* tracks I have been viewing and photographing for the past thirty minutes and the imperceptible tracks the golfers are leaving on the turf of the golf course. Many animals leave tracks—some should be remembered, others quickly forgotten, along with any corresponding double or triple bogeys. As I watched the faces of the golfers as they record their scores, I am certain that they would definitely vote for the latter.

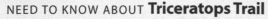

NEED TO KNOW ABOUT **Triceratops Trail**

DIRECTIONS From Denver, head west on US 6 to Golden. Travel past Colfax Avenue, the C-470 interchange, and then Heritage Road. Turn right at the signal at Nineteenth Street. After about a hundred yards, turn right on Jones Road. Follow this short road around to the right and park in the small parking area (holds about four or five cars). Walk south (to your left) on the Bike Path/Main Trail for about a quarter-mile to the Trailhead.

From C-470 north, take the Morrison Road Exit (CO 74). Drive into Morrison and turn right on County Road 93. You'll pass by Red Rocks Park on your left and then go under I-70. The road now becomes US 40. Turn left onto Heritage Road and then left onto US 6. Turn right at the signal at Nineteenth Street. Follow the directions above.

CONTACT INFORMATION Be sure to get a copy of "A Guide to Triceratops Trail at Parfet Prehistoric Preserve" ($2.00) from:
Dinosaur Ridge Visitor Center, (Friends of Dinosaur Ridge), 16831 W. Alameda Parkway, Morrison, CO 80465; (303) 697-3466; www.dinoridge.org

FEES None.

HOURS Open 7 days a week—sunrise to sunset.

BEST TIME TO VISIT Any time during the year—spring, summer, and fall are best.

CAMPING/LODGING There are literally hundreds of hotels, motels, inns, B&Bs, and campsites in the greater metropolitan Denver/Golden area. You'll find everything from "ultra cheap" to "ultra expensive" (and a lot in between).

ACCESS Triceratops Trail is wheelchair accessible. Please note that the steps down into the clay pit at Stop #2 can be difficult for physically challenged individuals.

RATING Easy. The trail can be traversed (from beginning to end and back again) in about half an hour.

NOTES If you're looking for something that is short and will keep both children and adults engaged, then this is a place for you. The trail is only about a quarter-mile from start to end, but at the end you must turn around and retrace your steps back to the beginning, thus resulting in a total hike of half a mile. The interpretive signs are brief, but quite informative.

Kids will be particularly interested in the tracks at Stop #2 and Stop #5 (be sure to bring your camera along). Adults will find some of the geological information and history of clay mining to be fascinating. For an all-inclusive (and very memorable) "dinosaur day" be sure to combine this very easy hike with a tour of Dinosaur Ridge, as well as a visit to the Morrison Museum of Natural History in nearby Morrison (where you'll find the skull of a Triceratops). It will be a day you and your kids will not soon forget.

CHAPTER 11

The Queen of Dinosaur Poop

UNIVERSITY OF COLORADO, BOULDER

My flight into Denver had been delayed by a series of Midwestern storms that hovered over Chicago and fouled up hundreds of family vacations and untold business trips. I waited patiently for my luggage to slide down the chute at DIA and onto the slowly revolving carousel. As my bag was the last to arrive, I grabbed the handle and hurried to the waiting area outside the terminal and to the van that would transport me to the off-site rental car location.

"Hello, I have a reservation for an economy car," I said when I arrived at the rental office.

"Hey, it's been a busy day and we have no economy cars available. I can give you a somewhat larger car for the same price." The agent was obviously not a happy camper today.

The weariness of travel and the change in time zones punctuated my reply. "Okay, I'm late for an appointment, so I'll just take anything you have."

"Fine. I'll enter your information into the system," he said, dismissively.

Without glancing in my direction, and obviously bored with his low-paying and semi-intellectual job, he dutifully began typing my address, driver's license information, and a host of other data into his computer.

"You here on business?" he asked in a distinctly robotic manner.

"Yes. I have an appointment this afternoon to see a paleoscatologist at the University of Colorado."

"A paleo ... *what?*" he asked, now looking up from the computer.

"A paleoscatologist," I replied, somewhat more slowly this time.

"What the hell is a paleoscatologist?"

"She's a scientist who studies fossilized dinosaur feces."

"Say that again," he responded, this time with a distinct note of incredulousness in his voice.

"She's one of the world's leading authorities on dinosaur dung. She studies fossilized dino poop in order to learn how and what dinosaurs ate, where they lived, their habits, lifestyles, and the geology and geography of prehistoric times," I replied.

"Oh," he said, as he tossed me my keys. "Your car is in space E-15."

I grabbed my bag and rolled my way out the door. As I did, I heard the agent remark to a nearby colleague, "Boy, and I thought I had a crappy job!"

Boulder, Colorado is a city of incredible diversity—a colorful panache of long-time locals and recent California transplants tired of the urban jungle. It's as if someone had captured Berkeley in the '60s and gently placed it into the foothills of the Rockies, carefully preserving a panoply of left-of-center college students and a kaleidoscope of social and environmental activism for another millennium. Streets hum with the constant whirring of pedals—78 percent of Boulder's arterial streets are equipped with bike lanes, and 16 percent of all commuter trips are made on bicycles in this city of 103,000 people. Strip malls of franchised restaurants and subdivisions of student apartments greet you as you enter the town via US 36. Insightful political slogans emblazoned on multi-colored T-shirts ("Somewhere in Texas a village is missing its idiot!"), iPoded pedestrians, and the mix of spit-polished Range Rovers and decaying VW's searching for non-existent parking spaces on Broadway lets you know you've arrived in academia. For it is the University of Colorado that is the centerpiece of this free-wheeling and very laid-back town.

On my way to the Museum Collections Building—a nondescript edifice that hugs the southwest edge of the main campus—I am nearly run over by a cyclist of Olympic proportions, who barks something at me as she speeds by on the bike path. It is then that I see that there is a walker's lane and a bi-directional biker's lane. The lanes are clearly marked (although, obviously, not always noticed) with icons indicating a "walker" and a "biker." I quickly move to the left just before a small band of in-line skaters, most likely political science majors, whizzes by me with reckless abandon.

I'm here to learn about coprolites, more specifically dinosaur coprolites. The term "coprolite" was first used by an Englishman, one William Buckland of Oxford University,* who studied fossils on the southern coast of England in the early 1800s. On several of his excursions, Buckland noticed spiral objects in the sand. Most scientists thought they were larch cones, but Buckland believed they were the fossil feces of ancient sharks. He proved this with an unusual demonstration. He poured cement into the intestines of sharks (presumably the sharks had gone to that "great aquarium in the sky" before having their gastro-intestinal tracts filled with permanently constipating concrete). When the cement hardened, it produced objects that were identical to the fossils he discovered on the beach.

In 1835, Buckland coined the term "coprolite" as the scientific name for the objects he found. Copro means "dung," from the Greek word *kopros*. The ending "lite," from the Greek word *lithos* (e.g. stone) is a common ending for fossil or mineral terms. So, linguistically a coprolite is "stone dung." Paleontologists have long studied the coprolites, or fossilized remains, of ancient animals looking for clues about their behaviors, eating habits, or migration patterns. However, the specific study of dinosaur coprolites is a relatively recent sidebar to the field of paleontology, and one practiced by a very small cadre of investigators.

My guide into the world of dino dung is Dr. Karen Chin. Karen is a paleontologist, or, more specifically, a paleoscatologist—someone who studies

---

*Professor Buckland had a pet bear that he would bring to several university functions. I imagine that the mere presence of this ursine companion in the lecture hall would be sufficient to prevent most, if not all, students from nodding off.

prehistoric and fossilized animal droppings. As you might imagine, paleoscatology is a narrowly defined field, yet Karen is one of its demigods. One writer has even referred to her as "The Queen of Dinosaur Poop" (which, I am sure, would make for some very interesting and very collectable business cards).

Karen is waiting for me when I arrive at her second floor office. She is wearing a black flowery dress, silver jewelry and low-cut heels—hardly the uniform of a stereotypical lab scientist who works with non-stereotypical dung. Her dark hair flows freely over her shoulders, accenting an angular face and a welcoming smile. She is personable, outgoing, and makes me feel very much at ease.

As a young girl, Karen was always interested in science, specifically the life sciences. However, when she was in college she took a geology course, and her direction in life changed

Dr. Karen Chin at work in her office at the University of Colorado, Boulder.

dramatically. While in graduate school, she worked under the tutelage of famed dinosaur expert Jack Horner at the Museum of the Rockies in Bozeman, Montana. She was amazed to learn that, under the right conditions, scat could turn to stone. Then she was given some suspected coprolites from the Two Medicine Formation in northwest Montana. Her careful analysis showed that these were indeed coprolites, and that they were the by-products of a large herbivorous dinosaur. At the time, she was one of the first paleontologists to analyze and categorize a dinosaur coprolite.

Later, she attended the University of California at Santa Barbara where she continued her research into coprolites, eventually obtaining her Ph.D.

in 1996. Before joining the faculty at the University of Colorado, she worked as a visiting scientist for the U.S. Geological Survey in Menlo Park, California, conducting paleontological research through a succession of federal grants.

We are barely two minutes into our conversation when Karen tells me something I had not previously considered. "Dinosaur coprolites are very, very rare. There are only a handful of specimens that can reasonably be attributed to dinosaurs. It is much more common to find fossil feces from aquatic animals because you generally have to have rapid burials to preserve them. So for aquatic animals you can have hundreds of fish coprolites in a small area, but when you are talking about fossil feces from terrestrial animals they are very, very rare. Discoveries of dinosaur coprolites have been really, really few."

She informs me that there are two big questions that she must always ask herself when she looks at a suspected dinosaur coprolite. The first one is, "Is it actually fossil feces?" She says that, unlike teeth or bones, animal fecal matter comes in a variety of shapes. The shape of a single sample may be determined by what the animal ate as well as forces that act on the specimen over time. "People have brought me things and sent me things that I still am not sure if they are coprolites or not.* The difficulty is that fossilized feces don't have a set shape, like bones or teeth; they are malleable and they have a different composition depending on diet and diagenetic regimes, which change with geologic time."

The author proudly holds a *T. rex* coprolite (and, no, he didn't have to wash his hands afterwards).

*At this point I am imagining an endless parade of people, similar to those who wait for the start of PBS's *Antiques Roadshow*, forming long lines outside Karen's office with all manner and shapes of coprolites (or faux coprolites) in hand. They are hoping, as do all the Roadshow participants, that her analysis will set them up financially for life.

Paleontologist Jim Kirkland was one of the original scientists working at the Mygatt-Moore site outside Fruita (see Chapter 2). Kirkland is a colleague of Karen's, and she told him that, "if people found anything [at the site] out of the ordinary that they suspected could be feces to let me know." One day a package arrived from Kirkland containing various specimen blobs.

"I sliced through [the coprolites] and they were just jam-packed with plant material—just jammed packed! And all that was comminuted—chopped up," she told me excitedly. Indeed, what Karen discovered was an array of plant remains, including bits of leaves, stems, seeds, pollen, even stomata and other cellular details. One thin section sliced from one sample contained seeds from several gymnosperms, including ginkgo trees. Coiled fern sporangia showed up in other samples. Karen's knowledge of paleobotany helped place these specimens in their proper context. For example, she noticed that there were chopped up stems from *cycadophytes*, a type of plant that dominated the Jurassic Period (199.6-145.5 million years ago). That, plus the age of the surrounding sediments, led Karen to conclude that, "the best interpretation for these specimens is that they are little masses of fecal matter, Jurassic in age.

"It was a really beautiful, exquisite preservation," she exclaimed.

In a paper she wrote while in graduate school, Karen convincingly proved that dinosaur coprolites can exhibit a wide variety of morphologies. These may include spherical, cylindrical, fusiform, spiral, blocky, pancake-like, and amorphous forms (similar, I suspect, to the items you might find on the menu at any backroads truck stop). In her paper, she noted that there is also a great deal of variation regarding coprolite colors. Specimens may be colored brown, white, cream, orange, black, gray, or blue. Suffice it to say, these factors only complicate the coprolite identification process.

The second question Karen asks when looking at a suspected dinosaur coprolite is, "Who produced this?" She cautions that size is not always an accurate predictor and that interpretations based on size must be made very carefully. For example, a small dinosaur coprolite may have broken off a much larger sample. Also, it is quite possible for a large animal to produce small samples of fecal matter. A male moose, for example, which typically weighs in at around 1,500–1,800 pounds and stands seven feet tall at the shoulder, produces scat pellets the size of grapes. Thus, it is entirely possible for a large animal, such as an oversized dinosaur, to deposit very small droppings. On the other hand, small animals, such as household cats, do not typically produce large fecal masses (fortunately for those of us who must periodically empty out litter boxes).

Oftentimes Karen makes "some educated guesses because there may be a wide range of organisms that produce a suspected coprolite, especially mid-sized specimens, which can be produced by fish, crocodiles, or even small dinosaurs. With very large specimens, it is a little bit easier because you can assume that a little guy could not have produced a large amount of feces." As a result, she knows that coprolite size should be used primarily to infer *minimum* sizes of possible producers.

According to Karen, her questions about coprolite composition and probable producers, and the fact that they don't have easy answers, are "the primary reasons why we've identified relatively few dinosaur coprolites."

Dinosaur coprolites are fossils (specifically, they're known as trace fossils*) and fossils have long been objects of fascination for paleontologists. However, several conditions must be met for something to fossilize. First, there must be a rapid burial. A swift burial prevents decomposition, since organic material breaks down very quickly in the presence of oxygen. When a layer of earth or sediment covers organic material, oxygen often cannot get to it. This creates an anaerobic (without oxygen) environment. In these conditions, the decomposition process may be slowed or stopped completely.

Over long periods of time, the constant action of wind and rain on the surface of the earth (e.g. weathering) wear away tiny bits of rock. Eventually, these microscopic bits are washed into streams, rivers, lakes, and ponds. Flowing rivers and currents in lakes move the minerals along. When the water slows down or stops moving, the minerals and sediments settle out. If there is some organic material nearby (e.g. bones, leaves), the dissolved minerals may seep into the material and replace the organic, decomposable

*Trace fossils provide proof of life from the past and include things like footprints, burrows, and coprolites. The other type of fossilized material—body fossils—includes any part of an actual plant or animal. These may be things like bones, teeth, shells, or leaves.

material with inorganic compounds. This slow and constant replacement is the process we know as fossilization. This process results in a heavy rock-like copy of the original object. In essence, a fossil is a facsimile of the original—it is not the actual object itself.

Although fossils have the same shape and size of the original item, their color, density, and texture are often different. A fossil's color depends on the minerals formed inside it. Usually, fossils are heavier than the original. That's because they are created entirely of minerals. However, it's interesting to note that fully 99 percent of prehistoric animals did not fossilize—they simply decayed and were forever lost from the fossil record.

Throughout our conversation, Karen deftly reminds me that the fossilization of dinosaur dung was very rare. Unlike hard objects, such as bones, soft piles of fecal matter evaporate, wash away, get stepped on, seep into the soil, or are carried off by other animals. In a nutshell—nothing remains!

Luckily, however, dinosaurs occasionally left their droppings on floodplains. A floodplain is a wide flat area near a river—an area where flooding is likely to occur. It's also an environment conducive to preservation. Other places where droppings were preserved include watering holes, ponds, swamps, and similar muddy areas. Assuming that a pile of poop was quickly covered by sediment (from a flood, for example), then there was a chance, a very small one to be sure, that it could eventually turn into a coprolite.

Interestingly, coprolites form in much the same way as bone fossils. Dissolved minerals in the surrounding water begin to fill tiny spaces inside the feces—a process that also takes millions of years. The organic materials in dung may be replaced with those minerals. The minerals inside the microscopic spaces sometime grow into crystals. These minerals may include silica, calcite, or pyrite. The minerals act like powerful glue, cementing the whole mass of dung together. Eventually the entire mass may harden into rock. The soft dinosaur dung has now become a coprolite.

The preservation of dinosaur feces was often a matter of environmental luck, for it was dependent on many things. These include the amount of organic materials in the dung, and its water content. (If there is significant water in the dung, then it is less likely to fossilize.) Another preservation factor includes where the dung was deposited and its method of burial. Also crucial is the chemical composition of the sediment surrounding the scat and the internal temperature of the poop. Fossilization may also be affected by the acidity of the surrounding water. The pressure of several layers of earth on the scat is another considerable factor. Becasue so many events must be in place for dinosaur droppings to fossilize, coprolites are more rare than bone fossils.

Paleontologists are scientific detectives; however, unlike with modern-day detectives all of the usual suspects have been dead and gone for millions of years. Unfortunately, an investigator such as Karen can't grill a suspected poop-etrator ("Listen here Mr. *T-Rex*, or whatever your name is, did you or did you not leave this pile of poop on the flood plain last night at approx-

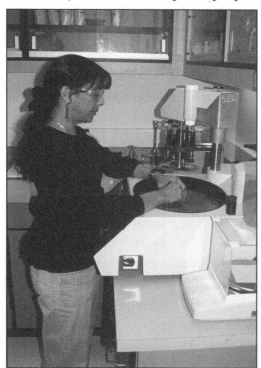

imately 10:30?"). But she can use her powers of observation, deduction, and scientific intuition—detective skills that would rival any gumshoe in a Leonard Elmore novel.

In 1995, a team of paleontologists from the Royal Saskatchewan Museum unearthed a suspected dinosaur coprolite in Canada's Frenchman River Valley. The specimen, one of the largest carnivore coprolites ever found, measured 44 by 16 by 13 centimeters (approximately 17 by 6 by 5 inches), with an estimated volume of just over 2.4 liters (approximately 2.5 quarts). In

Dr. Chin Performs a number of scientific tests on every sample of fossilized dung (or suspected dung).

order to determine if it was a dinosaur coprolite, it was turned over to Karen for examination.

First, Karen performed a number of tests on the fossil to determine the chemical components of the suspected coprolite. Next, during an intense visual inspection, she noticed tan bits of dinosaur bone embedded throughout the matrix of solid calcium phosphate, or apatite—the building block of bone. This suggested that the coprolite had been produced by a meat-eating (and bone-chomping) creature.

Her preliminary tests provided her with some valuable, though limited, scientific evidence on the specific beast that would have deposited the poop. But now she was forced to use her powers of deduction to narrow the field of possible suspects. Karen knew that the sample had been removed from sediments deposited during the Late Cretaceous Period (99.6–65.5 million years ago). Most of the carnivores that inhabited what is now southern Alberta during that time period were small theropod dinosaurs, such as *Elimisaurids, Leidyosuchus* and *Troodons,* as well as a few mid-sized crocodilians. However, there was one very large carnivore. Based on the overall size of the coprolite, the geological context in which it was located, and the fact that it was chock-full of bone fragments, she concluded that the best candidate for the pooper was *Tyrannosaurus rex.*

Now that the suspect was identified, Karen wanted to learn something about the apparent victim(s). Using some of the smaller coprolite samples that had eroded downhill from the main mass, she cut ultra-thin slices across various blobs. With the assistance of comparative anatomist Gregory Erickson (now of Florida State University), she noted that the bone fragments in the slices lacked distinctive growth rings typically associated with carnivorous dinosaurs. In addition, there was an absence of bone replacement or healed stress fractures. The distribution of bone fibers and blood vessels in the bone led them to deduce that the ingested animal (represented by body bits distributed throughout the coprolite) was a sub-adult herbivorous dinosaur.

Then the two researchers looked at the thickness of the bone walls inside each of the slices. This was an important factor—one which indicated that the bone fragments most likely came from limb bones. Precise measurements of those fragments suggested that the victim was about the size of a modern day cow and weighed around seven hundred kilograms (three hundred pounds). Working back to the herbivores that inhabited this area at that time helped them conclude that the unfortunate victim was either a small *Triceratops* or an *Edmontosaurus*.

The evidence of bone fragments in the *T. rex* coprolite also suggested that this "terrible lizard" was able to pulverize bone as it bit down on huge chunks of meat. Equally interesting was the secondary discovery that many of the bone fragments scattered throughout the coprolite had been partially dissolved. This action typically results from gastric acids working on the bones as they pass through the digestive system. Most carnivores digest bone to some extent, although crocodiles are the only modern-day creatures able to completely digest the skeletons of their victims. The partial digestion accomplished by *T. rex* seemed to suggest that the ancient predator, much like its modern-day reptilian counterparts, obtained some nutrients from the prey's bones.

The mid-afternoon sun filters in through the plate glass window that takes up part of one wall in Karen's office. As I glance toward the west, I can see the majestic Rockies arch up from the horizon like hump-backed goliaths with white-capped backs. I am reminded that where we are now talking was once a prehistoric rainforest crawling with predators and prey alike. My imagination kicks in, and I can almost see a *Tyrannosaurus rex*, hungry for a slow-footed herbivore, sloshing around the shoreline of an imaginary Jurassic swamp just across the street. I am quickly jolted back to reality by the tinkling of a bell. An ice cream truck passes by on the street outside, and just like any humanoid predator of frozen dairy products, my mouth begins to salivate.

Knowing that Karen has been trained as both a botanist and an ecologist, I ask her about paleolandscapes, specifically what she has learned about prehistoric geography based on her analysis of dinosaur coprolites. I am curious about the relationship between the contents of a dinosaur coprolite and the territory in which an ancient depositor may have roamed.

She tells me a story about the Two Medicine Formation in northwest Montana—the area where her mentor, Jack Horner, has unearthed the nesting sites of *Maiasaura* ("good mother lizard"), a duck-billed dinosaur that lived about seventy-five million years ago. Among other clues, Horner found the bones of hatchlings and juveniles lying together in and around their nests. This led him to conclude that the hatchlings stayed in the nest while their parents fed and protected them. This, as you might imagine, was a radical departure from more common assumption that dinosaurs provided no maternal or paternal care for their young.

It was 1989, and Karen, just at the beginning of her doctoral studies, was looking for a reasonable research project. Horner presented her with a most unusual present—several nondescript and amorphous blobs broken into a variety of sizes. In the laboratory, Karen subjected the chunks to several scientific tests. First, using a super sharp knife, she obtained several thin slices cut across the face of the fossilized dung. She meticulously examined each slice under a powerful microscope. Almost immediately, she made several startling discoveries.

One slice contained a small grouping of seeds. Further examination revealed that these seeds were from gymnosperms. This group of plants includes cycads and ginkgo trees—plants that have been around for millions of years. These prehistoric trees are still found in many tropical and subtropical regions of the world. Several fern parts turned up in one sample. Ferns are found throughout the world today and were also common in prehistoric times.

Most amazing, however, was her discovery of leaf blades from cycad-like plants. Cycad-like plants typically have thick leaf blades. As Karen tells me, "when you get a plant with a thick blade that is a good indication of a more arid environment." I ask her if there is a relationship between these plants and the succulents, or desert plants, we have today. "No," she responds. "That's because it is not so much succulence as it is sclerophyllous, which means that it is tougher resulting in less water loss [Sclerophyll literally means "hard leaves."]. In some of them we actually found cuticles. Cuticle is the waxy covering on plants … and I did some separations and was able to mount pieces of those cuticles [on slides] and discovered very distinct little projections on them that are called papillae. When you get a lot of these papillae, that is another characteristic of plants that grow in arid environments, because it's another way of reducing some of the water loss."

I watch as a sly smile crosses her face—the kind a college student might display if offered the keys to a beer delivery truck. "I know this is a little bit of a bone of contention with some of the other paleobotonists," she says. "That's because they have interpreted some of these environments as being more wet." Generally speaking, many people presume that the age of dinosaurs was also an age of subtropical or tropical environments.* However, Karen's coprolite evidence seems to confirm geological times and geographical places in which the climate was considerably more arid than originally thought. Her scatological detective work has opened up some new interpretations and new views on prehistoric environments.

We move over to a notebook filled with photographs of the Two Medicine coprolite slices. Karen points to "little white things" sprinkled throughout some of the slices. She tells me that these are pyroclastic bubble shards or volcano ash from some ancient volcanic eruption. She explains that the ash from a prehistoric eruption would have coated plants and fallen onto the surface of drinking holes. As animals ate the plants or drank the water, some of that volcanic debris would find its way into their dung. When I ask if she has been able to trace the location of the volcanic eruption, she says that the size of the volcanic shards in the coprolite slices suggest that the volcano ranged in height from one kilometer (with a low velocity wind) up to four hundred kilometers in height (with a high velocity wind). The precise location of the volcano, however, has not yet been determined.

By this point in our conversation, I am completely enthralled. As we scan additional pages of photographs, Karen points to several mysterious winding burrows tunneled through many coprolite samples. Some of the burrows are very small, while others are up to an inch and a quarter in diameter. Most of the tunnels were hollow, but others were filled with fine plant debris or sediment. The obvious question was how did the tunnels get into the dung? The answer was more intriguing than I could have ever imagined.

*In fact, most traditional illustrations (in textbooks, popular magazines, and children's books) of dinosaurs in prehistoric environments feature a dazzling array of tropical plants, swamp-like conditions, and distinctly sultry settings.

Dr. Chin points to some of the features that make a coprolite unique.

To help solve this part of the puzzle, Karen turned the sample over to an entomologist. It was then that the mystery of these coprolites began to unravel. After a long and careful examination, it was determined that the burrows had been created by prehistoric dung beetles. This was not expected. That's because scientists have long believed that dung beetles are modern-day creatures.

If you visit Africa or Australia you will soon discover that dung beetles are quite common throughout each of these two continents. These beetles are valuable insects because they get rid of large quantities of dung. Working in pairs, dung beetles gather bits of animal dung (for example, from elephants, giraffes, antelopes, lions, and zebras) on the ground and roll them into balls. The dung balls may be as small as a marble or as large as an apple. These balls are then rolled to another location and buried in the ground. The female beetle lays her eggs inside the dung ball and when the eggs hatch, the larvae eat their way out (how's that for a baby's first meal?). Believe it or not, the fecal matter provides the young larvae with all the nutrition they need during the first critical days of their lives.

However, scientists long believed that dung beetles didn't originate until the rise of large mammals (that's because large mammals tend to leave large amounts of dung!). And, large mammals didn't appear on the earth until long after the extinction of dinosaurs. But, the presence of dung beetle tunnels in the coprolite samples proved that dung beetles were prehistoric creatures, too. In other words, long before they were collecting the dung from African or Australian animals, these beetles may have been rolling balls of dinosaur dung across a prehistoric landscape. It seems that dung beetles have been around much longer than originally thought.

The dung beetle tunnels in the coprolites also revealed another fact. Extended examinations revealed many different sized tunnels in the sample. As a result, Karen and other paleontologists think that several different species of beetle lived on the dinosaur dung. At this juncture, they just don't know for sure. But, here's something else—modern day dung beetles only use the dung from mammals. We now know that prehistoric dung beetles utilized reptilian dung. This discovery in samples of fossilized feces changed scientists' ideas and perceptions about several prehistoric animals—insects as well as reptiles!

The dung beetle tunnels may also be proof of a prehistoric food chain. For example, most dinosaurs were herbivorous. Those creatures left behind blobs of dung full of vegetative matter. Like modern-day beetles, the prehistoric dung beetles needed the dinosaur's dung to survive. And, prehistoric plants needed the nutrients in the dung. The cycle looks like this:

> Dinosaur eats plants ▶ deposits dung ▶ dung found by beetles ▶ beetles lay eggs in dung ▶ dung fertilizes nearby plants ▶ plants grow ▶ dinosaur eats plants

In other words, there may have been a prehistoric cycling and recycling of organic material, just as there is today. Think about it this way—recycling may not be a modern-day idea. We now suspect that this process may have been taking place in nature for at least seventy-five million years.

According to Karen, a study of the plant parts in dinosaur coprolites often reveals fascinating information. For example, the digestive process of many modern-day herbivores is often incomplete. Some types of plant materials, such as cellulose, do not completely break down during the digestive process. Instead, these materials pass from one end of the digestive system to the other with little or no decomposition. As a result, they often have limited nutritional value.* Consequently, many species of herbivores need to eat large quantities of plants in order to survive.

The Two Medicine coprolite revealed vegetation from many different species of plants. This suggested that the animal that produced the now fossilized dung had a wide and varied diet. It appears that this animal did not feed on a single species of plant. In fact, it probably learned to survive on many different kinds of plants.

A detailed analysis of the plant parts in a coprolite also can tell us something about the time or era in which those plants lived. Certain plant species in a

---

*A day or so after a summertime barbeque of hamburgers, potato salad, and corn-on-the-cob, you have undoubtedly noticed little kernels of corn sprinkled throughout your feces. Those corn kernels cannot be broken down by your body's digestive process simply because they are encased in a film of cellulose, which is impervious to stomach acids. Thus, they pass from top to bottom (excuse the pun) intact and undigested.

coprolite help us match the time period in which a dinosaur lived with the time period in which a plant species lived. This provides more critical information about the dinosaur, as well as information about prehistoric plants. Interestingly, there are plant parts in coprolites that are related to modern-day plants. There are also plant parts that are a permanent record of species now extinct.

Examining embedded plant parts solved part of the mystery of the Two Medicine coprolite. We know, for example, that the animal that produced it was an herbivore. It ate a wide variety of plants and it had an incomplete digestive process. This meant that the creature that produced it was not a *Tyrannosaurus rex* or *Allosaurus*—both of which were carnivores. However, to narrow her choices, there was another piece of detective work Karen needed to do. But, first, a dietary side trip.

Here's something you don't think about very often—eating celery. So, let's imagine you're eating a single stalk of celery. While eating celery is not something you really think about, it could provide a scientist (who was studying *you*) with lots of information about your eating habits. For example, you may bite into a stalk of celery with your front teeth. If you do, then there will be a distinctive bite pattern straight across the stalk. Or, perhaps you bite into a celery stalk with the teeth on the sides of your mouth. If so, there would be an angular bite pattern on the stick of celery. Grazing animals, for example, often bite with the teeth on the sides of their mouths. This makes it easier for them to chew thick or woody materials.

Okay, now let's imagine that a certain herbivorous dinosaur deposits a mass of feces in a stream bed. Imagine, too, that the area where that dinosaur lived and ate and pooped was alongside a great inland sea. It's now millions of years later and the dino dung has been transformed into a coprolite. Now, imagine that paleontologists discover various skeleton bones of the dinosaur at a "dig." Several neck bones and hip bones are also unearthed. Nearby they also discover the fossilized feces.

The coprolite is sent to Karen in Boulder. There, she uses a special saw to remove a very thin slice from the face of the hardened dung. She then prepares a slide from the thin slice and slips it under a powerful microscope. With a practiced eye she discovers several items embedded within the specimen.

One of the first things she sees is woody plant stems. These plant parts are scattered throughout the sample. But it's not the plant parts that are necessarily important. It's what they look like. These pieces reveal clues as to how the plants were eaten.

She notices lots of angular breaks in the woody fibers. This suggests that the plant material may have been chewed up. Think back to that piece of celery that you ate earlier. You may have bitten into it with your side teeth. If you did, you may have created a few angular bites on the stick of celery. This is just what Karen saw on the plant fibers in the coprolite sample. This provides Karen with critical information about how a dinosaur may have chewed its food.

But other mysteries still remain. Karen still doesn't know whether the plants found in the coprolite were part of the dinosaur's regular diet. It's possible that the plant samples were inadvertently eaten while browsing among other plants. Nevertheless, the coprolite has confirmed for us the fact that the dinosaur was an herbivore.

When Karen studies coprolites, she is interested in many things. She wants to learn something about the animal that created the dung and she also wants to know about where it lived. She can often do that by analyzing the minerals in a coprolite. Coprolite minerals often reveal information about the region in which an animal roamed. For example, there may be a high concentration of calcium in a coprolite. If so, then Karen might speculate that there were lots of shellfish near the dung when it was deposited. That's because shells have significant levels of calcium.

Other minerals in a coprolite can also tell her about the geology of the land. There may be iron, magnesium, or lead throughout a coprolite. These provide Karen with information about the minerals that may have been around long ago, although it's also possible that the minerals were washed into the area from another place. These clues are important, and may suggest some of the geological changes that took place over long periods of time. Frequently, they also raise additional questions for Karen and other scientists to explore.

Sometimes, Karen will bombard a coprolite sample with X-rays—a process known as X-ray diffraction. The angles at which the X-rays bounce off the materials inside a coprolite sample reveal critical information about the minerals. Each mineral has a different diffraction factor or angle of bounce. By recording those angles, Karen can often determine the specific types of minerals inside a coprolite specimen.

Coprolite samples can sometime reveal high levels of phosphates. We know that bones are rich in phosphates. We also know that meat-eating animals frequently chew on the bones of their victims. This may suggest that a coprolite sample was deposited by a carnivore rather than an herbivore. Interestingly, the presence of phosphates in a carnivore's diet also helps in the fossilization of its feces. In other words, the more minerals in dinosaur dung, the easier it was to turn into stone.

Due to the high levels of phosphates in their dung, carnivore coprolites are more abundant than herbivore coprolites. Yet, we also know that carnivorous dinosaurs were much more rare than herbivorous dinosaurs. In fact, most dinosaurs discovered so far (via body fossils) have been plant-eating species. In an interesting paleontological twist of fate, there was less dung from carnivorous dinosaurs available for fossilization, but more of that type of dung was actually fossilized.

Coprolites can help us solve additional mysteries about dinosaurs. For example, when people first started studying ancient creatures they were mainly focused on dinosaur bones. That is still the primary focus of many paleontologists because, through those bones, we learn about what an animal looked like. But coprolites can help us answer questions that the bones can't. For example, a coprolite may have tiny food particles inside it. This could mean the dinosaur chewed its food into small bits before swallowing it. Some food particles may be large. This suggests that the dinosaur ate its food in large chunks.

Analyses of coprolites provide many intriguing answers about the life and times of dinosaurs. So too, do they present paleoscatologists such as Karen with even more questions to answer. For example, when the Two Medicine specimens were further analyzed, approximately eighty snails showed up in the slides. Did this mean the dinosaur regularly ate snails? Probably not. Karen tells me that the snails may have been sticking to leaves swallowed by the dinosaur and the herbivore would have inadvertently eaten them. Or, the snails may have gathered on the feces after it was deposited. Some questions were answered, but new ones continue to arise.

A varied collection of dinosaur coprolites.

Karen and I are discussing the future of paleoscatology, and I am curious as to why someone would want to specialize in this relatively obscure and unglamorous field. "It is important to recognize that when we look at the fossil record we are trying to reconstruct all aspects of life," Karen says. "One important aspect is defecation because it's the way our body gets rid of things we don't need. It also provides mechanisms to recycle things back into the environment. Often times, what we see in movies of dinosaurs are the dramatic parts of their lives—the predation and the running. So, when people first hear that I study feces it takes them aback because it's not a romantic subject, but it is a very real subject."

Admittedly, "romance" and "animal poop" are not terms I have often used in the same sentence. However, Karen is quick to point out that scientists study aspects of feces and defecation in order to learn about different physiological processes in animals. She punctuates this by stating, "I am just taking this back into prehistoric times—trying to learn the real life of animals—not necessarily the glamour aspects."

As we conclude our conversation, Karen finally asks me the question I have been waiting to hear. "Would you like to see some dinosaur coprolites?" With unsteady feet I follow her into the adjacent laboratory. She unlocks and opens the doors to a steel gray cabinet in the corner. There before me lay row upon row of the most incredible sight I have yet to witness in my journalistic career. Neatly arranged and carefully labeled were stone-cold masses of … of … of dinosaur turds. My heart was racing, my breath was shallow, and my hands were trembling—I had, at last, reached The Promised Land!

CHAPTER 12

Return to the Oven

MYGATT–MOORE QUARRY DIG

Throughout all my prehistoric journeys across the deserts and mountains of Colorado I met several paleontologists—both professionals and amateurs. I was always taken, not just with the breadth and depth of their knowledge, but also by their passion for this seemingly "dead" field of scientific inquiry. I have long believed (and this trip did nothing to dissuade me from this belief) that a scientist is simply a person who asks a lot of questions, and goes out to find the answers to those queries.

Paleontologists, I quickly discovered, probably had (and continually have) more questions than perhaps any other field of science. The unfortunate (or fortunate, depending on your point of view) thing is that the answers to their questions are not always found in scientific literature or dusty library tomes tucked deep in the bowels of some university library. The answers to their questions often have to be teased from the minutest fragment of a dinosaur bone, the impression left in a slab of weathered rock baking in the piercing summer sun in a remote desert location, or the fragments of skeletal remains that had been smashed, weathered, or subjected to incredible geological pressures over tens of millions of years.

Just as the questions are not easy to answer, so too are the answers both difficult and trying to locate. Paleontology is an inexact science. There are many pioneers who have paved the way, but their discoveries may be tenuous or temporary—to be discounted or disproved with the discovery of yet another piece of the paleontological puzzle known as dinosaurs. In short, dinosaurs reveal their secrets grudgingly—the answers have been secreted away in ridges of hardened sandstone, gigantic blocks of mudstone, and sweeping expanses of uninhabited territory that lack creature comforts and demand rigorous and hardy (and, probably, slightly foolish) souls to explore their hidden treasures. I believe that paleontologists are the heroes of modern science—or to paraphrase the opening line from the TV series *Star Trek*—they boldly go where no one has gone before. That boldness is evident in both matters cerebral and matters physical.

Out of my respect and admiration for these men and women of science, I wanted to dip my proverbial toes into the proverbial waters of paleontological research—even if I was only a temporary visitor to this complex field. And so, I signed up for the Dinosaur Expedition Program sponsored by the Museum of Western Colorado. This one-day expedition visits the Mygatt-Moore Quarry out at Rabbit Valley (see Chapter 2). There, for a fee of $125.00, up to twenty "wanna-be" paleontologists can join with a professional paleontologist for a day of digging and sweating and digging and sweating and … Although I had walked the "Trail Through Time" out at Rabbit Valley many times previously, I had yet to experience the overt thrill of backbreaking excavations, energy-sapping temperatures, and scientific progress measured in millimeters rather than feet and yards. This was my chance to fulfill a lifelong dream—to be a real scientist … if only for a day.

Before setting out on this prehistoric trek, I made arrangements to interview John Foster, the resident Curator of Paleontology at Dinosaur Journey Museum in Fruita, and the leader of the expedition several days hence. Like many paleontologists, John didn't set out to intentionally become a paleontologist. It wasn't like he had a cosmic revelation and stood up one day to announce, "I want to be a paleontologist!" Like many before him, John fell into the field quite by accident. And, also like many before him, the route had any number of twists and turns and bends.

John's initial plan was to be a marine biologist. Growing up in southern California he had, for most of his life, been obsessed with sailing, the ocean, and especially with sharks. He thought that biology would be a natural major considering his background. While he was pursuing his biology degree he decided to take a course in geology—and his life plan was immediately altered. He soon changed his major.

(Photo courtesy Dick Hodgman) ·

However, "While I was in geology, I found that biology still influenced me because we'd be out doing geologic mapping or research and we'd be finding corals or trilobites out in the Mojave Desert. Professors would come along and say, 'Hey, got to get back to mapping.'"

By the time his senior year rolled around, John got the notion that he wanted to be a paleontologist. "My major professor [is] the one who is partly responsible for getting me into this, but he was also trying to warn me that it was fairly impractical, job-wise." However, John was well into completing his geology degree, so he decided to complete that degree and then do his paleontological studies in graduate school. He was accepted at South Dakota School of Mines, but decided to take a year off and travel throughout Europe.

After returning from the Continent, he completed his Masters degree and started working for about a year and a half while waiting for the next round of graduate school applications. Afterwards, he attended the University of Colorado for his doctoral studies in paleontology. Later he worked on a series of temporary grant-funded positions, including an approximately six-month paleontological survey in southern Utah and at the University of Wyoming, where he served as curator for two years. In Laramie, he spent his time re-cataloging and updating the curation of 40,000 museum specimens. But, the grant money was quickly running out.

He kept looking for a permanent position. "Then this job [Curator of Paleontology] came up just as I was three days into unemployment. I started here about seven and a half years ago. Here I'm curator—which means, technically, my responsibilities are for the paleontological collections, but since we're a fairly small museum I'm basically responsible for the collections and exhibits and labs and site manager for the [Mygatt-Moore] quarry. I'm also responsible for coordinating the maintenance and some administrative stuff. Never a dull moment 'cause I'm always switching from one of those things to the other."

I ask John what he hopes folks will come away with when they visit Dinosaur Journey Museum. I'm also curious as to the goals of the dig that I'll be participating in out at the quarry. John tells me that one of the primary goals of the museum is to provide visitors with information that may not be readily apparent from reading books or watching TV specials. A lot of the museum exhibits are interactive, so that provides visitors with unique opportunities to "get up close and personal" with dinosaurs. While he assures me that an appreciation for the history of life in the Colorado Plateau or Rocky Mountain region is paramount, he hopes folks will also discover something that surprises them.

He goes on to tell me that the intent of the field experience out at the Mygatt-Moore Quarry is for participants to learn a fair amount about excavation techniques and appreciate the work that paleontologists do day in and day out. There's also the hope that people might find something out there. That's the really exciting part for professionals and amateurs alike. As John points out, "It happens to us even if we've been doing it for twenty years. Any new bone, no matter how mundane it is, when you first uncover it—that's the first light of day it's even seen in 150 million years. There's always a certain amount of that excitement. And, allowing the dig participants to have that is really most gratifying."

John is, however, quick to point out that that doesn't always happen. Most of the time there are no discoveries at all. The work may involve trenching around a big jacket or picking at the mudstone around the end of a bone that was exposed sometime in the previous season by another visitor. (The week before my visit, a professional crew of paleontologists removed a jacketed bone from the quarry—something they'd been working on for the past two seasons.) But, for most people, those too can be enjoyable experiences because they know they are making an honest contribution to scientific discovery. On the other hand, on the same day someone, just out of pure chance, finds a theropod tooth. According to John, "they're practically jumping all over the place."

The point John continues to emphasize is that everybody's experiences are going to be a little bit different, and that what they find is going to be a little bit different—hopefully everybody has fun with whatever particular aspect of the quarry work they do. He also underscores the fact that people are not out there long enough (seven and a half hours) for them to really learn a whole lot about dinosaurs. The most valuable information about dinosaurs can be better obtained through the exhibits at the museum. And that's just a result of the fact that quarry work is really slow. John puts it this way:

> There's not always gigantic progress that happens. People aren't necessarily going to be able to see an entire skeleton uncovered as we go—it's almost glacial the speed at which we get things done. Lots of times it's hit and miss. Sometimes we don't jacket stuff on any particular day, other times we do and its almost random chance the day people happen to show up. If somebody shows up and ends up jacketing something they'll get that fun part, but they haven't seen all the work in trenching it. So it's kinda hard to get that full experience unless you're out there for three weeks or something. So we can't really demonstrate everything involved with field work, but hopefully the little taste of it they get gives them some indication. And, hopefully they find something that is fairly exciting—gives them a little flavor of what keeps us going through all the heat and boredom the rest of the time. There's a possibility that the next rock you turn over may have an Allosaurus tooth in it. That's what gets you through it being 109 degrees with gnats biting you and it's raining.

Knowing that the one-day expeditions out to the Mygatt-Moore Quarry will undoubtedly attract an interesting cross-section of the American public, I ask John why the so-called average person on the street should be interested in paleontology. He explains that even a rudimentary knowledge of paleontology gives one a greater understanding of (and undoubtedly an appreciation for) the possibility of any future extinctions. He also shares how even a rudimentary knowledge of paleontology provides an appreciation for today's animals—that is, modern-day species survive in ways that were already being done more than 150 million years ago. Today's herbivores, both large and small, obtain their food in much the same way as prehistoric herbivores did. Modern-day carnivores, such as lions and sharks, use many of the same techniques to feed themselves as did the dinosaurs of the Jurassic Period. As John so eloquently puts it, "Folks may be surprised to learn that many of the behavioral habits of today's animals had their roots in the animals of long ago. They may be entirely different species (and totally unrelated), but in many cases there may be more similarities than differences between animal species separated by tens of millions of years of existence."

As John talks, I realize that here is a scientist captivated by story. It is not the plethora of dinosaur facts and figures that John wants folks to walk away with while participating out at the dig. To John, it's not the names of the dinosaurs, or the geologic periods in which they lived, or even the variety of dinosaur types that lived in this little corner of the world that are important. Much more important is an appreciation for the stories that lie buried beneath the sand and dirt and centuries-hardened mudstone of western Colorado. "So the types of dinosaurs aren't so much the story, the really well preserved ones are nice, but they're not really the story. The story out of that site is what was going on that preserved so many skeletons that got so completely scattered all over the place."

John talks about the interweaving of stories with an excitement and passion that is contagious. Each of the stories is like a small mystery—solve one and you may have a clue for another. Some of those mysteries revolve around why some bones were chewed and why others were broken in place. How did so many carnivore teeth wind up in the same place? How did some of the chunks of ribs wind up being rounded at both ends? "Why do some bones have breaks in them that are completely right angles ... I mean there's no wear on the corners at all?" It's that combination of discoveries and their attendant mysteries that keeps the excitement high. It's the story he wants to share with the lay public, too.

John is equally eager to point out that paleontology is "really a slow process." He notes that major discoveries are often separated by months, if not years. Collection at the site has been taking place for more than twenty-five years and even though some significant finds have been unearthed, there's also the time needed to carefully and systematically examine those finds and put them in an appropriate context. "We just have to be patient and know that, for the taxonomic study of this site, we've been collecting stuff here for twenty-five years, and just the process of going through and compiling all the data on these bones over the years will take several years." He underscores the importance of patience as an essential element in any paleontological work. One-day visitors only get to see a small slice of that process—not the years that may come before or after the discovery of a significant find. As John puts it, "There's patience in the field, there's patience in the lab, and there's patience in the research."

I ask him if he would say that patience and paleontology go hand in hand. He responds by saying, "My old advisor at South Dakota used to tell people that when we were going out digging—patience is the number-one tool that you need."

It's about 8:00 a.m. on a Wednesday morning. The day has dawned crisp and bright and I'm standing outside the Dinosaur Journey Museum in Fruita, waiting for my fellow amateur paleontologists to join this "expedition" to the Mygatt-Moore Quarry. Three or four cars pull up and discharge

One of the official greeters outside the Dinosaur Journey Museum.

IMAGINE A TIME LONG AGO.
Imagine a time millions of years ago—
a time when dinosaurs ruled the world.
Imagine a lush and verdant swamp. Clumps of ferns
choke the shoreline. A grove of Dryophyllum trees is clustered
near one end of the ooze. Their branches arch out over the water.
Willow trees poke their branches into the hazy afternoon sky.
Large dragonflies flit in and out of water plants clustered along
the shore. The hum of tiny insects and the flutter of prehistoric
wings break the stillness of the marshy landscape.

Nearby, a forest of Artocarpus trees, a broad-leafed flowering
species, lines the western edges of the swamp. Small crocodilians
and an occasional Brachiosaurus meander through this verdant
territory. The air is humid and punctuated with the squeaks and
rumblings of many different creatures coming to the watering
place to drink. There is an immense diversity of life and sound.

Along a slow moving stream, an Ankylosaurus browses on
a patch of low-growing herbs. Ankylosaurus is an armor-plated
dinosaur that lived during the Late Cretaceous Period (99.6–65.5
million years ago). These dinosaurs reached a length of twenty-five
feet and an overall weight of two to three tons. Their name means
"fused reptile"—referring to the solid mass of armor plates on their
backs. Their equally armored sides were protected by spines and
bands of circular plates. At the end of the tail was a heavy, bony
club that they may have used for protection when attacked.

Look closely and you will also see one or two Allosaurus
dinosaurs lurking in the shadows of nearby trees. With their over-
sized heads, stout bodies, and short three-fingered forelimbs, they
are fearsome predators. Of moderate length (thirty feet), they have
large and powerful hind limbs and long, heavy tails. These were
creatures at the top of the food chain—their prey often consisted
of slow-moving herbivores that frequented the watering hole.

The Allosaurs *survey the various creatures that come to drink. They dismiss the* Ankylosaur *as too dangerous an opponent. Still, their muscular jaws open and close slowly. Their large sharp teeth are ideally suited for ripping flesh. Their powerful jaws can easily crush the skeletons of their victims. They watch … they wait … as a small herd of sauropods approach.*

The predators slowly scan the herd. They are searching for the youngest members of the group. Their brains are readied for the kill. The solitary bleating of a nearby herbivore echoes across the still waters as the predators charge and attack. They simultaneously clamp their great jaws onto the neck and hind leg of an unfortunate juvenile and rip out fat masses of flesh. The young dinosaur collapses to the ground … another meal for the hungry carnivores.

their passengers. Then a very large van emblazed with "Telluride Academy" pulls into the parking lot, and fifteen ten-year-olds pile out with backpacks, hats too big for their heads, and a constant chatter that is both endless and vibrant. Ah, I think to myself, a day in the desert with *Mr. Roger's Neighborhood.*

Registrations are carried out by John and his very capable assistant, Alex. John will be driving one of the museum vans, and Alex the other. I have the good fortune to be in Alex's van with some of the young paleontologists, along with a young mother (Dina) and her six-year-old son, Sam.

On our way out to the quarry, I chat with Dina and Sam. They are both from Loveland, Colorado, and this is their second time out at the quarry. Dina has worked as an editor and also has her Master's in Science. Sam has had a fascination with dinosaurs ever since … well, ever since he could remember. He has been to the Field Museum in Chicago as well as the Denver Museum of Nature and Science. Sam tells me that, "The first dinosaur I learned about was *T. rex*. And I know that a *T. rex* has teeth as big as steak knives." Far be it for me to even doubt the word of a six-year-old

The crew of young paleontologists begins gathering all the necessary tools to begin the day.

paleontologist, and so I ask him what his favorite dinosaur would be. "That would be the *Velociraptor*," he responds with pride. "I collect a whole bunch of dinosaurs and I have a *T. rex* tooth at home." His mother tells me that he fully intends to become a paleontologist when he grows up. In talking with him, it is evident that he's more than halfway there already.

Shortly after our arrival at the quarry, Alex gathers all the kids around her for a short introduction to dinosaurs and the work before them for the day. Even as Alex is trying to describe the various fossils discovered here, as well as the work that goes into that discovery process, the kids are peppering her with every kind of imaginable question. Like any seasoned classroom teacher, it is a lesson in trying to herd cats.

"What do we call a dinosaur with three toes?" Alex asks.

One kid quickly raises his hand and answers, "A three-toed dinosaur." The seven adults in the group are trying to quash their laughter as Alex, with just the faintest image of a smile on her lips, responds, "No, it's a theropod."

With a great deal of patience, good humor, and lots of information geared specifically to the age group of the kids, Alex provides these young scientists with valuable data necessary to put the days' proceedings in the proper context. Most important, she informs them about the "Five Rules of the Quarry":

Rule #1: If you find a bone, leave it in place so we can verify it.

Rule #2: Don't move bones out of their original position in the quarry.

Rule #3: We never dig straight down into the rock. That often has a tendency to break the bone.

Rule #4: We like to keep our areas clean.

Rule #5: Use the hammers very carefully.

The kids (and small cadre of adults) are each assigned basic paleontological tools, including a screwdriver (to be used as a makeshift, though very efficient, chisel), one small brush, one large brush, a claw hammer, and a dustpan (for gathering up debris). As we saunter over to the quarry site, we note that there's some excavation already taking place. A few adult volunteers (Zach, Kay, and Ray) are already hard at work chipping, trenching, and jacketing selected specimens in the large pit that's dug into the side of a small hill.

With Alex providing direction and supervision for all the youngsters, John comes around to each of the adults and assigns them their various responsibilities for the day. He points out a big chunk of rib and another small fragment off to the side. However, he wants me to work around a bone that's been outlined in the mudstone by a previous volunteer. He informs me that the bone looks like it might be part of an *Allosaurus*, but that won't be known until its been dug out more and is in 3-D relief. He tells me to get the area around the bone swept off very carefully. He then shows me how to properly use my hammer and screwdriver to remove very small bits of mud from around the bone fragment.

My task at this point is to remove particles of mudstone without causing any disturbance to the bone or any other fragments that may be buried underneath or off to the side. "What you want to do," John tells me, "is try and get through here and try to get this rock out without moving this one which will be a little bit tricky ... you'll have to go slow and take really small pieces out. You're going to basically use your hammer to tap this ... you want to make a little bit of a trench through here ... and we'll probably wind up taking these two together in a small jacket, then we'll worry about this one. I'd like to get this in so we can find out what it is."

I wedge myself into a somewhat comfortable position against the side of the quarry pit. My left leg is shoulder high and braced against the wall.

The *Allosaurus* bone being worked on by the author.

My right leg is at an odd angle with my foot resting on a stone block. I'm sitting on a carpet square with my cache of tools and a large bucket on my left. I bend over between my legs and with screwdriver and hammer in hand begin tapping on the *Allosaurus* bone.* I'm hoping that by the end of the day I will have removed enough rocks so that this specimen is ready for jacketing. The contortions I have to make are a little difficult for a sixty-one year old. But I'm trying to get in a position that will allow me to clear out some of the surrounding debris without damaging the dinosaur bones or causing undue harm to my own, somewhat fragile, bones. I'm now a paleontologist!

Although my body geometry is sure to remind folks about the pretzels in the showcase at their local Auntie Annie's pretzel store, I'm finding it pretty exciting to be (officially) excavating a paleontological site. I'm especially thrilled to be working on a fellow carnivore—an *Allosaurus*. Throughout the day I'm learning, bone by aching bone, that the key is be very *very* patient and very careful. It takes a long time to chip away just the tiniest bit of stone from around a fossil. These things have been buried for tens of millions of years—this is not the time to hurry the excavation process.

While I'm chipping, some kids are working in teams to remove debris from a recently dug trench. Others are prying loose some bits of rock surrounding a crushed bone. They're chattering back and forth, and every once in a while one of the kids will shout, "I found something!" It seems as though their discoveries are being made by the minute rather than by the weeks or months.

It's now time for a mandatory water break. The temperature has risen to the low nineties and we need to keep our bodies hydrated. The kids all dash to the van where they grab their cups and begin to gulp enormous quantities of water. Meanwhile, the three of us—Pru (a fellow adult novice paleontologist), Kay (a volunteer for the Museum of Western Colorado), and myself—try to untwist our bones and unfreeze our muscles. With a few grimaces and an occasional shared grin, we extricate our contorted bodies from the pit and saunter (or, in my case, shuffle) over to our stashes of water bottles.

*At this point I'm wondering if this could possibly be one of the recruiting moves required in auditions for The Peking Acrobats ("The internationally acclaimed ensemble of twenty-two remarkable performers with their astounding, centuries-old feats of physical skill…."). If not that, then I could certainly become the poster boy for the American Chiropractic Association's advertisement in the next issue of the *AARP* magazine.

During a brief discussion Kay tells us about some of the paleontological clues that we should keep our eyes open for. These include the fact that dinosaur teeth will stand out from the soil like a new car—shiny and black. They will be, she says, "… almost as shiny as obsidian." Pru and I also learn that plant material has a waxy feeling to it. According to Kay, it's "… like rubbing your fingers over a crayon or candle." Bones, on the other hand, do not feel like that at all.

Too soon, the break is over and we must ease ourselves back into our contorted positions back in the quarry. As I resume my yoga-like position, Sam and his mother Dina are just off to my right. I hear Alex explaining to Sam that he's found a 150 million-year-old pebble at his specific spot. "Hey, Sam," she says. "You're the first person in the entire world to have actually seen that pebble." His smile is a mile wide!

The sun is continuing to beat down. Fortunately, the tarp stretched over the quarry protects us from the direct rays of the sun. Even so, it's starting to approach triple-digit temperatures. At this point, it seems as though my progress is being measured not in inches, but in teeny tiny millimeters. Little by little, bit by bit, I'm chipping away minuscule bits of

Excavation at the quarry is slow and laborious . . . and lots of fun!

rock from around the end of my *Allosaurus* bone. (As is the case with any paleontologist, I have now taken over ownership of this specific bone—it is now *my* bone!) The progress is extremely slow, pedantic, and repetitive. Even after several hours there seems to be little progress to show. Fortunately, I'm a patient paleontologist.

Kay keeps talking to Sam, giving him lots of encouragement. Sam is totally immersed in all the action. Kay shows him a leaf impression and encourages him to rub his fingers over it. After a minute, she asks him, "Does this feel like a candle?" Sam gives a vigorous nod and realizes that he's correctly identified a plant. Just as important, he has also located the end of a bone sticking out from the quarry face. With his practiced hand he delicately brushes the debris away from the bone to expose it just a little bit more. After this cleaning, a preservative will be applied over the end so it will harden and can be safely removed from its multi-million-year-old mudstone prison. Quite an experience for a six-year-old paleontologist!

My work is measured in very tiny steps. Chip, chip, chip. Brush, brush, brush. Chip, chip, chip. Brush, brush, brush. The *Allosaurus* bone is fragile and I am constantly aware of even the slightest shift in the tiny stones around it. I am using a very small paint brush to clean up my site every five minutes or so. Tiny step by tiny step, the bone is standing out in greater relief—but it's been here for 145 million years and is in no hurry to extricate itself from its stony imprisonment.

It's time for another water break (or, as those of us on this end of the quarry call it—"The Hydration of the Ancients"). We stumble and creak to our water bottles once again and watch as the kids engage in a quick game of water tag. We're reminded that these water breaks are mandatory —every forty-five minutes to an hour—and a necessary part of any paleontologist's existence (and survival) in this arid environment.

Back at the pit, young Sam is working with increased levels of intensity and devotion. With his tongue sticking out of his mouth, he is diligently using the hammer and chisel as though he has practiced this art on a regular basis. With his mother working by his side, his work ethic is putting us older members of the team to shame. He is, in so many ways, in a total world of his own.

Off to my left, Kay is assisting Pru with a new discovery. "Look at this bone," Kay exclaims, "it looks like it's headed down under this one. I think its two different bones and I think this one is diving under this one. I would take this layer right here first. I'd leave that for now. Take this layer then you can begin on here. Wow, that is very interesting! So you're going to start tapping on it with your awl. When you're tapping over here, make sure this isn't moving. Maybe you want to go that way so you're tapping away from it."

Kay turns to me and shows me how I should be deepening the trench around the *Allosaurus* bone. She demonstrates how to widen the trench I've been working on all morning without affecting the position of the specimen. There's a certain degree of precision necessary here. I need to make sure that the trench that cuts in and around the bone provides enough room for the inevitable jacketing that will occur many weeks hence.

The progress is in one very small increment after another. It's enduring an arid environment, contorting oneself in an obscene acrobatic position, and continually chipping away at rock. Chip, chip, chip. Chip, chip, chip. Chip, chip, chip. Shuffling papers in an air-conditioned office might seem to have more drama than the back-breaking work out here. It would certainly be a lot more comfortable ... but it's considerably less satisfying.

The quarry is open for the general public to visit, and it's not long before a couple from southern California and two young men from Switzerland show up. Each of them is asking lots of questions about our work, any new discoveries made, and the slow and steady progress taking place. It's interesting that now I'm on the other side of the paleontological divide so to speak—responding to those questions as though I might be the resident expert in charge.*

The two young men are quite curious about all the work taking place here. With their thick German accents, they pepper Pru, Kay, and I with a host of questions. We describe all the work that has been taking place this morning, and I tell them, "Well, we do have some extra tools here." And one of them replies, "Well, then have a good time."

Shortly thereafter, an announcement for lunch is made. There's a spread of meats, cheeses, bread, tomatoes, lettuce, chips, cookies, and sodas that

*Lending additional credence to the infamous quote from the eminent philosopher P.T. Barnum: "You can fool some of the people all of the time!"

Alex has laid out on a table adjacent to the pit. The kids are halfway through their peanut butter sandwiches by the time the adults shuffle up the rise to pile their plates with sandwiches, fruit, and cookies. Each of us tries to find just the right place under the tarp that will guarantee us forty-five minutes of shade (although not necessarily forty-five minutes of peace and quiet).

A stop at the restroom, several swigs of water, and an additional body lubrication of SPF50 later, and we are back in the bottom of the quarry to continue our paleontological duties. By now, the kids are beginning to feel the effects of both heat and pedantic work, and their interest levels are slowly waning. However, Sam, with his tongue just poking out the side of his mouth, is very much into his little paleontological corner of the world.

The bone that Pru uncovered on my left is now being measured and placed on the quarry grid that John maintains. John has a tape measure that stretches down one side of the quarry. He uses this to plot the actual position of the bone on a permanent grid that records, graphs, and illustrates each and every discovery here. This is a new one and must be accurately plotted so it can be examined later in its appropriate context.

It's time, once again, for a mandatory drink, and we drink mightily! The water is warm now, but we hardly notice—it's wet and its necessary. It's about 1:15 in the afternoon, and the temperature has risen above the triple-digit mark. By now, I have a pretty good idea of what a Thanksgiving turkey or my wife's delicious pot roast feels like.

As we return to our specific specimens, two college students arrive at the quarry. They stand near the end—the spot closest to Pru—and pose some questions about her work on the newly discovered bone. Pru invites them to use the hammer and screwdriver to chip away at some rocks. One young man carefully descends into the pit and crouches down on his haunches. Pru hands him the necessary tools and a few instructions, and he begins his work. The smile on his face is enormous and it's quite evident that he is totally enthralled with the process. He can barely hear our conversation as he slowly chips away at the end of Pru's dinosaur bone. A new paleontologist has been created and is completely enthralled with the entire discovery process. He continues for nearly fifteen minutes before Pru almost has to wrestle the tools out of his hands and continue her own work.

A few questions later and the two of them slowly walk back down the road. It is certain that at least one of them has a very permanent smile eternally plastered on his face.

It's now about 1:45, and the sun overhead is brutal. The tarp over our heads offers little comfort and a questionable amount of shade. The kids, for the most part, are pooped out and are shuffling around trying to make their own entertainment. The slow progress of work accomplished in a confined environment (and perhaps even the lack of video games) may have taxed the limits of their patience. The pit is virtually empty now, although Pru and I are still picking away at the small bits of rock surrounding our specimens.

Two o'clock rolls around, and John and Alex decide its time to call it a day. As tools are being packed away, boxes loaded, and the quarry covered over with a layer of dirt and debris (to discourage vandalism), I take the opportunity to chat with Kay Fredette, who has gently guided us throughout the day. She is also one of the many volunteers who works here on a regular basis.

Kay tells me that after her kids had "left the nest" she decided she wanted to volunteer at the Museum of Western Colorado with the thought that she might become a docent. However, the folks at the museum had other ideas and invited her to work in the paleontology lab. From her first day there, she was hooked. "I just love working with the small stuff, although I work on the big stuff, too. You know, the first time you see a bone you're the first human being who ever laid eyes on it!"

She recalled that before her kids were born she had been a dental assistant in an orthodontist office for four years. As a result, she had the necessary fine motor skills because she had not only worked closely with the dentist, but also worked in the lab bending appliances for kid's braces. The work in the paleontological lab was ideally suited for her skills and experience.

So she began her paleontological "career" in 1986 and has been at it ever since. She still considers herself an amateur even after twenty-two years of work in the field. "After twenty-two years, what keeps you coming back to the quarry two to three times a week?" I ask her. A small smile creeps across her face as she tells me that it's the excitement of finding something new and the pleasure in knowing that she can do it carefully and accurately. "It's a warm fuzzy," she notes with pride.

I'm interested in knowing about any memorable experiences during her tenure at the quarry. Again, an infectious smile creeps over her face as she tells me about an incident several years ago when she was assigned to work with two youngsters at another nearby quarry. It was part of a five-day expedition that the museum runs each summer. Over the course of four days, the three of them uncovered three little ring bones—short limb bones from an unknown dinosaur. She and the kids were able to trench completely around the bones during that time period. On the fifth day she took the kids into a nearby trailer and worked with them cutting burlap into long strips in order to jacket the ring bones. She and the kids mixed up the plaster and began laying the strips over the bones. By the end of the day, the bones had been completely excavated, jacketed, and shipped off to the lab for further analysis. She emphasizes that it was a most unusual experience—since paleontological work never happens that fast. "Nevertheless," she says with pride, "it was an experience those kids will never forget!"

The entire crew—kids and adults—piles back into the two vans for the journey back to Fruita and the museum. The sun continues its non-stop baking of both land and road—we are driving through a virtual oven set on "blistering." It seems as though the air conditioning just can't work fast enough. However, in less than thirty minutes we pull up in back of the museum and begin to unload some of the supplies.

So I can understand the importance and impact of this excursion for the general public, I speak with Alex Morrow, who is the museum's Field Coordinator for the summer. Alex has also previously worked as a preschool teacher, a nanny, and a babysitter, so she comes equipped with a tremendous gift of patience —a necessity when dealing with a flock of pre-adolescents and some creaky (not creepy) adults.

After sliding some boxes into the museum, she and I locate a small alcove off the main paleontology lab. I'm most curious about the impression she wants people to leave with after they've been on one of these one-day paleontological adventures. "If they're children, I want them to know that they can do this ... that when they grow up they can be paleontologists. When I was growing up, there were no female paleontologists. When I was four years old, I said, 'I want to be a paleontologist!' Now, here I am."

Alex goes on to tell me that this expedition can have tremendous value for adults as well. She tells me that a trip like this will give people a good sense of what is involved in the fields of geology and paleontology.

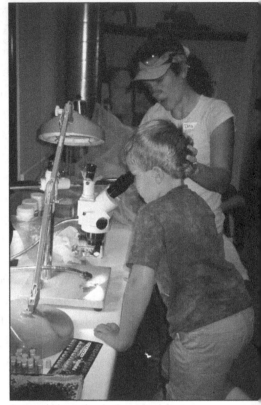

Sam and his mother in the paleo lab at Dinosaur Journey.

She realizes that a lot of adults still are confused about the differences between archeology and paleontology. A trip like this can help them understand the significant differences that exist between these two scientific fields. She also wants them to walk away with an understanding and appreciation for the history of the earth and how that history was dominated for so long by prehistoric creatures, which are just now being uncovered. She concludes by telling me that she hopes to take her degree in paleontology and eventually get her teaching certification. Her ultimate goal is to become a high school science teacher. I have no doubt that she will be an excellent role model for all her young charges.

After leaving Alex, I catch up with Sam and Dina. I thought it might be interesting to get his overall impression of the venture—simply because this was his second time out at the quarry and he was sort of an "old hand" at all this paleontology stuff.

"What did you enjoy most today out at the quarry, Sam?" I ask.

"I found bones. It looks like I found another rib that was matched to that one rib," Sam replies with the air of an accomplished six-year-old paleontologist.

"What do you think is going happen to that rib?"

"It might come back to the museum one day."

"How did you learn so much about dinosaurs?" I inquire.

"Well, because I kept liking them and liking them and I kept reading more about them."

"What could other kids learn about dinosaurs?" I ask.

"That dinosaurs are really interesting and my favorite dinosaur is *T. rex.*"

I decided to ask Sam one final question.

"What are your three favorite things in the world?"

Sam ponders the query very carefully (with a characteristic stroking of his chin). After a few moments he proudly says, "My three favorite things in the world are dinosaurs, football, and chocolate!"

It's clearly evident that this is one six-year-old with his priorities very much in order!

NEED TO KNOW ABOUT **Mygatt–Moore Quarry Dig**

DIRECTIONS From Grand Junction, head west on I-70, and take Exit #19 (Fruita). At the stop sign, turn left onto CO 340 and head south. Go around two traffic roundabouts and continue driving south. Look on your right side and you'll see a McDonald's Restaurant, and just after that will be the Dinosaur Journey Museum (two imposing dinosaurs will greet you as you enter the short road to the parking area).

CONTACT INFORMATION Dinosaur Journey, Museum of Western Colorado, 550 Jurassic Court, Fruita, CO 81521; (970) 858-7282; http://www.museumofwesternco.com/dino-digs/
(Be sure to log on to the website to obtain the latest information and current schedule of expeditions out to the quarry.)

FEES There are several dinosaur expeditions available. These include a half-day, full day and three day dig at the Mygatt-Moore Quarry; as well as a five-day Utah expedition. Please call (1-888-488-DINO, ext. 212) for the latest fees.

HOURS The one-day dig at Mygatt-Moore is from 8:15 a.m. to 4:00 p.m.

BEST TIME TO VISIT The half-day, one-day, three-day and five-day digs are scheduled for various dates throughout the summer months. It is important that you check out the actual dates for each trip at http://www.museumofwesternco.com/dino-digs/.

CAMPING/LODGING Fruita has a half-dozen hotels and four campgrounds (check out www.gofruita.com). Grand Junction (www.visitgrandjunction.com) has nearly four dozen hotels, inns, B&Bs, motels, and campgrounds. There are plenty of accommodations in all price ranges.
  The Comfort Inn (970-858-1333), Super 8 Motel (970-858-0808) and La Quinta Inn (970-858-8850) are all on Raptor Road—an easy walk to Dinosaur Journey.

SERVICES   There is an enclosed pit toilet at the site. The museum provides transportation to and from the quarry, lunch, drinks, and excavation tools. Participants will need to bring sunscreen, a hat, insect repellant, a water bottle, and a camera.

ACCESS   The site at Mygatt-Moore would be appropriate for physically challenged individuals. However, you may want to check with the museum (888-488-DINO or 970-242-0971) before scheduling any trips.

DIFFICULTY RATING   Moderate. Although there is no walking or hiking involved, a certain degree of physical activity is involved. Long periods of time in less-than-comfortable positions are not unusual. Be prepared.

NOTES   For me, this was the trip of a lifetime. I intentionally saved this venture as the final destination on my journey across the length and breadth of Colorado—and I was not disappointed. Although I can't (technically) post any paleontological credentials on the wall of my office, I can with certain pride announce at any number of cocktail parties and other social functions that I have done serious paleontological work in the wilds of Colorado. I can accurately describe my "discovery" of an Allosaurus bone and how I advanced the frontiers of science with my painstaking and serious attention to a 150 million-year-old fossil (Applause, Applause).

This is not a trip to miss. Whether you go as an individual, as a couple, or as an entire family, this trip will spark countless stories and foster an incredible array of memories that will be shared at school, at work, and in living rooms for quite some time. This is certainly not book learning—but a unique opportunity to "get down and dirty" with dinosaur fossils. Piercing summer sun and the thought of keeping your local chiropractor gainfully employed for some time should not deter you from this journey back in time. Take your kids, take your spouse, take a friend, but make sure this trip is on your schedule for any visit to, or in, Colorado—particularly the Western Slope. You will be forever changed—guaranteed!

CHAPTER 13

Not Quite the Last Chapter

S can the *New York Times* Best Seller list and what do you find? Romance, intrigue, adventure, sex, how to be a more complete person by including more romance, intrigue, adventure, and sex in your life ... and so on. But, has anybody ever come out with a best selling novel about scientists? No! For the most part, popular authors tend to eschew scientists as primary characters in their books. Scientists are often relegated to minor roles (if they have any roles at all) or are portrayed as lackluster figures without a hint of romance, intrigue, adventure, or sex in their lives.

So, I wondered, what would it be like to ask some of the more well-known authors of our time to create stories about real life scientists? Since I know "somebody who knows somebody who knows somebody," I was able to secure some previously unpublished manuscripts penned by several authors. Herewith are two samples of those compositions.

Them
by
Stephen K_____

He could feel the terror coursing through every fiber of his being. The nauseating swells that pulsated through his body were back again. His head thumped in tune with his heart beat. The air rushed past him at a breakneck pace, intensifying the pain that wretched his gut. A sickening taste crept into his mouth, full of acid—eating away at the remnants of his sanity. He was imprisoned by his own fear—a fear that permeated his conscious mind as though some ancient and powerful sorcerer controlled him.

He wanted to run. He wanted to yell. He thought he could escape the monster inside him, but he knew the consequences if he did. A hideous, mewling scream began to form in his throat, almost choking him. He tried to back up, but the demons that held on to his mind would not allow him to move. The black hissing that echoed in his ears intensified, blocking out other sounds and pulling at the corners of his mind. He knew he wasn't demented, but the creatures that managed him now were more powerful than he had ever imagined. They were unrelenting in their power—seeping into every cell of his being.

The fear was blinding him; clutching at his senses. It would have to be faced, he thought, but the sickening images before him only grew larger. His breath came in short gasps now—he heard himself panting. He knew the sickness would not pass—once again the horror was taking over every fiber of his body. Finally, with hands trembling so badly they were almost out of control, he reached out and opened the door of the laboratory. "Damn, damn, damn," he muttered. "Another day spent washing those stupid Petri dishes."

The Promise and the Warmth
by
Danielle S_____

She could hear his footsteps long before he entered the room. The echoes always brought back sweet memories of their times together. He was unlike all the others. A strong, rugged man in his early thirties, he always had a gentle smile. Sometimes, when he walked by her she could smell a musky scent—a scent that often filled her with unabated joy. Once, she saw him with his shirt slightly unbuttoned and her mind soared on a flight of uncontrollable fantasy.

She sometimes wondered what he thought of her—whether his kind words and soft voice concealed a secret past. He was often silent, but that made him all the more appealing. Strong, silent types were the men she was most attracted to. Like Bobby, her high school sweetheart, who had always brought her flowers and gently taught her things she would never read in books.

As soon as he entered the room, she could feel the flutter in her heart. She didn't know what it meant or why it lasted so long, but it pleased her nonetheless. She could feel the color rise in her cheeks and she tried not to look directly at him. He started to speak in that deep baritone she loved so much. Each word he said was like a symphony—sweet and poetic. As usual, they talked about the things that mattered most to her. Their conversation was always easy and relaxed and she was comfortable in his presence.

Somehow she knew that this meeting was going to be different. Perhaps she saw it in his cobalt-blue eyes or in the way he walked into the room. The thought of it made her quiver slightly and she began to feel a strange sensation throughout her body. Their initial conversation over, she waited, not knowing what to expect. The room was suddenly quiet, only the rain made a soft patter on the window panes. The hands on the clock barely moved. It was then that he said the words she had waited so long to hear.

"Dr. Thompson," he began. "I was finally able to adjust the thermostat in your lab." At that moment she knew she had found the best custodian in the entire science complex.

One of my favorite "Far Side" cartoons by Gary Larson shows a group of dinosaurs standing outside a cave. The dinosaurs are lighting up some cigarettes and furtively glancing in several directions. The caption reads: "The real reason dinosaurs became extinct." I like that cartoon for several reasons, but primarily because it illustrates the fun that can be had with science. Although Larson gave science and scientists a gentle jab every now and again, he also demonstrated how science is a part of everyday life.*

I realize that to many people scientists appear to be dry, dull folks who devote their lives to dry, dull subjects. Each semester, I offer an undergraduate course on "Teaching Elementary Science" to juniors and seniors who are preparing to become elementary classroom teachers. Sometime during the first week of the semester I invite students to write a "Science Autobiography." Here is part of that assignment:

> Frequently, we bring preconceived ideas and beliefs to our science learning and teaching experiences. These are formed by our direct experiences with science, the people we meet who work in science, and the publicity science receives. Please think about your own personal experiences with science, scientists, science in the media, and science teachers.
>
> Relate your earliest memories of science and your reactions. Write about your experiences with science, explaining what you think the study of science involves. What have you grown up to believe about the scientists themselves? Who are they and what do they do?

The responses generated by this assignment are, at the very least, instructive for both the students and myself. They reflect both truths and misconceptions about the role of science in students' lives and the impact science has had throughout their education. Here are some selected responses from a recent class:

- "Growing up, I've always been under the impression that scientists were 'different' yet extremely smart. I've always looked at scientists

---

*Another favorite "Far Side" cartoon illustrates an enormous creature's eye (perhaps a dinosaur) reflected in the right side view mirror of a car speeding down the road. Clearly spelled out on the bottom of the mirror is the following: "Objects in mirror are closer than they appear."

as people who discover new ideas and elements and are eager to explore more to get different findings."

- "Scientists were always geniuses to me. They were very smart and discussed topics that I didn't understand and had no interest in. I never understood why anyone would want to be a scientist or have anything to do with science."

- "A scientist to me is a person who studies something and tries to find answers to questions they set forth and discover why things are the way they are. They pose questions and find answers by providing scientific and actual evidence as to why something occurs."

- "I think of scientists as being incredibly intelligent, but not really knowing how to 'dumb' their conversation down so that everyday people understand. I also see scientists as finding the cures for rare diseases and putting long hours in labs, looking at rats."

- "I think scientists themselves are very observant and intelligent. Anyone can be a scientist by just studying/observing/ figuring out how things work."

- "I've grown up to believe that scientists are incredibly smart individuals and are very dedicated to the area in which they study."

It is always interesting to note common themes that thread their way through these essays. Those include: scientists are incredibly intelligent; scientists speak a language that is mostly unintelligible and incomprehensible to the rest of society; and scientists are individuals who seldom have a life outside of the laboratory or outside their area of specialty. I am convinced that these themes are not

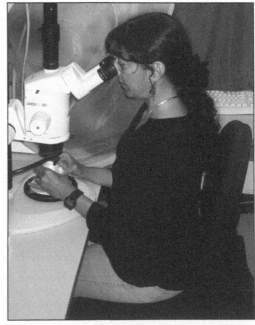

Scientists like Dr. Karen Chin are constantly searching for answers to tough questions.

Exploring the world can generate questions and provide opportunities to find the answers to those queries.

restricted solely to college students, but are equally reflective of beliefs held by the general public.*

Sometime during the second week of the semester I also invite each of the students to take out a blank sheet of paper and "… draw an illustration of a scientist." My intent is to tap into their perceptions (more accurately, their misperceptions) of what a scientist is and what scientists do. These are students who have gone through fourteen or fifteen years of education, been subjected to an untold number of science classes, been required to read more textbooks and view more grainy and yellowed filmstrips than they would ever care to admit, and seen any number of "B" movies and faux science programs on television.

The drawings of those "typical scientists"—almost every one—are distinguished by the following characteristic features: male figures, frizzy hair, lab coats, glasses, pocket protectors, inside a laboratory (typically bent over a microscope), and the characteristic blank and nerdy look on their faces.

*One of my extremely talented, dynamic, and creative undergraduate students recently wrote in response to this assignment, "In my personal experience, science is the exploration and investigation of any and every aspect of the world around us; seen or unseen, explained or unexplained. To study a science field is to strive to reasonably explain the previously unexplained phenomena of the world around us." Wow! How would you like to have her as your child's classroom teacher?

The stereotypes reflect the general public's perception of a "typical" scientist as much as the perceptions of college students. After discussing these illustrations with the class I ask if scientists could ever be female, work outdoors, have well-quaffed hair and a "Live Strong" bracelet on her wrist, or wear a tank top with the perpetually smiling face of Mylie Cyrus on the front. They all look at me sheepishly and mutter, "Yes" under their breaths. These students discover that they, like much of the general public, have assigned scientists to their own little sociological niche which exists just this side of "Nerd-dom."

One of the constant themes I perpetually share with my students is the fact that everyone can be a scientist. Anyone who has ever been around a four year old knows that they are noted for asking a perpetually endless string of questions. This age group is naturally curious about the world around them ("Why is the sky blue?"; "Why do geese fly south?"; "Where do babies come from?"). It can be safely said that four year olds are prone to inflict a never-ending series of questions on any and all adults in their immediate vicinity.

I tell my students that, for me, a scientist is quite simply "someone who asks a lot of questions and goes out and discovers the answers." The point I try to make is that anyone—no matter their age, education, or social standing—can be a scientist. While the media has often presented us with a stereotypical view of what scientists look like (i.e., the portrayal of Dr. Frankenstein [by Gene Wilder] and his hunchback lab assistant [portrayed by Marty Feldman] in the Mel Brooks movie *Young Frankenstein*), where they work (old musty castles cloaked in a veil of foreboding mist and surrounded by irate villagers holding fiery torches in the middle of the night), and the experiments they conduct (creating big, breathing, balding androids out of an assembly of mismatched body parts disinterred from the local cemetery), scientists are, no more, no less, people who ask questions ... lots of questions.

When I began this journey across the length and breadth of Colorado, I had a thousand questions. By the end of that quest, I had answers to 999 of them. More importantly, however, I had unique and singular opportunities to "get down and dirty" with science in general and with paleontology specifically. I met museum curators, lab technicians, fossil preparers, field site supervisors, tour guides, university professors, and a plethora of just-plain-folks from every corner of the country. Each of these individuals overflowed with questions about prehistoric life ... each of them sought to discover rational and accurate answers. Whether professional or amateur, these were people who had never lost their childhood fascination with dinosaurs, nor with the surfeit of mysteries, questions, and "unknowns" surrounding these prehistoric beasts. It was, in many ways, a fraternity of searchers, a coalition of seekers, and an army of scientists that found, and continues to find, both intellectual pleasure and personal satisfaction in learning the "hows," "whys," and "whens" of Colorado's most ancient creatures.

Conversations with this legion of explorers and discoverers yielded far more information—and dispelled far more myths—than I ever would have been able to cull from library books and outdated websites. John Foster, the Curator of Paleontology at the Dinosaur Journey Museum in Fruita, says that part of his mission is to dispel misperceptions and stereotypes, not only of scientists (paleontologists specifically), but also of the field of science in general. He told me that his "mission is to open up science for the public—make it more accessible and let people know that many of the things that scientists do on a daily basis are part and parcel of what anybody who

Sometimes you have to dig deep for the answers—like 500 feet underground in a Colorado cave.

is accomplished in their profession does: solve problems, ask pertinent questions, seek a multiplicity of solutions, and work in harmony."

Lois Oxford, who led me past the awe-inspiring exhibits and dramatically posed fossils at the Dinosaur Depot Museum in Cañon City, was adamant about the need for dinosaur museums to be interactive, rather than passive, establishments. "People—whether they are adults or kids—learn so much more," she told me, "when they are encouraged to ask questions and when the resources are available for them to discover, on their own or with staff assistance, the answers." The same can also be said of all of the outdoor sites I visited—sites that provide first-hand experiences into the intriguing world of paleontology as well as the opportunities to discover the unanswered questions that still remain in sandstone beds or mudstone outposts.

One of my "rules" for this book was that it would concentrate on the "outdoor museums" of dinosaur fossils and paleontological discoveries throughout Colorado. However, as I soon discovered in my travels, questions were continually generated at each venue and every "dig" I explored. I often found the need for some additional backup data in order to put my adventures into a proper perspective. And so I sometimes crossed an invisible line—I went indoors!

I visited the American Museum of Natural History in New York ("One of the premier attractions … is the museum's series of fossil halls, including its two famed dinosaur halls. The museum is home to the world's largest collection of vertebrate fossils, totaling nearly one million specimens.") There, I battled crowds of schoolchildren who, like a determined swarm of honeybees, surged through the exhibits with a constant drone of high-pitched activity. On two separate occasions, I stood in awe while gazing at more than one hundred specimens, including *T. rex*, *Apatosaurus*, *Triceratops*, and *Stegosaurus*—all of which have Colorado roots. I wandered through the Hall of Saurischian Dinosaurs and the Hall of Ornithischian Dinosaurs and took an endless series of notes, scribblings, and musings as part of the research for this book.

In the middle of a brutal winter, I traveled from my home in Pennsylvania to the National Museum of Natural History at the Smithsonian Institution in Washington, D.C. There, I wove my way between myriad clusters of inquiring children and their equally inquisitive parents to the Hall of Paleobiology. ("How did life and all its wondrous forms come about? The story begins almost 3.5 billion years ago and unfolds in this exhibit. This exhibit includes Dinosaurs, Life in the Ancient Seas, Fossil Mammals, and Fossil Plants.") The skeleton of a *Tyrannosaurus rex* and a *Triceratops* (more Colorado natives) greeted me as I entered the always-crowded hall. I stood transfixed by the scientifically posed fossils and the wealth of information offered at each display.

I journeyed to the Field Museum in Chicago ("From the dawn of life to towering dinosaurs and our extended human family ... How did life on Earth evolve? Explore the awe-inspiring process and the science that reveals it...."), where I met Sue—arguably the world's most famous *T. rex*. I dodged legions of students—both elementary and high school—on field trips and stood transfixed by the work of the folks in the Fossil Preparation Laboratory, where several fossils were being readied for scientific study. I boned up on my geology at the Earth Sciences exhibit and learned something new about genetic research at the DNA Discovery Center. Most importantly, I visited the dinosaurs that Elmer Riggs had located far away from the Windy City deep in the hillsides of western Colorado.

No scientific expedition into the wilds of Colorado would be complete without a journey to the wilds of Denver—specifically the Denver Museum of Nature & Science and their Prehistoric Journey Exhibit ("...one of the premier natural history museums in the country ... which features a *Stegosaurus* fossil discovered near Cañon City by a high school teacher, and an *Allosaurus* skeleton found by a thirteen-year-old girl in Moffat County.").

As you walk inside "Prehistoric Journey" on the third floor of the museum, you are greeted by a continuously playing movie about prehistoric life from the beginnings of the earth. Inside the doorway, one of the

THE DAY IS MISTY AND COOL. *A light fog hovers over the valley. An early summer rain has formed small puddles everywhere and the trees have been washed by a bath of constant raindrops.*

A family of hadrosaurs browses through a prehistoric forest. They are plucking leaves and stems and whole branches from the overhanging vegetation. Because of their size they must eat constantly. This group has settled in among a forest of coniferous trees that has grown up alongside a riverbank—a river that is now swollen with swift-flowing waters from the recent storm.

The creatures continue to reach up into the uppermost branches of the trees. They use their teeth to strip the branches of leaves in a single pass. There is little time for chewing—the food is swallowed just as quickly as it is stripped. The leaves pass down the digestive tract and into the stomach. There they are mixed and crushed by stones and small rocks that these huge creatures occasionally swallow.

One of the slow-moving members of the group succumbs to the ravages of old age. He slumps into a shallow mud puddle. Later in the day, another summer flood washes through the area. The carcass is covered with a layer of sediment. Over the course of several years, additional floods wash through the area adding more layers of mud. The remains are sealed, and along with it a thousand different secrets.

initial displays explains the fossilization process using a piece of wood as an example. For instance, sometimes a piece of wood may become buried in a jacket of mud. That mud may harden into a thick coating of rock. After many years, the wood may decay, and a detailed mold is left like a pocket inside the rock. As is sometimes the case, mineral-rich water seeps into the mold, where it collects and forms a piece of rock in the shape of the piece of wood. This kind of fossil seldom preserves any details of internal structure.

It may be that a deposit of minerals fills the empty spaces in the wood in the same manner as water fills up a sponge. In this instance, some of the wood's original structure may remain as part of this "replacement fossil." Or, if the replacement process keeps on going, the remaining wood may dissolve away and be replaced by other minerals from the water. In this case, the details of internal structure are frequently preserved.

Additional displays in "Prehistoric Journey" describe the Mesozoic Era—251.0 to 65.5 million years ago—a time when dinosaurs appeared, some reptiles began to fly, flowers evolved, shallow seas periodically flooded the center of what is now North America, and the super-continent Pangaea began to break up. Other interpretive signs inform visitors about the Jurassic Period, when the climate was warm with wet and dry seasons, and the Cretaceous Period, when dinosaurs diversified into many new and varied forms including the world's largest land carnivore.

I turn a corner and come face to face with a familiar face—a *Stegosaurus* specimen that was discovered in 1937 near Cañon City. It was exhibited for over fifty years in a famous, and we now know, incorrect pose before being moved and rearticulated into its current pose.

The exhibit hall was relatively quiet—just a few families passing through. I had thoughtfully decided to visit during the middle of the week in the middle of the summer—a time when the crowds would be considerably smaller and the noise considerably lessoned. I was staring at the *Stegosaurus* exhibit, clipboard in hand and pen at the ready. Occasionally, I would jot down some notes, impressions, or random thoughts onto the legal pad I always had ready. While I was recording some ideas, a young couple and their seven-year-old daughter approached the exhibit. The young lady watched me with rapt attention for several minutes. Finally, her curiosity could stand it no more and she questioned me.

"Who are you and what are you doing here?" she asked.

"I'm learning about dinosaurs," I replied.

"I know a lot about dinosaurs," she offered with a note of pride.

"That's great! So do I."

"Are you in school?" she inquired.

"No, I'm visiting here because I'm writing a book."

Without missing a beat, she responded, "I'm a writer, too! I learned this year. I didn't have to wait until I was old like you."

Further conversation, I knew, would be fruitless. I humbly slunk into another section of the museum and began to read about the KT boundary, which marks the end of the dinosaurs and many other species, and a geographical border where the oldest rocks from the Tertiary Period lie on top of the youngest rock from the Cretaceous Period.

Later I come upon other displays describing changing climate patterns. Also described was the death of many previous species of animals and plants and how they paved the way for the period of time that scientists called the Cenozoic (65.5 million years ago to the present). Nearby is an engaging display geared specifically for children, "Sherlock Bones and the Case of the Found Fossils," which describes the work of taphonomists—scientists who discover what happens to an animal from the time of its death to the discovery of its fossilized remains.

The museum is alive with exhibits hanging down from the ceiling—skeletons of prehistoric creatures—and rooms that are open and inviting. I observe, with a certain degree of caution, *Allosaurus* and *Stegosaurus* doing battle with an eighty-foot-long *Diplodocus* towering above them. I stroll past Jurassic Period landscapes covered with brambles of bennettite bushes and tree ferns. I wander along prehistoric habitats and examine ancient plants. Indeed, there's a panoply of displays and presentations of every shape and color—a veritable feast for any scientist's (young or old) eyes.

After a full day of scrutinizing workers in the paleo lab, gawking at "old friends" in fierce combat, and observing a healthy slice of prehistoric life, its time for a turkey sandwich, energy bar, and bottle of water at the museum's appropriately named snack bar—the *T. Rex Café*.

What I learned at these world-class museums confirmed not only the data I had collected in the field, but also underscored my belief that anyone—adults and kids alike—can be a scientist. All one needs is an insatiable curiosity and a bank of questions waiting to be answered. I began this book

Scientists come in all shapes and sizes (and ages)!

with a list of queries that had no easy answers, and I finished with a respect for the folks who journey forth and, day in and day out, search for the answers. In many ways I felt a kinship with these individuals—like them, I never really knew what I was going to discover around the next bend or just over the next hill, but I was always eager to make the trip. Like any scientist worth her or his salt, I got my hands dirty and my mind filled with new possibilities and new discoveries.

I saw that same insatiable thirst for knowledge in the many folks I met along the trail or in the laboratory. People from all over the country and from every possible socio-economic group joined me on this journey. Together we dug in distant locations, we surveyed ancient river beds, we poked and prodded through long-abandoned quarries, we stared at enormous skeletons that towered well above our heads, we rode dusty roads and long asphalt highways, and we posed countless questions each and every step along the way. Sometimes we found the answers, sometime not. But, as the old saying goes, it was the journey that was more important than the destination. We were fellow adventurers, fellow explorers, and fellow travelers. We were held together by a common bond and a common quest. We were scientists!

Sure, there will be more roads to travel and more dinosaurs to find (hence the title of this chapter), and I hope that an unlimited supply of unanswered questions will always prod those ventures. While I certainly hope that my own fossilized skeleton is not exhibited in some futuristic museum (as were the many prehistoric "friends" I discovered on this educational voyage), perhaps, just perhaps, somewhere down the line I might receive a letter like the following:

Dear Mr. Author:

I just finished reading *Walking with Dinosaurs: Rediscovering Colorado's Prehistoric Beasts*. Well, all I can say is that your depiction of scientists as everyday people and your on-site explorations of Colorado dinosaurs were both delightful and delicious. It just so happens that I work as an itinerant producer in Hollywood. I turned your book over to the studio and they had the same reaction as I did. Which all boils down to this: They would like to turn your book into a major motion picture. In fact, they've begun some initial inquiries and are seriously considering a famous actress (Julia Roberts?) to play the part of the self-effacing, yet alluring, kindergarten teacher who wants to give up her part-time nightclub career as a ventriloquist to become a nomadic paleontologist on the Western Slope. I understand that they are also negotiating with several actors (I hear George Clooney might be available) to play your role of the rakishly handsome, though prematurely balding, college professor who must moonlight as a tattoo artist in Aspen in order to pay "hush money" to the mob regarding an incident with a canary, a bar of soap, and a lady from Boulder who wears multicolored socks and suede earrings. The lawyers are drawing up the contracts now and you should be hearing from them shortly. As soon as it's ready they'll want to start production. They're hoping you'll be able to fly out to "tinsel town" to serve as the movie's (highly paid) advisor.

Sincerely,

Larry Moencurley

Big Budget Motion Pictures

CHAPTER 14

Phenomenal Colorado Dinosaur Facts

More dinosaur fossils have been discovered in Colorado than in any other state.

- *Coelophysis* has been discovered, not only in Colorado, but also in the African country of Zimbabwe.

- The first discovery of dinosaur bones in Colorado was made in 1869 or early 1870.

- *Ornitholestes*, a dinosaur of the Late Jurassic Period found in Colorado, means "bird robber." However there is no evidence to show that it ever caught any birds.

- The first *Triceratops* ever discovered was found near Denver in 1887.

- After *Diplodocus* was discovered, Andrew Carnegie had ten copies made of all 300 bones. He gave the skeletons as gifts to museums around the world.

- The first *Stegosaurus* ever found was discovered near Morrison, Colorado.

- The largest dinosaur discovered in Colorado was the *Supersaurus,* uncovered in Dry Mesa Quarry. Its total weight would be equivalent to 426,666 Big Macs.

- *Supersaurus*, an enormous dinosaur also unearthed at Dry Mesa Quarry in western Colorado, would have had a body length equivalent to three large school buses parked end to end.
- The longest set of fossil footprints in the New World can be found in Colorado. This trackway of footprints goes continuously for a distance of 705 feet.
- *Stegosaurus*, the Colorado state fossil, had a tail as long as its body—twenty to twenty-five feet.
- *Allosaurus* was first discovered in Colorado in 1869. It has also been unearthed in Utah, Wyoming, Oklahoma, South Dakota, Montana, and New Mexico.
- More than thirty different species of dinosaurs have been discovered in Colorado. These include, but are not limited to, the following:

Dinosaur	Period	Dinosaur	Period
Albertosaurus	Late Cretaceous	Epanterias	Late Jurassic
Allosaurus	Late Jurassic to Early Cretaceous	Haplocanthosaurus	Late Jurassic
Apatosaurus	Late Jurassic	Iguanodon	Early Cretaceous
Barosaurus	Late Jurassic	Marshosaurus	Late Jurassic
Brachiosaurus	Late Jurassic	Ornitholestes	Late Jurassic
Camarasaurus	Late Jurassic	Ornithomimus	Middle to Late Cretaceous
Camptosaurus	Late Jurassic	Othnielia	Late Jurassic
Ceratosaurus	Late Jurassic	Stegosaurus	Late Jurassic
Coelophysis	Late Triassic	Stokesosaurus	Late Jurassic
Coelurus	Late Jurassic	Supersaurus	Late Jurassic
Deinonychus	Early Cretaceous	Torvosaurus	Late Jurassic
Diplodocus	Late Jurassic	Triceratops	Late Cretaceous
Dromaeosaurus	Late Cretaceous	Tyrannosaurus	Late Cretaceous
Dryosaurus	Late Jurassic	Ultrasaurus	Late Jurassic
Fruitadens	Late Jurassic	Velocirapter	Late Cretaceous

- Three of the largest dinosaurs ever discovered in the world were found in Mesa County, Colorado.
- *Ultrasaurus*, discovered at Dry Mesa, Colorado, was tall enough to look into the sixth-floor window of a building.
- The Fruita Paleontological Area has produced some fossils of adult dinosaurs that were smaller than a chicken.

Colorado has more dinosaur fossils than any other state in the country.

- *Camptosaurus*, which have been unearthed throughout the Morrison Formation, were able to chew plant food thoroughly before swallowing it. Most herbivores plucked and swallowed their food to be ground up by gastroliths in the stomach.
- The brain of a *Stegosaurus* only weighed two and a half ounces—about 1/250,000 the weight of its body.
- *Diplodocus*, a "popular" dinosaur found throughout Colorado, was ninety feet long (the length of 864 average-sized paper clips laid end to end).
- The Denver Museum of Nature and Science has displayed a *Tyrannosaurus* skeleton that is constructed of hollow fiberglass. It is so light that it can stand on one leg.
- *Apatosaurus*, like an elephant, had thick pads of gristle behind its toes that acted as cushions. It had a brain no bigger than a cat's.
- From 1909 to 1922, approximately 350 tons (700,000 pounds) of dinosaur bones were extracted from Dinosaur National Monument and shipped to the Carnegie Museum in Pittsburgh.

- Each of the horns on a *Triceratops* may have been more than three feet in length.
- *Allosaurus*, which lived throughout Colorado, had teeth that worked like steak knives. It was able to move its upper and lower jaws back and forth, tearing its food between them.
- Approximately 33 percent of Colorado has surface rocks from the Mesozoic Era. Nearly four-fifths of those are from the Cretaceous Period alone.

Apatosaurus, many of which have been unearthed in Colorado, had feet quite similar to a modern-day elephant.

- *Fruitadens*, one of the world's smallest dinosaurs, was discovered near Fruita, Colorado. Its total weight would be equivalent to eleven Big Macs (estimate).
- From 110 million years ago to about 65 million years ago much of Colorado was underwater (the Western Interior Seaway).
- *Triceratops*, which has been discovered in various locations throughout Colorado, lived to the very end of the Age of Dinosaurs.
- *Brachiosaurus*, a massive dinosaur that lived in what is now Colorado, had a head that was forty feet (four stories) above the ground.
- *Ultrasaurus* weighed ten times as much as an average bull elephant (five tons).
- The largest dinosaur bone in the world was found in Dry Mesa, Colorado. It consisted of hip bones and several attached vertebrae. It measured six feet high and four feet, six inches long. It weighed 1,500 pounds.
- *Tyrannosaurus*'s front limbs were so tiny that they could not touch each other. Yet they were able to lift 450 pounds.
- A skull of *Pentaceratops* (similar to a *Triceratops*), a Late Cretaceous dinosaur discovered near Rangely, Colorado, was almost ten feet long. It's the biggest skull yet uncovered of any terrestrial dinosaur.

- The Morrison Formation, a treasure trove of most dinosaur discoveries in Colorado, is made up primarily of deposits of sand, mud, and volcanic ash deposited over more than eight million years.
- *Mymoorapelta*, uncovered at the Mygatt-Moore Quarry in 1990, is the first Jurassic Period ankylosaur (short, squat herbivores, some with large clubs at the end of their tails) discovered in North America.
- *Triceratops* remains have been discovered on the Front Range, but none have been uncovered on the Western Slope.

The "Dinosaur Freeway" goes through Colorado—preserving life in an ancient time.

Colorado Dinosaur Museums

Denver Museum of Nature and Science

2001 Colorado Blvd.
Denver, CO 80205
(303) 322-7009
www.dmns.org
Hours: Daily: 9:00–5:00
Admission: Adult $12.00; Junior $6.00; Senior $8.00.

If you're looking for an informative and interesting display of prehistoric life, then run (don't walk) to the DMNS! This is one of those wonderful museums where there is literally something for everyone. No matter if you are a casual observer, an amateur paleontologist, or a wanna-be scientist, you have to see Prehistoric Journey on the third floor. Kids will gasp and parents will be dazzled by the incredible displays.

Dinosaur Depot

330 Royal Gorge Blvd.
Cañon City, CO 81212
(719) 269-7150
www.dinosaurdepot.com
Hours: vary throughout the year, but typically 9:00–5:00 every day throughout the summer, and 10:00–4:00 Wednesday through Sunday the remainder of year.
Admission: Adult $4.00; Child (4–12) $2.00; Child (0–3) Free

As it says on its website, "The Dinosaur Depot Museum is a GEM…." And boy is it ever! Small in size but big in heart, this jewel is packed to the rafters with exhibits, displays, and information that is both captivating and exciting. What I enjoy so much is the personal touch—the volunteers are ready to answer your every question, folks in the paleo lab will take time from their duties to explain what they do, and the staff will literally go out of their way to provide you with data and details that will amaze, delight, and inform. This is a true "visitor-friendly" museum. It is most definitely worth a stop!

Dinosaur Journey Museum

> 550 Jurassic Court
> Fruita, CO 81521
> (970) 858-7282
> www.dinosaurjourney.org
> Hours: Monday through Saturday 10:00–4:00; Sunday 12:00–4:00
> (October–April); Monday through Sunday 9:00–5:00 (May–September)
> Admission: Adult $8.50; Senior $6.50; Children $5.25

Watch out! This place is filled with robotic dinosaurs that will make loud noises, swing their heads in menacing ways, and even spit water at you. Kids will watch in awe as these life-sized replicas bring the world of dinosaurs to life. This is a true wonderland of exhibits and displays that will open up eyes and delight the senses as few places can. This place sparkles with imagination and dazzles with information. Good luck trying to drag the youngest members of the family out of this museum—they'll want to stay here for at least an era … or perhaps a millennium.

Dinosaur Ridge Exhibit Hall

> 16831 West Alameda Parkway
> Morrison, CO 80465
> (303) 697-3466
> www.dinoridge.org
> Hours: Monday through Saturday 10:00–4:00; Sunday 11:00–4:00

Take a "Trek Through Time" with this well-displayed prehistoric journey. Dynamic artwork of dinosaurs and other critters, floor to ceiling murals of life in ancient times, and informative details about each of the major periods of the earth's history will keep you enthralled. There are activities and projects for kids and plenty to discover by adults. Make this part of your walk around Dinosaur Ridge and you'll be a full-fledged paleontologist in no time!

Morrison Natural History Museum

501 Colorado Highway 8
P.O. Box 564
Morrison, CO 80465
(303) 697-1873
www.mnhm.org
Open daily 10:00-5:00
Admission: Adult $7.00; Senior $6.00; Youth $5.00; Children Free

This is one of my all-time favorite Colorado museums! It's small, but it's jammed-packed with all kinds of up-close-and-personal dinosaur fossils (don't forget to pet the *T. rex*), as well as a wealth of information for dinophiles of every age. Here you can get a personal, hands-on tour with extremely knowledgeable guides where you'll learn about contemporary dinosaur discoveries, regional geology, and living native reptiles. Don't miss this one—it is definitely worth the journey!

Rocky Mountain Dinosaur Resource Center

201 S. Fairview St.
Woodland Park, CO 80863
(719) 686-1820
www.rmdrc.com
Hours: Monday through Saturday 9:00-6:00; Sunday 10:00-5:00
Admission: Seniors $10.50; Adults $11.50; Children (5-12) $7.50; Under 5 Free

The RMDRC bills itself as "Ancient fun for everyone!" Here you will be able to see unique and spectacular dinosaurs, giant pterosaurs, breathtaking marine reptiles, huge carnivorous fish, and realistic life restorations. They also have an interactive children's area, a fossil preparation lab, an enormous gift shop, and guided tours on a daily basis. This is a place the entire family will enjoy ... and talk about for years.

University of Colorado Museum of Natural History

Fifteenth and Broadway
Boulder, CO 80309
(303) 492-6892
www.cumuseum.colorado.edu
Hours: Monday through Friday 9:00–5:00; Saturday 9:00–4:00; Sunday: 10:00–4:00
Admission: Free (but "…the museum appreciates donations")

The University of Colorado Museum of Natural History houses the largest natural history collection in the Rocky Mountains. Currently, more than four million objects are categorized into five disciplines: Anthropology, Botany, Entomology, Paleobiology/Geology, and Zoology. The Museum's Discovery Corner allows children of all ages to explore natural history through hands-on activities with specimens and artifacts. "Fossils: Clues to the Past" is one of the most popular exhibits.

Select Reading List

Colbert, Edwin H., 1984. *The Great Dinosaur Hunters and Their Discoveries*. Dover Publications, New York.
This book takes you inside the lives of the men and (very few) women who blazed paleontological trails across the American West and around the world with their discoveries and explorations. This is the human side of the world of dinosaurs—and a most readable side it is.

Fair, Erin, Tempel, Joe, and Moklestad, Tom. 2008. *A Guide to Triceratops Trail at Parfet Prehistoric Preserve*. Friends of Dinosaur Ridge. Morrison, CO.
This brief but thorough guide to Triceratops Trail is chock full of valuable information for anyone planning a visit to this site. The descriptions are clear and the directions are easy to follow—a perfect combination for any amateur paleontologist.

Fiffer, Steve. 2001. *Tyrannosaurus Sue: The Extraordinary Saga of the Largest, Most Fought Over T. Rex Ever Found*. W.H. Freeman. New York.
From its discovery in 1990 in South Dakota, through an incredible sequence of legal battles, to its place of honor at the Field Museum in Chicago, this tale has all the elements of a good crime story—but it is truly science at its best! Get it and savor every delicious detail!

Foster, John. 2007. *Jurassic West: The Dinosaurs of the Morrison Formation and Their World*. Indiana University Press. Bloomington, Indiana.
Throughout the American southwest, the Morrison Formation has given up some of the most compelling information about dinosaurs. Written by eminent paleontologist John Foster (see Chapter 12 of this book), this is the story of life in an ancient world that continues to amaze and confound.

Horner, John, and Gorman, James. 1988. *Digging Dinosaurs*. Harper. New York.
Noted paleontologist Jack Horner chronicles his seven-year investigation that eventually demonstrated that species of dinosaurs raised their young and lived in herds. Horner was the first to discover the first large-scale concentration of baby dinosaur fossils and nests.

Jenkins, John, and Jenkins, Jannice. 1993. *Colorado's Dinosaurs*. Colorado Geological Survey. Denver, CO.
Although some of the information is slightly outdated, this is a most valuable guide to the various dinosaur sites throughout Colorado. Its seventy-four pages are filled with insightful information and lots of easy-to-read science.

Johnson, Kirk and Troll, Ray. 2007. *Cruisin' the Fossil Freeway*. Fulcrum Publishing. Golden, CO.
This is the story of a delightful journey across the American southwest by a paleontologist and an artist in their never-ending search for fossils. There are adventures galore and an infectious sense of humor that will keep readers enthralled to the very end.

Lockley, Martin; Fillmore, Barbara; and Marquardt, Lori. 1997. *Dinosaur Lake: The Story of the Purgatoire Valley Dinosaur Tracksite Area.* Colorado Geological Survey. Denver, CO.
A thorough and complete guide to one of the country's most amazing and intriguing sites. Full of history, sociology, anthropology, paleontology, and geology, this guidebook will provide you with an incredible array of data in an easy-to-read format. Read it and be amazed!

Lockley, Martin. 2001. *A Field Guide to Dinosaur Ridge.* Friends of Dinosaur Ridge. Morrison, CO.
This is a "must-have" guide to Dinosaur Ridge. The author provides visitors to the fascinating site an inside look into the history, geology, and paleontology of this remarkable and unique area. Be sure to read this before any planned visit.

Long, John. 2008. *Feathered Dinosaurs: The Origin of Birds.* Oxford University Press. London.
Paleontologist John Long provides a stunning visual record of these extraordinary prehistoric creatures, illuminating the evolutionary march from primitive, feathered dinosaurs through to the first true flying birds.

Manning, Philip, 2008. *Grave Secrets of Dinosaurs: Soft Tissues and Hard Science.* National Geographic Society. Washington, D.C.
In 1997, a high school student discovers a nearly complete dinosaur mummy. This sets off a chain of events that would rival any detective yarn. This book reads like a novel, but is packed with more science than you can shake a stick at.

Mitchell, W.J.T. 1998. *The Last Dinosaur Book.* University of Chicago Press. Chicago.
Mitchell, an eminent cultural historian, puts dinosaurs in their proper place, both as sociological icons and as scientific curiosities, in this heavy though very informative book. In 320 pages, he answers that pervasive question: Why are dinosaurs so popular?

Novacek, Michael. 2002. *Time Traveler.* Farrar, Straus and Giroux, New York.
This is a captivating account of how one scientist's boyhood fascination with dinosaurs took him to almost every continent in search of prehistoric creatures—both reptilian and mammalian.

Parker, Steve and Mertz, Leslie. 2008. *Extreme Dinosaurs.* Collins. New York.
This is a very readable and thorough examination of the Age of Dinosaurs. Each of the chapters is brief, but chock-full of interesting facts and incredible data. This is a "must-have" for any dino-phile!

Paul, Gregory. 2003. *The Scientific American Book of Dinosaurs.* St. Martin's Griffin. New York.
This book provides a complete portrait of dinosaurs' existence, including how they evolved, what they looked like, where they lived, how they behaved, and why they went extinct. The most sensational finds and the latest theories are covered in this comprehensive tome.

West, Linda, and McKnight, Clint. 2001. *Dinosaur: The Dinosaur National Monument Quarry.* Dinosaur Nature Association. Vernal, Utah.
This is another "must-have" guide to be read before setting off for Dinosaur National Monument—the quarry that Earl Douglass made famous. Although the quarry is closed (at the time of this writing), this informative guide (along with captivating photos) will succinctly provide readers with all the necessary information.

Acknowledgments

While this book was being copyedited in the summer of 2009, I had the opportunity to stop by the offices of Johnson Books to introduce myself to my intrepid editor and the staff of this incredible publisher. I walked in the door and presented myself to the first person I saw. She immediately turned around and announced to all within earshot (including half of downtown Boulder), "That old fossil guy is here!" I knew, then and there, that I had the perfect publisher for this tome.

On its journey to publication, this book was enhanced by the contributions of many people. From patient scientists to die-hard dinosaur buffs, many folks willingly shared their wisdom, dedication, and curiosity to the creation of this book. Without their assistance (and not infrequent paleontological hand-holding) this project could never have been completed. I owe an immeasurable debt of eternal gratitude to each and every one—whose names are, now and forever, associated with one (slightly fossilized) author.

Many thanks to Vince Matthews, state geologist and director of the Colorado Geological Society, who directed me to the "Major Chronostratigraphic and Geochronologic Units" of the USGS, which helped me maintain order and consistency in my frequent references to prehistoric times. An incredible note of appreciation is also extended to "King Kong" who was much more than an inspiration for Chapter 1—as far as I am concerned, he is the original (and only true) American Idol!

Thanks to Chuck (no last name) during my first visit to the Mygatt-Moore Quarry (in 2002) for orienting me to this magnificent site and to Lindsey Lennek at Dinosaur National Monument, who provided me with some delightful statistics.

I am forever indebted to John Foster, the Curator at Dinosaur Journey Museum in Fruita, for his expertise and insights about paleontology in general and the Mygatt-Morre Quarry specifically. His contributions were invaluable in the composition of Chapters 4 and 12. I am equally thankful for the assistance of Bruce Schumacher, the Rocky Mountain South Zone Paleontologist, who clarified some significant points about the work being done at the Fruita Paleontological Area.

My visit to La Junta was considerably enhanced by my conversations with Ty Sisson (and the great food at Mexico City Restaurant); the insights and deliberations of Justin Simon, a volunteer with the U.S. Forest Service; and the delightfully informative details about the Purgatoire tracksite offered by Kevin Lindahl, the Visitor Information Assistant, also with the U.S. Forest Service. Any visit to La Junta would be incomplete without conversation with these individuals.

In Cañon City, I was treated to a wonderfully informative conversation with Lois Oxford, the Volunteer Coordinator with Dinosaur Depot Museum. The day was further enhanced with on-site visits to Skyline Drive and Garden Park Fossil Area under the expert tutelage of the energetic Pat Monaco. These two are, most certainly, the "First Ladies of Paleontology." Thanks also to Jon Stone, Museum Director of the Dinosaur Depot Museum, for helping to set up my visit.

At Dinosaur Ridge, Tom Moklestad, the Education and Operations Director, provided me with passionate insights and insightful data about this dynamic site. Kudos and "high fives" are also due Chelsea Hutson, a Museum Assistant at the Morrison Natural History Museum, who shared her love for this small, but amazing, museum.

No amount of appreciation could ever be sufficient for the contributions of Dr. Karen Chin (of the University of Colorado) to this project. She willingly gave up valuable research time to meet with me on two separate occasions (2002 and 2007) and opened up her lab so that I might fully understand the significance of paleoscatology to the study of dinosaurs. Her expertise and dedication to the field of paleontology is without equal.

During the summer of 2008, I had the honor of working with several individuals at the Mygatt-Moore Quarry. Amateur paleontologists all, we dug and examined and contorted our bodies in various configurations, just to look at 65-million-year-old fossils. I am indebted to Kay Fredette, a volunteer with Dinosaur Journey Museum, and Alex Morrow, the Field Coordinator for the museum, who willingly shared their wisdom and enthusiasm for on-site paleontology. Many thanks are due Dina Baird and her six-year-old son, Sam ("The World's Next Great Paleontologist") for spending the day and sharing their thoughts about dinosaurs … and dinosaur discoveries.

I am particularly indebted to my son, Jonathan, who, at the last minute, was able to don a paleontologist's hat and set out to shoot new photographs and collect pertinent research necessary to update some of the information in this book. His enthusiastic willingness to go "above and beyond" is to be both celebrated and cheered.

In the world of publishing there are many heroes … but few as wonderful as Mira Perrizo, my editor and publisher of this book. Her continuous and enthusiastic support of this project, her deft editing of the manuscript, and her dedication to the highest ideals of book publication are to be celebrated, cheered, and applauded. (Hell, she deserves a standing ovation!) She is the consummate editor (other authors should be so fortunate), and I have been honored to have had her as an integral part of this literary venture into the wild and wonderful world of Colorado paleontology.

PUBLISHER GENERAL'S NOTE: The Publisher General has determined that any individuals inadvertently excluded or inconveniently "misplaced" for the Acknowledgments section of this book are to be accorded all the same rights and honors of those previously mentioned (along with our sincerest apologies). Any exclusion is undoubtedly due to the brain fossilization (or overall decomposition) of a certain author and should not be construed as any sort of personal affront. Appropriate corrections will be made in future editions.

About the Author

Phyllis Disher Fredericks

Anthony D. Fredericks

Okay, let's get one thing straight—this guy is no enchanted prince. After all, he wears glasses (he hasn't quite figured out how contacts work), he's balding on top (the result of a dip in the wrong gene pool), and he pals around with a dog (a clue as to who his best friends might be). True, he does have that perpetual smile plastered on his face, but so do a lot of insurance salesmen and used car dealers.

Here's what we do know about Tony: His background includes experience as an elementary teacher, reading specialist, storyteller, and college professor ("Oh, no, not one of those!"). In addition, he is the author of more than one hundred books. These include more than seventy teacher resource books and nearly three dozen award-winning children's books. His education titles include the best-selling *Science Fair Handbook (3rd Ed.)*, which he co-authored with Isaac Asimov, and the hugely popular *Frantic Frogs and Other Frankly Fractured Folktales for Readers Theatre*. His award-winning children's titles include *Under One Rock: Bugs, Slugs and Other Ughs*; *The Tsunami Quilt: Grandfather's Story*; and *A is for Anaconda: A Rainforest Alphabet*.

Additionally, Fredericks is the author of several adult trade books including the perennial favorite *How Long Things Live*. Currently, he is a professor of education at York College, York, Pennsylvania, where he teaches elementary education methods courses and creative writing classes.

Tony and his wife Phyllis (truly an enchanted princess) live in Dover, Pennsylvania. They have two children, Rebecca (who lives in northern England) and Jonathan (who lives on the Western Slope of Colorado).